Planning for Basic Needs: A Soft Option or a Solid Policy?

A Basic Needs Simulation Model Applied to Kenya

ROLPH VAN DER HOEVEN

A study prepared for the International Labour Office within the framework of the World Employment Programme

Gower

Aldershot · Brookfield USA · Hong Kong · Singapore · Sydney

Published by

Gower Publishing Company Limited
Gower House
Croft Road
Aldershot
Hants GU11 3HR
England

Gower Publishing Company
Old Post Road
Brookfield
Vermont 05036
USA

ISBN 0 566 05680 1

Printed and bound in Great Britain by
Athenaeum Press Limited, Newcastle upon Tyne

329128

Contents

CONTENTS

Tables

Figures

Preface

This book presents a basic needs model applied to Kenya as part of the project financed by the Government of the Netherlands, "A socio-economic framework for basic needs planning", embracing basic needs models for Colombia, Sri Lanka and Kenya, which was carried out within the framework of the World Employment Programme of the International Labour Organisation (ILO). A preliminary version of the present model, with a discussion on how a broader basic needs model ought to be developed, was prepared in 1981. For that paper, and in the course of the preparation of the present version of the model, I received comments and observations from many people.

Advice received from Henk Bos, Hans Linnemann and Syamaprasad Gupta, who formed part of the steering group of the basic needs modelling project, was above all appreciated. They prevented me from going into never-ending dark alleys and often challenged my perception of the laws of economics.

In Kenya, Mr. H. Mule, Permanent Secretary for Finance and Planning, Mr. F. Masakhalia, former Permanent Secretary for Planning, and Professor T. Ryan, Director for Planning, all showed interest in the study and allowed access to data sources. This was greatly facilitated by the open attitude of Mr. Singh and Mr. Agunda, past and present Directors of the Central Bureau of Statistics, and their staff, who have always been extremely helpful. Comments received from Mr. Wasonga of the Ministry of Finance and Planning on an earlier draft of this book have also been most helpful. Leopold Mureithi, of the

Faculty of Economics at the Univerity of Nairobi, also shared his ideas with me, and many fruitful observations were made at a staff seminar on the proposed work.

Arne Bigsten, Paul Collier and Jan Gunning have shared their research findings with me and made various comments upon earlier parts of the work, for which I am grateful.

Irma Adelman and Ole Norbye commented upon the first version. Their observations on the inherent mechanisms of basic needs and societal development was a stimulus for further work.

Erik Thorbecke and Mohendra Shah have always been helpful in discussions and sharing their work with me.

At the ILO, I owe special gratitude to Richard Anker for discussing his model with me, for allowing some of his source material to be used, and for giving, together with Vali Jamal and Michael Hopkins, a critical reading to an earlier version of this manuscript which helped to improve the final text. A special "thank you" is due to R. Scott Moreland, as my first steps in the modelling field were done with his Bachue-International model. Some parts of the demographic subsystem in this model system still bear a resemblance to his work. Kristina Boudjenane and later Eric Zbinden gave me advice and provided a helping hand with the many intricacies of programming large-scale models.

Mary Dominguez, Jane Barrett and Christine Alfthan deserve a special tribute for making my illegible scribble readable to the outsider, and for always remaining good-humoured when I tried to take advantage of ever-increasing word processing facilities. Caroline Hartnell took great care in editing the manuscript.

But most of all, I am grateful in this undertaking to Jan Vandemoortele, who provided tremendous support for this work, and was often a perfect trait d'union between day-to-day life in Kenya and the ivory tower in Geneva. Without some of his background studies this work would be greatly deficient.

An earlier version of this basic needs model was presented at an ODI/IDRC seminar on "Stabilisation policies and income distribution", held in Nairobi, Kenya, in 1984, to an Arab and International Meeting on Modelling for Development Planning held in Rabat, Morocco, in April 1985, and to the Seminar on "A socio-economic framework for basic needs planning" held in Lucknow, India, in August 1985. Participants on these occasions made valuable suggestions.

Last, but by no means least, I would like to thank Harold Banguero, Effie Gutkind and Michael Hopkins for the many discussions we had on basic needs modelling and for the seemingly endless arguments as to how reality could best be represented in formulae in their models as well as in this one.

However, none of them is (or presumably would like to be held)
responsible for the outcome of this work.

About the structure of this book

The purpose of this book is to investigate whether basic needs policies will be effective both in the short and in the long run and how the outcome of basic needs policies relate over the long run to other policies, by looking in detail at interaction between economic and social aspects of development. In order to do so, a basic needs simulation model is constructed and applied to the situation in Kenya.

This book is divided into three parts. Part I provides an introduction to the development of the concept of basic needs, its critics, and how ideas concerning policies for basic needs should be translated into a model. Part I ends with a short description of the characteristics of the Kenyan economy and some aspects of basic needs satisfaction.

Part II discusses in detail the various components of the model and describes how the parameters of the model have been derived. The last chapter in Part II describes how the results of the model are presented within the framework of a social accounting matrix. This part of the book is also intended to provide modellers and basic needs analysts with building blocks for their work.

Part III describes the outcome of the modelling exercise. It discusses the base run trend of the model, aspects of validation, and some experiments with policies aimed at increasing or decreasing basic needs satisfaction. The influence of the external situation is also discussed. The final chapter of Part III evaluates the various scenario experiments comparatively and provides a general conclusion to the work.

Six appendices discuss some more technical aspects of parameter estimation in further detail.

PART I
INTRODUCTION

1 Development of the concept of basic needs and various criticisms

1.1 Introduction

A presentation of the development of the concept of basic needs can perhaps best be organised around three types of development strategy which were respectively introduced in the mid–1960s, in the early 1970s and in the mid–1970s – a growth strategy, an employment and anti-poverty strategy and basic needs strategies. It is around these that discussions on development issues have centred.

The growth strategy emphasised the development of the (capital–intensive) modern sector as a principal vehicle of development. This modern sector also required a relatively high degree of skill formation on the part of the workforce. Justifications for the growth strategy were based upon a number of premises. One of the most important was perhaps the observation that this strategy had brought earlier industrialised market economies to their present welfare levels. A further justification was that although poverty alleviation should, of course, be a matter of concern for governments, the best vehicle for poverty alleviation was a redistribution of income increases resulting from growth. It was also thought that in the long run better results could be achieved by growth strategies through rapidly building up capital stock and infrastructure; perhaps not immediately but certainly later on the poor would benefit more from such strategies.

PLANNING FOR BASIC NEEDS

This intertemporal concept of development was often supported by reference to the work of Kuznets (1963), who investigated the development of income inequality over time by looking at the historical process in some European countries and by making comparisons between countries (both developing and industrialised) with different GDP levels. Income distribution in Europe had become more unequal during the growth process in the nineteenth century, but became gradually more equal in the middle of the twentieth century. Among developing countries Kuznets found that both low-income and high-income countries had less income inequality than medium-income countries.

A theory which was often cited in support of the growth hypothesis was Lewis's theory of the labour surplus economy (Lewis, 1954; but see Lewis, 1979, for a retrospective look). The principal characteristic of the labour surplus economy (see also Fei and Ranis, 1964, 1966; Jorgensen, 1961) was that, given the existence of surplus labour in the rural and artisanal sector, labour would move from rural to urban areas, where slightly above subsistence wages were paid; the urban areas would develop by investing surpluses from the rural areas and from the urban areas themselves. Once sufficient absorption from rural areas had taken place wages and incomes in the labour surplus sector (which would no longer be a labour surplus sector at that point in time) would rise and a broader interaction between the two sectors of the economy would take place.

For the process to work at a relatively fast rate, however, a number of pre-conditions would have to be met which were absent in reality. Streeten (1981) summarises some findings of the literature on the theory of the labour surplus economy and groups them around four elements. First of all, the differences between urban and rural incomes were much greater than the labour surplus theory presupposed. Colonial heritage, trade union influence and skills related to a higher level of technology often caused higher income differentials and resulted in faster migration than predicted and so prevented rapid absorption of the labour force (Harris and Todaro, 1970). Low standards of living in the rural areas acted as a further push factor. Migrants were often among the better educated, thus depriving the rural areas of trained manpower. To what extent this is a positive or negative factor does depend on the relationships migrants maintain with their rural hinterland. Return flows of incomes and return of migrants themselves are shown by Collier and Lal (1984) to have a positive impact on rural development.

Second, the capacity expansion in modern industries often took place with imported, labour-saving technologies. This

4

also prevented absorption of the labour force, while the nature of the technology often tended to create large wage differentials between skilled or managerial workers on the one hand and unskilled workers on the other (Bhalla, 1975).

Third, and perhaps most important, the breakthrough in agricultural technology and productivity (either through investments and/or through land redistribution) benefiting the entire agricultural sector, which had occurred in some more successful countries, had been lacking in most countries (Adelman, 1984).

Finally, population growth was more rapid than in any comparative situation in the development of Western Europe, making the creation of gainful employment for those entering the labour market extremely difficult.

Dissatisfaction with the employment-creating and distributional record of the growth strategy, together with research findings that many pre-conditions for this strategy were in fact lacking, resulted in increasing attention to other strategies. A first reaction was the so-called employment strategy, which emphasised programmes to increase employment in the modern sector. This often involved investigating institutional constraints and biases in the choice of technologies. However, given the small size of the modern sector, attention quickly shifted to include problems in the urban informal sectors and the rural sectors. But a major conceptual difficulty arises in analysing problems in the informal and rural sectors, which is that the concept of employment is unclear or undefined in these sectors. Productivity or income per head proved a much better yardstick. Hence attention shifted from a pure employment strategy to an anti-poverty strategy, which would affect a much larger part of the population. Such a strategy should incorporate many more programmes for small-scale rural households, for rural infrastructural works and for redistribution of land, as in many cases productivity on small plots proved to be higher than on large holdings. Furthermore, programmes were added to improve incomes in the urban informal sector. In order to make labour more productive in all sectors such programmes also emphasised basic schooling and simple vocational training. Inequalities in the modern sector were to be tackled through redistributive fiscal measures.

Well-known examples of anti-poverty strategies are to be found in the 1972 report of the ILO to the Government of Kenya (ILO, 1972), and the joint study by the University of Sussex and the World Bank on redistribution and growth (Chenery et al., 1974).

One disadvantage of the anti-poverty strategy was that

attention was predominantly given to incomes, which often resulted in an overemphasis on the demand side as compared to the supply side. Indeed, research showed that improved income distribution would not automatically result in increased access to basic needs such as education, health and water supply. Examining the relationship between basic needs indicators and other variables, including income level and income inequality, for a sample of developing and developed countries, Sheehan and Hopkins (1979) did not find income or income distribution to be important for most indicators. By separating low-income and middle-income countries and using simple correlation coefficients Leipziger and Lewis (1980) show that in low-income developing countries income level is more important than an equal distribution of income for improving basic needs performance, while income distribution seems more important in middle-income developing countries. Ram (1985) uses a more recent and better data base for low- and middle-income countries than the above studies, but reaches similar conclusions, namely that while income level seems to be important in both low-income and middle-income developing countries, the only factor significantly affected by more equal income distribution appears to be protein and calorie intake in middle-income countries, and even this relation appears to be less significant than was found by Leipziger and Lewis (1980).

It thus appears that more equal income distribution does not guarantee increased satisfaction of basic needs. This does not mean that income redistribution is not in itself a good thing. But additional policies and structural changes are necessary if increased satisfaction of basic needs is to be assured.

Furthermore, most analysis is carried out in terms of country averages as regards basic needs satisfaction, as comparative data on access of different social groups within countries are lacking. Although it is uncertain to what extent inclusion of such data would affect the conclusions, it is important that the different position of the various socio-economic groups should be taken into account.

A second disadvantage of an anti-poverty strategy was that some quite important and essential elements in the well-being of a household were left out, i.e. those that are usually provided partly or completely outside the market mechanism (education, health, water supply, housing). These factors resulted in growing attention to basic needs strategies.

Strategies are used in the plural here as there is more than one strategy for arriving at stated basic needs objectives. Following Hopkins and van der Hoeven (1983) and Stewart (1985), a distinction is made between basic needs strategies and a basic needs approach. We speak of a basic needs approach when the objective of the policy or policies is to satisfy basic needs within a (reasonably short) finite planning horizon. This can be arrived at through different types of development strategy. A basic needs approach is thus concerned with the objectives of a development process while precise policy instruments used to arrive at this objective are part of a particular strategy. However, as we will see later, a number of policy instruments lend themselves almost without exception for inclusion in a basic needs approach.

The document of the 1976 World Conference on Employment, Income Distribution and Social Progress and the International Division of Labour, Employment, growth and basic needs: A one world problem, is often cited as the first complete treatment of the subject (ILO, 1976). However, although the World Employment Conference and the Conference document triggered off widely held debates, especially within the various fora and bodies of the United Nations, ideas for planning for basic needs were already current.[1] Two examples of applications of certain elements of basic needs policies which date from before the World Employment Conference (one from India and one from a global world model) will now be discussed as they can be shown to have particular relevance to the interpretation of the concept.

1.2 Some examples of an early application of a basic needs approach

India was the first country to make the satisfaction of minimum (or basic) needs a focus of its plans. The "minimum standards of living" or the "minimum needs" approach first emerged in the early 1960s. An Indian Perspective Planning Division (PPD) document emphasised the concepts of absolute poverty and a minimum income level. This was in direct contrast to the implicit way of including relative levels of poverty in the Indian First and Second Plans. At the same time, the PPD document showed awareness of the limitations of the approach, stating that "redistribution on this scale is operationally meaningless, unless revolutionary changes in property rights and the structure of wages and compensation are contemplated" (Srinivasan and Bardhan, 1974).

It is in the draft of the Indian Fifth Plan that the theme of the elimination of poverty and the achievement of a minimum level of living first appear as central goals. In this document it was maintained that if "one has to rely on growth alone without directly tackling the problems of unemployment and income distribution, it may take another 30 years or 50 years for the poorest sections of the people to reach a minimum consumption level" (Government of India, 1972, p. 1).

In the Fifth Plan itself, poverty objectives take on clearer dimensions. The National Minimum Needs Programme explicitly sets out eight elements of basic needs, although there is no indication as to which should be given priority.[2] However, implicit assumptions of the National Minimum Needs Programme are:

(a) that combining of the most essential social services into a whole would be more viable than treating them separately;

(b) that the physical convergence of facilities at growth centres would lead to a reversal of the trend of "over-urbanisation"; and

(c) that levels of income that remained low, despite increases in the overall rate of growth, would have to be supplemented (Baji, 1975).

The Revised Minimum Needs Programme of the Sixth Plan[3] differs from the Fifth Plan's Minimum Needs Programme only in terms of norms; the eight items of basic needs are the same.

Conceptually, two approaches are possible with the minimum needs concept in a finite planning horizon. One is to estimate a minimum income (or, rather, consumption) target adequate to meet minimum needs (a poverty line) and then calculate how much inequality in incomes needs to be reduced by the end of the planning period in order that, given average income and consumption levels, even the poorest groups can achieve the minimum targeted consumption levels. Alternatively, given the minimum targeted consumption and unchanged income distribution, a required average national consumption level can be derived and planned for so that even the average consumption of the poorest groups is sufficient to satisfy basic needs. The former approach assumes some redistribution of income but the latter does not. The Fifth Plan chose the first approach, even though an earlier document prepared by the Planning Commission (Srinivasan and Bardhan, 1974) was based on the second approach. The Sixth Plan took a mixed approach.

The final version of the Sixth Plan (Government of India, Planning Commission, 1980) discussed two main scenarios for poverty alleviation. The first would reduce poverty solely through growth in aggregate income. The second would take specific measures to emphasise both growth and reductions in income inequality in order to meet the minimum needs consumption target. In this scenario it was calculated that the percentage of persons below the poverty line would drop to 30 per cent (instead of 38.9 per cent in the first scenario) by 1984-85. Estimates for consumption expenditure and sectoral outlays are, therefore, based on two sets of assumptions, namely one of unchanged inequality and one of a reduction in inequality.

Another early application of a basic needs approach can be found in the work of the group of scholars in Bariloche, Argentina (Herrera et al., 1976). This work was undertaken as a response to the well-known earlier publication of Meadows et al. (1972), carried out for the Club of Rome. The Bariloche report rejected the mechanistic way Meadows projected the world's future and argued that the most important problems facing society are not of a physical but of a socio-political nature. These problems are rooted in an unequal distribution of power between nations as well as within nations.

The Bariloche group showed that, in the near future, the environment and natural resources will not present absolute physical limitations to arriving at such a society. This was done with a mathematical optimisation model which had as its objective function the satisfaction of basic needs,[4] rather than the usual indicator of gross domestic product.

Having examined various options with the model the group emphasised the following points:

(1) Models which predict future catastrophes in the world take into account in only a limited way the fact that most people in the world already live in a catastrophic situation.

(2) Developing countries cannot develop themselves simply by copying the development path of the developed countries.

(3) The wasteful exploitation of natural resources and the destruction of the environment result largely from consumption by developed countries and by privileged minorities.

(4) Policies to protect the environment, including a decrease in the consumption of natural resources, will be difficult to realise on a world-wide scale in a situation in which not everybody has attained an adequate standard of living.

(5) The more privileged groups, especially those in developed countries, should restrain their economic growth in order to lessen the pressure on natural resources and the environment.

An important element of such a viable new world order, according to the Bariloche group, is an egalitarian society, both nationally and internationally. The fundamental principle is that every human being, by virtue of his very existence, has an unchallengeable right to satisfy his basic needs – nutrition, housing, health, education. Such a society would not be a consumer society, but a society where production is determined by social needs[5] rather than profit.

1.3 Interpretation of basic needs policies

These two examples of a basic needs approach show that basic needs policies can be interpreted from various angles. In the Bariloche model satisfaction of basic needs is seen as a development goal of society replacing traditional goals. It can be interpreted as a yardstick against which maximisation of the gross domestic product can be measured. This implies at a global level a redistribution from the wealthy North to the poorer South as well as a redistribution at a national level from rich to poor. There is also an emphasis on moving away from a consumer society towards one where production is geared to needs.[6]

The approach in the Indian planning models was much more pragmatic. Here a so-called poverty line was calculated, and an extrapolation of growth with constant income distribution showed the percentage of the population below the poverty line at a given target date. This percentage could be lowered either through higher growth or through reducing income inequality, or through a combination of both. However, as Rudra (1978) stated:

> It has treated the minimum private consumption part of the strategy too much in terms of expenditure and paid too little attention to individual commodities in qualitative and quantitative terms ... It boils down to a sequence of calculations all starting from the key figure of a minimum per capita private consumption target.

Alagh added that:

> the redistribution targets of the plan are set on a priori grounds, and explicit links with regional investment, output generation and employment strategies do not exist. Thus poverty removal on basic needs-oriented planning remains in a virtual cul-de-sac. There are programmes but since major basic needs, like food, clothing and shelter would remain largely a by-product of income and employment generation aspects of the economy and only the public

'basic needs' like education and health are largely
amenable to programme foci, this aspect of Indian
planning needs considerable attention. (Alagh et al.,
1984).

1.4 Elements of a basic needs approach

Some important elements of a basic needs approach are the
identification of and the specific attention for target groups
in the planning process, the use of corrective measures by the
government (through asset or through factor reward redistribution) if the development process does not reach the target
groups sufficiently, and the use of the government budget to
deliver non-marketable needs to the target and other groups.
Another important element is that of participation of all
members of the society, not only in formulating targets for
themselves but also in finding creative solutions as to how to
reach these targets.

An essential aspect of the basic needs approach is target
setting. This involves various questions: first, the question
as to which needs have to be considered as basic needs, and
second the question of who decides which needs are included in
the basic needs bundle. Furthermore, needs have to be
translated into norms, which evokes a further question as to
what kind of norms should be chosen. All this is largely
country- and culture-specific; most questions should be
answered by the communities concerned in collaboration with
planners and experts. In order to measure progress indicators
– and more specifically indicators specifying needs satisfaction for the different socio-economic groups – have to be
chosen and calculated. Broadly speaking, we can distinguish
between input indicators (for example, the number of nurses
per 1,000 people) and output indicators (such as life
expectancy at birth). The aim is, of course, to improve the
latter indicators, while the former can be a useful guide as
to policy changes.

For those needs that are satisfied largely through private
expenditure a target income level could also be specified.
However, one should take care not to concentrate on incomes
only, for reasons discussed earlier, and to avoid problems
labelled in the beginning of this century in the United
Kingdom as secondary poverty, where poverty – especially
inadequate nutritional intake – prevailed among large groups
of households, despite receiving an income equal to or above
that of the official poverty line.

The whole process of determining elements, targets and
indicators is country-specific; it can be considered an
important part of the basic needs approach in so far as the

planning process emphasises the social and distributional aspects more than usually occurs in the traditional growth strategies.

When designing a basic needs approach it is important that the specific consequences of policies relating to the income and consumption levels of the various socio-economic groups are made explicit. Shortfalls for the various socio-economic groups can be overcome through different forms of policies such as:

(a) explicit growth policies, if it is certain that growth will trickle down;

(b) policies redistributing either income-earning assets or incomes or both; and

(c) provision of a certain number of services and goods to all or to certain target groups, not only by providing goods and services free, but also by subsidising goods or giving certain users preferential price treatment.

In the literature much debate has taken place as to what can be "properly" labelled basic needs strategies. We have already indicated that one should rather speak of an approach, and that different policies and strategies - as, for example, those briefly spelled out above - can be part of a basic needs approach provided that they result in a rapid increase in needs satisfaction, either through improved incomes or through publicly provided goods and services, and have the twin aim of improving not only the material well-being of the most deprived but also their place in society.

In this debate two mainstreams of thought concerning the basic needs approach can be distinguished, as has already been indicated in section 1.3. The first is based on the idea that redistributive efforts on the part of the government could neutralise the absence of a trickling down mechanism. Consequently, the redistributive effects of government programmes, fiscal policies and income transfers are emphasised and seen as sufficient.

The other stream of thought sees the problem of people not meeting their basic needs as more of a structural problem. Because of imbalances in the social and economic systems, certain groups do not receive an equal share of the fruits of development (Griffin and Khan, 1978). Although not opposed to the ideas of the first stream, the second sees "basic needs" more as an organising concept around which to analyse present and alternative structures of development (Standing and Szal, 1979). As one author says, "The 'basic needs' approach has therefore to be treated as an approach for social reorganisation around a core of quantitative economic targets, and not to be regarded as an approach towards arriving at these targets" (Rudra, 1978, p. 68).

1.5 Criticisms of the basic needs approach

Criticisms of the basic needs approach have often been raised. They usually belong to one or other of the following categories:

1. Attention to basic needs is retarding growth. Even if attention to basic needs is fruitful in the short term it will lead to decreased growth which will ultimately lead to worse results. The retardation in growth, according to critics, is caused by:

    (a) too much social expenditure (on education, health, water, etc.), which reduces savings and investments, with negative effects on growth;
    (b) redistribution of incomes and assets towards poorer groups, which increases consumption and decreases investment, resulting in lower economic growth.

2. A basic needs approach is nothing new and lacks analytical rigour.

3. A basic needs approach leaves out class analysis and underestimates political changes.

4. A basic needs approach leads to more state influence and reduces the flexibility in the economic system that is necessary to achieve high growth rates.

5. A basic needs approach will keep developing countries at a low level of technological development and impede the establishment of a new international economic order.

The question of the effects of social expenditure on growth is older than the basic needs debate; one line of investigation has been in terms of the human capital approach. Generally, the effects of education have been seen as most significant. However, Correa (1970), Galenson and Pyatt (1964) and Oshima (1967) have all demonstrated the importance of social investment in dwellings, health and nutrition as well as education for developing countries. Of more recent date is the work of Ram and Schultz (1979), which found that a 1 per cent drop in morbidity in India results in an 0.3 per cent increase in labour productivity.

The question of provision of basic needs versus economic growth has been examined mainly by means of cross-country analysis. The first study was that of Sheehan and Hopkins (1979), who used multiple regression and factor analysis for developed and developing countries jointly to study relations between basic needs, demographic phenomena, growth and income distribution aspects, and the interaction between them. The relation was mainly studied by considering the rate of economic growth and income distribution as explanatory variables. Their main conclusion was that neither income distribution nor economic growth had much impact on basic needs indicators (the exceptions being life expectancy, calorie consumption, and the number of doctors). One of the explanations for this lack of impact was that in most cases the absolute level of per capita GDP provided good explanatory power.

In order to eliminate the impact of the absolute level of per capita GDP on basic needs performance Stewart (1985), using a data set for developing countries, first regressed certain basic needs indicators on per capita income and then analysed the characteristics of countries below and above the regression line, called by Stewart "poor" and "good" performances. She notes the absence of a particular association with economic growth – although among middle-income countries poor basic needs performers had below average growth rates – and states that:

> there is no evidence for any conflict with economic growth. This is supported by the evidence on the investment ratio with no association between basic needs performance and investment ratio among middle-income countries and a positive association for low-income countries where in 1960 poor performers had below average investment ratios and in 1979 good performers had above average investment ratios. (Stewart, 1985, p. 97).

A relationship between growth and provision of basic needs may exist, in both directions, with growth and level of income influencing provision of basic needs and vice versa. In the above paragraphs we discussed mainly the first aspect, but especially in the light of our simulation modelling exercise we are equally interested in the second aspect.

Hicks (1979) tried to answer the question of whether basic needs satisfaction affects growth by regressing economic growth rates on a large number of variables, taking a sample of non-oil developing countries. He found that both schooling

14

and life expectancy were influencing per capita growth positively. In the case of life expectancy, collinearity between GDP and life expectancy is removed by "normalising" life expectancy, i.e. by investigating whether deviations in life expectancy that are unexplained by income levels are affecting growth. (This is basically the same method as applied by Stewart.) Hicks argues, however, that a positive finding may still not bring us to reject the possibility of a negative relation between basic needs expenditure and growth, as the formulation of the regression equation does not indicate to what extent growth was sacrificed during the period that basic needs were being improved. He therefore included in the regression not only the actual level of basic needs satisfaction but also its increment. If improving basic needs was growth-inhibiting, the latter would be expected to have a negative effect. But in this case, too, Hicks found a positive correlation. He also carried out a second test to see whether the investment rate would be negatively influenced by higher levels and higher increases of basic needs performance. Again this was not the case.

In all the examples given above, the issue has been investigated through ordinary regression analysis, although the authors were aware of the two-way relationships between basic needs performance and economic growth. Wheeler (1984) has rightly argued that a system of simultaneous equations might provide more answers, adding that the patchiness of the data has often prevented such an approach. Based upon an extended data set, Wheeler has developed a simple simultaneous four-equation model, relating the variables: output, nutrition, education and health.

The variables are mainly in percentage changes and the main equation is that of output growth which is determined by a Cobb-Douglas function with capital, labour and labour-augmenting technical progress as a function of health, nutrition and education.

Percentage increases in capital are proxied by investment and GDP data, on the assumption of a constant capital-output ratio. Percentage increases in labour are proxied by the stock and increase in the adult population. Percentage increases in nutrition are explained by the percentage increase and the absolute level of per capita income. Increases in literacy[7] also depend on per capita growth, while increases in health (life expectancy) depend on increases in output per capita, education, nutrition and a stock variable for medical personnel.

Unlike Hicks (1979) and also unlike Wheeler (1980), Wheeler (1984) did not find that life expectancy as a measure of health had a consistent impact on output growth. The health variable was consequently dropped from the system.[8] The results of the model exercise, which is carried out for 1960-70, 1970-77, and for a pooling of the two sets, indicate that basic nutrition and education do make a positive contribution to the explanation of output growth when changes in the basic factors of production (capital and labour) and simultaneity are taken into account. A 1 per cent increase in nutrition leads to a 0.6-1.0 per cent increase in growth, while a point increase[9] in adult literacy rates leads to a 0.01 per cent increase in growth.

Wheeler furthermore checked his results for regional outliers, for which he found no evidence. He also introduced export activities as a possible explanation for increased efficiency in handling resources[10] by adding to the production equation variables indicating the growth rate of manufacturing exports and the growth rate of imports. The growth rate of exports is fully endogenised in the model. The new specification, however, does not call into question the role of literacy, while the role of health remains limited.

The long-standing discussion of the effects of education has been reviewed by Psacharopoulos (1984), who argues that recent research substantially enlarges and reinforces the earlier evidence relating to the contribution of education to economic growth. Yet Streeten, in a paper on unsettled questions regarding basic needs, still calls for more research, as the evidence on the contribution of investment in human capital to economic growth is not always conclusive. Regarding the macro studies (such as Wheeler's), he questions the causality in econometric relationships between growth and investment in human capital. Micro studies can be inconclusive because investment in human capital may perhaps be a success for one group at the expense of another group. He argues, therefore, in favour of a combination of econometric (macro) and micro studies (Streeten, 1984).

The alleged adverse consequences of income and asset redistribution on growth have been investigated by various authors. The allegation is often based upon the observation found in the literature (for example Paukert, 1973) that cross-section data on income inequality, at different stages of development, tend to reveal greater inequality in the less developed countries than in the developed countries, and among the less developed countries less inequality in the very poorest countries than in the less poor ones.

It would, however, be erroneous to conclude that developing countries in their process of development will necessarily follow the pattern of change that can be inferred from cross-section analysis. Fields (1980) argues:

The evidence does show the highest relative inequality in the group of lower-middle income countries than elsewhere. However, this pattern is far from inevitable. Concerning the inevitability issue we should note how little of the variance in relative inequality is explained by income level. ... Further empirical research has shown that inter-country variations in inequality are systematically related to structural differences in the countries' economies (pp. 70-71).

Adelman (1978) suggests that inequality during the development process can be avoided by early asset redistribution, assets being redistributed before they become truly scarce in the development process, rather than trying to reverse the income inequality resulting from unequal asset distribution through income redistribution, which takes longer, as the experience of the present industrialised countries has shown. Assets to be redistributed are in the first instance land, and at a later stage education, as successful experience in China and the Republic of Korea has shown.

The second set of criticisms of a basic needs approach states that it is nothing new and lacks analytical rigour. We indicated earlier that the basic needs approach arose as a logical successor to other development approaches, as a result of the often unsatisfactory outcomes of development efforts aimed at poverty alleviation. It is true that many elements of the basic needs approach are not new; what is new is the emphasis on distributional aspects and the focusing of attention on the poorest groups (Ghai, 1978). This set of criticisms is thus based on the erroneous assumption that something like a single, definitive basic needs strategy exists, which we already rejected above. In fact work has been and is being undertaken (the present study also contributes to this) in order to test various strategies as regards their objective of fulfilling basic needs targets.

A third criticism of a basic needs approach is that it gives an impression that alleviating poverty is easy, and that important political and class analysis is left out. From the foregoing it may be clear that an increasing focus on poverty is not the same as solving all poverty problems. What some initial basic needs calculations have shown is that given existing resources and incomes an increase in basic needs satisfaction is possible, provided structural changes take place (see, for example, the discussion on the Bariloche model). This in no way nullifies the existence of political problems, and these have to be taken into account. In fact the basic needs approach has underlined the importance of political and social problems - to the extent that another set of criticisms even argues that, in the words of Streeten (1981), "the basic needs approach is used as the Trojan horse of communism".

A fourth criticism is that basic needs policies lead to more state influence. This is perhaps best expressed by Lal (1983). Lal's criticism of basic needs policies, as well as of other poverty-focused policies, is based on what he calls the Dirigiste Dogma - which is the preoccupation development practitioners have with various forms of government control to promote economic development. Lal sees those who support basic needs policies as proponents of the Dirigiste Dogma. His basic argument is that the basic needs philosophy gives equal importance to growth and redistribution, and values, although often implicitly, slow growers/good distributors above fast growers/bad distributors. According to Lal the last group should receive more attention, as they will ultimately provide better conditions for all the different strata of the population. Lal reproaches the basic needs propagandists with having paid too much attention to dirigiste regimes such as Sri Lanka and the United Republic of Tanzania.

His criticism is to be taken seriously, as basic needs policies certainly have sometimes given more weight to distribution and welfare policies than to economic growth. However, basic needs policies do not try to dismiss growth as something secondary; rather they place growth in the context of a social welfare function, which includes not only income but other aspects of quality of life, distinguished for different socio-economic groups. The way to achieve growth and redistribution depends very much on the social structure of the country. Taiwan (China) and especially the Republic of Korea, are quoted by Lal as success stories both in terms of growth and in terms of quality of life. However, both Taiwan (China) and the Republic of Korea undertook far-reaching programmes of land redistribution and increases in education during the 1950s and 1960s. These, together with a rather dirigiste investment policy, laid the basis for fast growth at a later stage, which was fairly equally distributed as the productive assets on which growth was based had been distributed at an earlier stage (Adelman, 1978).

The fifth set of criticisms relates to the idea that basic needs policies by emphasising attention to the poorest groups and by stimulating asset redistribution, will, in effect, condemn countries to backward technologies and hamper modern sector development. Although a basic needs approach would indeed put more emphasis on redistribution and poverty alleviation, it has been argued that "it would surely be unwise not to use the modern sector as a creator of income to be channelled, much more than hitherto, to the urban informal and rural traditional sectors. Highly sophisticated industries can be stimulated not to create employment, but to create more income, which through taxation can be channelled into the sectors of the economy which are labour intensive" (Emmerij, 1978, p. 36).

That increased attention to poverty will delay the establishment of a new international economic order is, as explained by various authors, a question of semantics used in political debate. Basic needs policies should not replace or delay the establishment of a new international economic order, but on the contrary contribute to it. This was the clear message from the work of the Bariloche group (Herrera et al., 1976), as discussed in section 1.2. The World Employment Conference document (ILO, 1976) was sub-titled "A one-world problem", and a large part of it was devoted to discussing international strategies (trade, international division of labour, transfer of technology and the role of multinational enterprises). According to Streeten, increased attention to basic needs would help foster increased self-reliance among developing countries (Streeten, 1982). What critics who make this criticism usually have in mind is that donor agencies in developed countries, through attaching conditions to development aid, reduce independent policy formulation in developing countries, and are also able to avoid important discussions on and necessary changes in global trade and financial flows. This, however, has little to do with the concept of basic needs strategies itself but more with the attitude of developed countries towards development issues.

1.6 Conclusions

In the previous paragraphs we have indicated why a basic needs approach was a logical reaction to earlier development strategies. Earlier strategies had excluded explicit attention and targeting for the poorer groups in a society, or had included them only as regards income, ignoring the non-monetary aspects of real living standards (such as adequate education and access to health, water and housing). Earlier strategies had also failed to acknowledge the need for all groups in society to participate in the formulation and implementation of the development process.

The basic needs approach was also a response to the fact that despite respectable rates of growth in developing countries a large number of people were still living below the poverty line, and that projections showed that unless specific measures were taken the number of poor would increase.

Despite wide-ranging criticism, partly based upon

misconceptions, a basic needs approach still appears to be highly relevant.

Since such an approach pays more attention to the supply side, it can even be argued that in the present world recession a basic needs approach is even more relevant than in the mid-1970s when it was launched, and can contribute to the process of adjustment to external shocks which so many developing countries are currently undergoing.

The contribution a basic needs approach can make to this adjustment process also makes it clear that a basic needs approach should be seen as an approach that fosters structural changes in the economy, and not simply as a ploy for increasing social expenditure by the government.

Questions regarding the consistency of policy instruments and physical and financial constraints nevertheless remain open. We try to answer some of these throughout this book.

Notes

[1] Because space is limited, this discussion does not take into account studies and reports which demanded that more attention should be given to the physical well-being, especially adequate nutritional levels, of workers and of the population as a whole. This is thoroughly reviewed by Rimmer (1981).

[2] India's National Minimum Needs Programme spelled out the objectives for the target group more specifically, namely:

    (i) Provision of facilities for elementary education for children up to the age of 14 years at the nearest possible places to their homes.

  (ii) Ensuring in all areas a minimum uniform availability of public health facilities which would include preventive medicines, nutrition and adequate arrangements for referring serious cases.

(iii) Ensuring a supply of drinking water to villages suffering from chronic scarcity or having unsafe sources of water.

 (iv) Provision of all-weather roads to all villages with a population of 1,500 persons or more.

  (v) Provision of developed home sites for landless labour in rural areas (100 sq. ft. per family).

 (vi) Environmental improvement of slums.

(vii) Spread of electrification to cover 30-40 per cent of the rural population.

(viii) Nutritional assistance to special groups. (Government of India, 1972, pp. 5-9.)

[3] What was called the Draft Sixth Five-Year Plan, 1978-83, is now superseded by the Sixth Five-Year Plan, 1980-85.

[4] More specifically, life expectancy at birth was maximised, as life expectancy is highly correlated to other socio-economic variables.

[5] The report acknowledges that it is difficult to determine social needs and that these needs differ over time and according to new developments in culture, social organisation and technology.

[6] This was also the approach from which the development of the basic needs concept in the ILO started in the preparations for the World Employment Conference (see Hopkins and Scolnik, 1976).

[7] Since some countries have made tremendous progress in literacy rates, Wheeler does not use percentage changes in literacy rates, as the results would be completely biased towards a few countries which have, starting from a low base, steeply increasing literacy rates. He uses instead absolute differences in literacy rates and has specified the literacy change equation accordingly by measuring the marginal effect of per capita income growth on literacy as well as the actual effect of schooling of the age cohort which passes to adulthood in each period.

[8] Wheeler (1984) ascribes the positive outcome of his 1980 results to the addition of data for the end of the 1970s, but does not provide a proper explanation for the divergence from his earlier results.

[9] See footnote 7, explaining why absolute increases, rather than percentage increases, are used.

[10] But note his qualification in the earlier model that all resources are used at a constant level of efficiency as long as the capital-output ratio and labour force participation rate remain constant.

2 Some remarks on modelling basic needs and an overview of the Kenya basic needs model

Basic needs policies, as discussed in the previous chapter, involve giving particular attention to the poorer groups in society. These policies, briefly recalled, aim first to improve the income position of such groups through increases in productivity, through improving their access to income-earning assets, and through redistribution of incomes; the second aim is to provide increased access to essential public services such as education, health and water supply. The interaction between such policies and their effects on the various groups in society - leaving aside the complementary need for social reorganisation and structural change in many societies in order to make such policies operative - strongly suggest a general modelling approach to basic needs.

What kind of properties should a basic needs model have? This depends very much, of course, on the questions one tries to answer with the model. We will first discuss the questions which a model dealing with basic needs should answer, and then provide a brief description of the Kenya basic needs model.

2.1 Questions to be answered by a basic needs model

One important question is whether a trade-off exists between economic growth and provision for basic needs (Streeten, 1979); equally important is whether the trade-off is large or small. If it is fairly small, and if societal time preference is influenced more by the time preference of the poor, the trade-off could be seen more as an issue of varying time preferences than as a "pure macro question" (see Ahluwalia and Chenery, 1974; Stewart and Streeten, 1971). The need to deal with this question imposes certain characteristics on the model. It needs to be a long-term model in order fully to evaluate the trade-off. It must also distinguish between the various groups in a society in order to assess the poverty level and shortfall in basic needs satisfaction of the various groups - not only as an end in itself, but also to provide a distinct impulse for the behaviour of these groups and the functioning of the economy.

As many basic needs items have to be provided by the State, the expenditure patterns of the public authorities have to be included in the model. And it is not only the pattern and magnitude of government expenditure that is important; equally important are the way expenditure is financed and the consequences of changes in various tax rates on other variables which drive the economy, such as investment, private consumption, etc.

One of the alleged reasons for the need to think in terms of some sort of trade-off between basic needs policies and economic growth is that basic needs policies are more consumption-oriented and thus result in lower savings and investment. However, as elegantly shown by Quibria (1982) in a Ramsey-type optimal savings analysis, increased consumption may increase labour productivity. Certain elements of basic needs expenditure may be seen as investment in human capital, which contributes to economic growth as discussed in the previous chapter. Basic needs policies may also change the structure of production and as a consequence lower the capital-output ratio. When the economy is on a path of steady growth, this will in turn lower the rate of savings and investment needed to stay at the same rate of growth. The model should thus be able to deal with investible surpluses in the economy, and be explicit about savings-investment relationships as well as investment behaviour.

The external sector is also important - first of all to answer the question whether basic needs policies increase or decrease the need for foreign exchange, in case foreign exchange is a binding constraint. Certain advocates of the basic needs approach argue that basic needs-type activities actually lessen the need for imports (Ghai, 1980). However, a system of food distribution, without concomitant food production, may increase the need for foreign exchange. The model thus needs to be explicit as to how a possible deficit on the current account will be financed and what the consequences are of such financing on the long-term debt situation. In certain cases it may be important to make explicit the effects of increased aid flows, financing a part of the current account deficit, on investment behaviour.

As indicated above, structural changes should be taken into account. The model should, therefore, not only distinguish between various economic sectors. In most developing countries, urban-rural differences are marked (Lipton, 1978), and the split between urban and rural areas helps to explain poverty and relative deprivation and can also shed light on structural change. Another aspect of structural change is the variation in the composition and size of the socio-economic groups over time.

A basic needs model should, furthermore, capture the major characteristics of the economies of less developed countries. One such element is the difference in production structure between agriculture, industry and services; there is also a distinction between large-scale and small-scale activities within those sectors.[1]

A second element, as we mentioned earlier, is the existence of a range of socio-economic groups, partly characterised according to the sectoral and size-of-operation distinctions indicated above. Such groups have different consumption behaviour which should be reflected in the model. The composition and size of groups can change rapidly over time or might be static, depending on different social and economic conditions. It is thus important to capture not only the size and behavioural patterns of groups, but also the degree of mobility between them.

A third element is what we will, for the moment, label as structural rigidities in the economy; these prevent economies from behaving according to the textbook rules. Prices are often administered and production factors cannot move freely, so that a neo-classical equilibrium mechanism functions very poorly. Explanations for such disequilibria range from inefficiency (which is the consequence of low development levels and cannot be assumed away) to manipulation by the dominant classes (often through the State) in order to set product and factor prices and access to assets to their own advantage (Griffin and Khan, 1978). Nugent and Yotopoulos (1978) go as far as to state that existing "equilibrating mechanisms" can work, in a system of permanent disequilibrium, to the disadvantage of informal sector activities, and that special programmes for the poorer groups involved in such activities are called for.

But disequilibrium is not only a consequence of the organisation of a society. A transitory state from present economic management towards more basic needs-oriented policies can cause significant disequilibria in the economy. Signals from supply and demand sides may not react to each other in such a case (Griffin and James, 1979). Ignoring the existence of such disequilibria and the failure of policy measures to cope with them may well result in a return to the original system, rather than leading to the desired changes.

The question of disequilibrium is therefore important for the construction of a basic needs model. A model formulated on assumptions of continuous equilibrium and smoothly operating rules to overcome imminent disequilibria might well result in denying problems of continuous inadequate functioning of markets, market segmentation, and of poverty and lack of basic needs satisfaction. Taylor and Lysy (1979), for example, stress the political and economic considerations involved in choosing closure mechanisms for a model, and Rattsö (1982) equally stresses the importance of choosing the appropriate closure mechanism.

A further requirement of a basic needs model is, therefore, that it takes into account aspects of disequilibrium on various markets. However, for modelling purposes we need to distinguish between the ex ante disequilibrium on various markets which have to be resolved in the economic process at the end of the time period, and the consequences of the removal of these disequilibria on economic agents and the functioning of the economy. Since markets function inadequately in most developing countries it is therefore appropriate in a basic needs model to arrive at equilibrium within a time period by quantity adjustment, keeping in mind that existence of such intra-temporal disequilibria influence the behaviour of agents in future time periods. The mechanism for arriving at equilibrium on product and factor markets within one time period can best be described as a "convergency" mechanism, while the effects of these ex ante disequilibria on economic agents form an integral part of the dynamic aspects of the model.

The related term "adjustment" can then be reserved to describe the process in which the economy is coping with untenable deficits and shortages of foreign exchange, caused either by internal policy measures or by external shocks, and is trying to adjust to the changed circumstances.[2] This process will take place over time. The length of the adjustment period depends on the policy options chosen, and the source of the initial current account deficit. Demand contraction will often reduce current account deficits quickly. Unfortunately, this is often at the cost of reducing economic growth and decreasing living standards. Expansion of supply – especially supply of exportables – and replacement of imports could provide the necessary adjustment over time without jeopardising real income levels. Expansionary policies are not always feasible, however, as sustained or increased capital inflows (to stretch the financing of the

current account deficit, and indispensable to bridge the gap
before expansionary policies become effective) are not always
available.

The combination of contraction in demand and expansion of
supply will, therefore, cause deviations from a steady growth
path. In fact, if external circumstances and domestic policy
measures change too frequently steady growth may never be
attained. This process of adjustment should also be reflected
in a realistic model.

Besides analysing basic needs and macro-economic
development, the model should also be able to capture the
consequences of some more detailed micro-economic policies.
The Kenyan Fourth Development Plan (1979-83) (Republic of
Kenya, 1979) gives an overview of objectives and policy
instruments (table 2.1), which can be used as a useful
check-list for the construction of a model, although the
inclusion of all policy instruments mentioned in table 2.1 may
still be a distant goal rather than a practical guideline.

2.2 A brief overview of some macro
models applied in Kenya

There is no dearth of economy-wide models in Kenya. In
this section we discuss two recent general equilibrium models
applied to Kenya and two other macro-economic models, one
belonging to the Bachue group of economic-demographic models
(Anker and Knowles, 1983) and Gunning's general equilibrium
model (Gunning, 1979). Certain aspects of the latter models
have influenced the construction of our own model.

Dick et al. (1983) used a general equilibrium model to
test the short-run impact of fluctuating primary commodity
prices (the model they developed is not only used for Kenya,
but also for Colombia and the Côte d'Ivoire). Their model
belongs to the family of static general equilibrium models
(see also Dervis et al., 1982). For Kenya it contains 11
sectors of production and three production factors (labour,
land and capital). The GDP deflator is set as numeraire;
other prices in the model include prices for factors of
production, products, inputs and exports. Producers are
assumed to minimise costs with nested production functions
which express first the possibility of substitution between
imported and domestic goods, second the inseparability of
inputs and production factors, and third the substitution
between factors of production. Households maximise their
utility from a bundle of imported and domestically produced
goods subject to a budget constraint. Government demands for
commodities are simply linked to demand for aggregate
consumption. Commodity export demands are a function of

PLANNING FOR BASIC NEEDS

Table 2.1. Summary table of employment policies and instruments, Fourth Development Plan (1979-83)

Employment category	Objectives	Policy instruments and institutional framework
Modern sector	Alter relative cost of labour Produce appropriate manpower in sufficient numbers	Wages policy Trade policy Fiscal policy Education and training policies Kenyanisation policies Pricing policy Employment services
Small-scale agriculture	Raise income levels Increase labour productivity	Agricultural intensification Agricultural extension services and training Rural development policy Land policy Pricing and marketing policies Provision of basic needs
Pastoralists	Raise income levels Increase livestock numbers and quality	Pricing and marketing policies Development of arid and semi-arid areas Provision of basic needs
Rural non-farm	Increase productivity Increase labour absorption Produce some of the privately consumed basic needs goods	Rural development policy Appropriate training, e.g. the village polytechnic Review the existing legislation on rural non-farm activities and remove or amend those sections that are unnecessarily inhibitive Provide credit extension services and other support
Urban informal sector	Generate more employment Produce goods and services for low-income groups Produce skilled workers Increase productivity	Remove restriction on informal sector activities Provide basic infrastructure including the necessary support services

Source. Republic of Kenya: Development Plan 1979-1983 (1979), p. 39.

shifts in the world demand curve facing a particular export commodity together with the world export price.

The solution of this system of optimisation problems yields a system of commodity-demand equations for current production, household consumption and investment and a system of factor demand equations. Competing price behaviour is imposed by equations relating prices to costs for current production, capital creation, importing and exporting.

The model by Dick et al. (1983) is, however, a short-term model and contains no changes in behavioural equations. Since it is overdetermined, the model is closed by solving a number of variables exogenously. Capital and land, as well as the nominal wage rate, are set exogenously. Two different options are possible in the closure of the last variable, related to the resource gap. The first option is that, since total output is determined endogenously and is by definition equal to income, the resource gap should be arrived at by setting the balance of payments gap exogenously and determining domestic absorption endogenously. The second option is that total absorption should be set exogenously (through government policies not explicitly modelled) and consequently the balance of payments gap determined endogenously.

The main purpose of this model is to investigate, under the two different closure assumptions described above, the consequences of an increase in export prices on domestic prices, domestic output, labour demand, and exports and imports.

Although the model developed by Dick et al. does pay attention to the foreign resource constraint, which as discussed above could be impeding the implementation of basic needs policies, it is clear from the above description that for the purpose of our modelling work this model falls short on a number of grounds. First, it does not make a distinction between the various socio-economic groups; second, it is not dynamic. Furthermore, government expenditure is simply linked to aggregate domestic consumption. Another difficulty is the role of price-clearing mechanisms, which do not seem to take into account any rigidities in price formation – a common feature in developing countries, as we discussed earlier.

Gupta and Togan (1984) developed a similar model to look at the consequences of terms of trade shocks and slowdowns in export demand for semi-industrialised countries, populous low-income Asian countries and primary producing countries. For the latter group, stylised factors from Kenya are taken. Unlike the model discussed above, it contains three different homogeneous income classes (farmers, non-agricultural labour and capitalists). Farmers receive the land and labour income in the agricultural sector, and capitalists receive all capital income including that from agriculture. The number of sectors is, however, reduced to four: agriculture, consumer goods, other industry and services. The possible occurrence of two rigidities is recognised in this model, namely keeping the price of foreign exchange fixed or not (and applying foreign exchange rationing in the first case) and keeping the real wage fixed or not (and hence restricting demand for labour in the first case).

While this second model does include a distinction between the various different groups in society, and pays attention to some rigidities, it is still not dynamic and also the treatment of the public sector is rudimentary.

To treat the questions surrounding basic needs policies we need much more disaggregation in the model, which furthermore needs to be dynamic and to include a number of institutional factors representative of the economy of the country. We will now discuss two models which have incorporated these elements.

The Bachue-Kenya model developed by Anker and Knowles (1983) is an economic-demographic simulation model with a long-run time perspective (10-30 years). Since it is a complicated model, no short description could do full justice to it. As the authors maintain, it can be considered to be part of a comprehensive country study approach to understanding economic-demographic relationships in Kenya. In-depth partial analyses of economic-demographic relationships in Kenya based on individual, household and district-level data (e.g. for fertility, mortality, migration, agricultural production, income transfers and female labour force participation) were done in order to increase knowledge on these relationships as well as provide a solid empirical base for the behavioural relationships in the Bachue-Kenya model. The model, in turn, provides a more complete picture of the full effects of changes in government policies and of different development paths on the population, on the economy, on employment and on income distribution. Bachue-Kenya consists of two parts, an economic part and a demographic part. The demographic part is modelled in great detail; it contains a large number of behavioural relations of the determinants of demographic variables (distinguished between urban and rural areas). As will become apparent, we have made use of these in-depth analyses and some of the relations developed for the Bachue-Kenya model are incorporated in the demographic subsystem of our own model. The economic sector of the Bachue-Kenya model basically determines output, demand and employment by sector of the economy and the degree of income distribution. A great many linkages exist between the economic and the demographic subsystems which give rise to feed-back effects from variables in one system to variables in the other.

The Bachue-Kenya model belongs to the category of simulation models which are solved recursively rather than to the category of general equilibrium models, and allows for the inclusion of a large number of structural factors. Earlier simulation models of this kind (see Rodgers et al., 1978) were demand-driven, i.e. final demand components were determined either recursively or exogenously with an exogenously imposed supply constraint on GDP growth. In the Bachue-Kenya model the level of agricultural exports/imports is sensitive to the balance between agricultural production and domestic consumption of agricultural goods, and the foreign exchange balance in turn constrains the overall rate of growth of the Kenyan economy.

A major difference between the Bachue-Kenya model and the Kenya basic needs model is in the size and detail of the demographic section, which is reduced in the Kenya basic needs model, and in the expanded economic section of the latter. In the Kenya basic needs model, income is distributed according to socio-economic groups in urban and rural areas (which became possible through the availability of new data) rather than to income deciles in urban and rural areas. Also, investment and government expenditure are treated endogenously in the Kenya basic needs model affecting, amongst others, the basic needs and the demographic subsystems. The endogenous treatment of investment and public expenditure in the Kenya basic needs model reflects endogenous constraints on capital formation and government expenditure, which must be included if the model is to capture simulation effects in savings and government expenditure aimed at providing basic needs.

As a consequence the Kenya basic needs model contains a formalised closing mechanism to reflect imbalances in the foreign exchange market, the product market and the capital market, and is able to equalise the savings-investment and the foreign exchange gap.

A formalised closing mechanism is also an element of the Kenya model developed by Gunning, of which a first version is presented in Gunning (1979) but which is still being experimented with. Gunning's model includes the main elements of a general equilibrium model (utility maximisation determines consumption; output in agriculture and in manufacturing is given by profit maximisation, and prices are related to excess demand), but it also has a number of non-neoclassical features to the effect that (a) some product prices, notably food prices, are controlled, in which case markets are cleared through quantity adjustment, (b) wages are not market-clearing, and (c) the distribution of land is fixed and rural financial markets are imperfect.

It is, furthermore, fairly disaggregated in a number of

sectors (using an input-output table), in agricultural products and in socio-economic groups (eight groups of urban households and 48 groups of smallholders).

The non-economic sector of the Gunning model is, however, rudimentary. Population growth is exogenous as are the educational endowments of urban households (no such distinction is made for rural households) and public consumption. Although the fact that these elements were exogenous did not matter for simulations with Gunning's model, which did not exceed a period of ten years, it would be of importance for the basic needs model.

The main question was, therefore, whether we should apply for our analysis a general equilibrium model, of the type developed by Gunning or a more structural model, of the type developed by Anker and Knowles.

As will be seen from the discussion of the model in the next section, we have tried to capture aspects of both models. However, as we have not formally included prices in our model (although we do have elements of prices which proxy price effects, as will be discussed in detail in Chapter 9), the basic needs model could be regarded more as a structuralist model than as a general equilibrium model.

2.3 Introduction to the Kenya basic needs model

The purpose of the Kenya basic needs model is to assess a reciprocal relationship between economic growth and social progress under various external conditions. This is done through tracking over time the effects of economic growth on levels of income and basic needs satisfaction among various socio-economic groups. A further purpose is to assess how macro variables like economic growth, investment and savings are affected by basic needs and income distribution policies as opposed to more traditional growth policies.

The following section provides a short description of the model. The various subsystems of the model are described in detail in Part II.

The Kenya basic needs model is a long-term simulation model belonging to the family of closed dynamic input-output models. It is a demand-driven model, where internal demand for investment and consumption is recursively determined, while external demand is exogenously determined. Demand-led growth can be constrained by growth of capacity of the economy, which is determined by investment, labour and technical progress, while supply-demand interactions affect certain variables in the model. The model runs over 25 time periods of one year.

Figure 2.1 provides an overview of the main relations in the model.

The model consists of seven subsystems:

1. a basic needs subsystem which provides an indication of the level of basic needs satisfaction of the various socio-economic groups; it also provides inputs into the other subsystems through changes in labour productivity and changes in consumption behaviour and by affecting demographic variables such as fertility rates and structure of the labour force;

2. a demographic subsystem which determines population growth and labour supply;

3. a supply subsystem which calculates, given the existing resources of the economy, possible supply on all markets of goods and services as well as on factor markets;

4. a demand subsystem which provides internal and external demand on all product markets;

5. an equilibrium subsystem which, through various convergency mechanisms, determines equilibrium on the foreign exchange market, the product markets and the factor markets, and provides the national accounts which are presented in the form of a social accounting matrix;

6. a foreign exchange subsystem which keeps track of foreign assets, debts and repayments;

7. an income distribution subsystem which allocates the various components of value added to the different socio-economic groups and which keeps track of income levels and poverty in each of the various socio-economic groups.

It contains 14 sectors:

1. small-scale agriculture [AGTRAD];
2. large-scale agriculture [AGRMOD];
3. mining [MINING];
4. food manufacturing [MANFOOD];
5. non-food manufacturing [MANNONF];
6. modern building and construction [BUCOMOD];
7. traditional building and construction [BUCOTRAD];
8. transport and communications [TRANSP];
9. modern trade [TRAMOD];

10. traditional trade and services [TRASETRA];
11. modern services [SERMOD];
12. general government services (excluding 13) [GOVPUADM];
13. government services relating to education and health [GOVEDHE];
14. ownership of dwellings [OWNSDWEL].

Small-scale agriculture is further subdivided into three categories of holding with different sizes.

The model further distinguishes between eight different socio-economic groups:

1. peasant farmers (subdivided into three categories of holding);
2. agricultural workers, skilled;
3. agricultural workers, unskilled;
4. agricultural employers and professionals;
5. non-agricultural informal sector workers;
6. non-agricultural formal sector workers, skilled;
7. non-agricultural formal sector workers, unskilled;
8. non-agricultural formal sector employers and professionals.

The model is designed in such a way that experiments with domestic policies and with changes in the external economic environment can be carried out in the form of scenario analyses. Scenario experiments, by definition, cause shocks to the system, and it is important to see how the system copes with these shocks. This is what we have labelled "adjustment" in the model. (For an introduction to the scenario analysis, see Chapter 12.)

The following paragraphs give a brief description of the subsystems of the model.

The basic needs subsystem first tracks how much is spent on various basic needs expenditure categories and how much each of the socio-economic groups is benefiting from expenditure on basic needs. Then, based upon these so-called input indicators, the system calculates to what extent the basic needs of the various socio-economic groups, as well as of the country as a whole, are being met. There are five basic needs categories in the model: primary education, secondary education, health, other publicly provided basic needs (water and housing) and nutrition.

Basic needs satisfaction has various linkages in the model: it affects mortality, population growth, skill composition of the labour force, labour productivity, value added shares in gross output and private consumption behaviour.

The demographic subsystem calculates population by age,

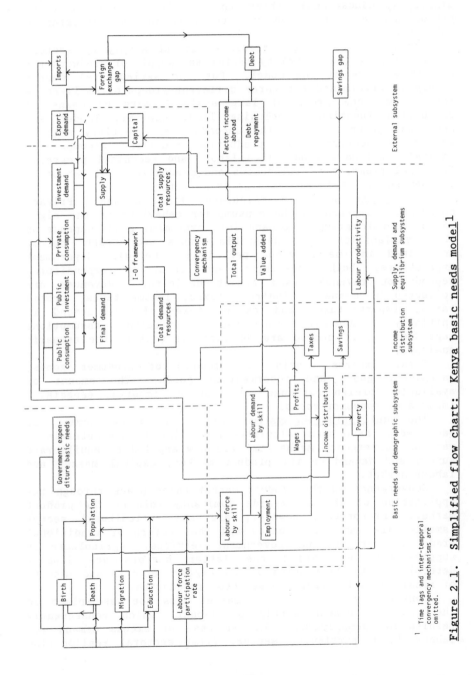

Figure 2.1. Simplified flow chart: Kenya basic needs model[1]

[1] Time lags and inter-temporal convergency mechanisms are omitted.

sex, location and educational status. Fertility, mortality, migration, educational achievement and labour force participation are all endogenously determined in the demographic subsystem.

The supply subsystem calculates labour supply by sector, capital supply (capacity) by sector and supply of products for the 14 sectors of the model. For the agricultural sector supply is determined for three different groups of small-scale farmers and one group of large-scale farmers by means of production functions, including land, capital, labour and technical progress. For the secondary and tertiary sectors supply is determined by production functions encompassing capital, skilled and unskilled labour and technical progress. Technical progress is autonomous and productivity of labour is influenced by levels of basic needs satisfaction.

The demand subsystem calculates final demand. Private consumption depends on the consumption behaviour of the eight socio-economic groups. Demand for investment goods depends on the availability of investible funds for each sector determined in the previous period (see below). Government expenditure, both investment and recurrent expenditure, depends on revenues (and budget deficits). Revenues are collected by means of indirect taxes, income taxes, profit taxes, import taxes and export taxes. Export demand is initially exogenously determined. Different assumptions regarding export demand are an integral part of the scenario analysis.

Total imports consist of imports of consumer goods, investment goods and intermediate goods. The amount of available foreign exchange may restrict imports, especially imports of consumer goods.

The equilibrium subsystem: After supply and demand for each sector have been calculated the model is overdetermined; various convergency mechanisms are now applied to equilibrate supply and demand on the product market, capital market and labour market.

Convergence on the product market takes place through the application of the short-side dominancy role of the product market. Exceptions, however, are the agricultural sector (small-scale and large-scale) and the sectors of traditional trade and services and government services. Agriculture is supply-determined, while the latter sectors are demand-determined. In the process of convergency exports and imports of final goods in tradeable sectors are adapted.

Convergency on the labour market does not take place in the case of excess supply of labour, which consequently results in unemployment. In the case of excess demand for labour in a particular sector, first sectoral reallocation takes place, after which shortage of labour will reduce capacity increase. Exogenous changes in wage differentials between skilled and unskilled labour as part of the scenario analysis influence the composition of labour demand.

Investment depends on the accelerator principle, i.e. the growth of sectoral output in the previous period. It also depends on whether excess demand or excess supply was prevailing in a particular sector in the previous period and on retained savings in the particular sector. Investments are restrained by the supply of investment funds. Supply of investment funds depends on household, public and business savings and on capital imports. The model allows for a savings gap, depending on a limit on external borrowing.

The foreign exchange subsystem determines first the maximum amount of allowable imports. If total demand for imports surpasses this maximum, imports of consumer goods are decreased. This may affect domestic final demand. This adjustment takes place before the convergency mechanism on the product market becomes operative.

The foreign exchange system also determines the final foreign exchange gap (which depends on imports net of tax, factor payments abroad, and exports) and the accumulation of debt (which depends on debt repayment and the foreign exchange gap).

Finally, the income distribution system calculates wages, profits, taxes and savings for all sectors.

The wage share for skilled and unskilled workers is determined behaviourally in the model. After the number of employed is determined, average wages for skilled and unskilled workers are calculated. Profits are partly paid out to entrepreneurs, partly sent abroad, and partly used to pay taxes, while the remainder is saved. After factor payments have been calculated, factor incomes (labour and profit incomes) are mapped on to socio-economic groups, for which transfers, taxes, expenditures and savings are also determined. Household savings for each group are determined residually as a difference between household disposable income and household expenditure.

The outcome of the equilibrium subsystem, the foreign exchange subsystem and the income distribution subsystem allows the calculation of the national accounts system and of the distribution over various socio-economic groups. This is presented in the form of a social accounting matrix.

The base year of the model is 1976, and most values of the model have been calibrated on 1976 figures, as explained in Chapters 4 to 11.

Although the model is expressed in constant 1976 prices there are "price"-influenced aspects in the model. Quantities adjusted in the convergency mechanism affect consumption and investment behaviour in the next period, thus capturing effects which are normally determined by prices. Furthermore, in the scenario analysis we allow changes in agricultural and non-agricultural terms of trade to affect incomes and production in the agricultural and non-agricultural sectors, while changes in the ratio of skilled to unskilled wages affect the composition of labour demand.

Notes

[1] The formal-informal distinction is also used, and is applied in the model. It should be mentioned, however, that although the issue of informal sector activities has been researched for quite some time (Sethuraman, 1981), the concept of informal activity still lacks clarity, comprising as it does, almost all activities which are for one reason or another not licensed - activities ranging from concrete small-scale undertakings, such as carpentry, etc., to petty trading and to activities which are on the fringe of being criminal. Discussion on the merits of the informal sector is usually confined to the first type of activity.

[2] We thank H.C. Bos and S.P. Gupta for this useful distinction.

3 An overview of Kenya's development since independence

This chapter discusses the main elements of Kenya's economic development in order to provide a background for the discussion in Parts II and III (for further discussion see, among others, Ghai et al., 1979; Hazlewood, 1979; Killick, 1981b). In the first part we deal with Kenya's attitude to development planning and highlight some aspects of the country's development. In the second part problems of income distribution and basic needs are treated in somewhat more depth.

3.1 Main characteristics of development planning

Kenya's overall economic growth in the first decade after independence was respectable. The annual rate of growth of GDP was 6.5 per cent between 1963 and 1972. However, the fruits of growth were not equally divided between all Kenyans alike. The 1972 ILO Employment Mission made the following observation:

> Since independence economic growth has largely continued on the lines set by the earlier colonial structure. Kenyanisation has radically changed the racial composition of the group of people in the centre of power and many of its policies, but has had only a limited effect on the mechanisms which maintain its dominance – the pattern of government income and expenditure, the freedom of foreign firms to locate their offices and plants in Nairobi, and

the narrow stratum of expenditure by a high-income elite superimposed on a base of limited mass consumption. (ILO, 1972, p. 11.)

The conclusions of this report influenced the Third Development Plan (1974-78), emphasising a change in approach that had already been noticeable between the First (1966-70) and Second Development Plan (1970-74). The First Development Plan focused strongly on a strategy to foster modern sector activities, which were supposed to have a greater potential for rapid growth than other sectoral activities. With the introduction of the Second Plan Kenyan policy-makers shifted the emphasis away from progress in a limited number of small sectors of the economy, resulting in income inequalities, to a more broadly based pattern of development. The strategy of the Second Plan aimed, through greater diversification of economic activities and services, to accelerate development in the rural areas.

The Third Development Plan (1974-78) recognised that "in spite of the rapid growth of the economy, in the first ten years of independence, the problems ... [of] unemployment and income disparities have become more apparent than they were in 1963". The Plan further acknowledged that "although the basic objectives (i.e. growth, employment, equity) remain unaltered, their relative importance has changed".

But it was not only the good intentions of the Government which changed the character of planning in Kenya. In the early phase of the Third Development Plan, Kenya suffered from the effects of the world economic recession and from rapid deflation. Indeed, the vulnerable character of Kenya's pattern of development, depending to a large extent on external forces, now became apparent. Kenya was forced to pursue more local, resource-based development policies. The world recession also affected Kenya's overall growth performance. GDP growth was still a comfortable 7 per cent in 1973, but in 1974 it was only 4 per cent and in 1975 less than 1 per cent. During the following two years Kenya was able to cash in on some benefits stemming from a combination of good weather conditions and a booming export market, despite the large increase in oil prices. GDP growth in 1976 was 5.6 per cent and in 1977 an almost record high of 8.8 per cent. But growth slowed down to 6.9 per cent in 1978, and in 1979 to a meagre 3.1 per cent. These growth rates have to be compared to a high rate of population growth which averaged, over the intercensal period 1969-79 about 3.4 per cent per annum (Republic of Kenya, CBS, Economic Survey, 1980).[1]

Drafted during the coffee boom of 1977, the Fourth Plan (1979-83) reflected the optimism which went with the boom. It was a well-written and well-argued document that stuck to the philosophy of the Third Plan, paying attention to diversification of industry and exports and proposing·policy packages to accelerate agricultural growth and improve smallholder living standards.

The Plan's growth target was ambitious. Overall GDP was to increase by 6.3 per cent per year, with agriculture growing at 4.7 per cent per year. Government revenues were supposed to grow by 7 per cent, while an export growth of 6 per cent would keep the current account deficit within manageable limits. The increased resource base was also to finance an important package of basic needs policies (discussed further in section 3.2, see also table 3.2).

Killick (1981a, p. 107) comments as follows upon the Fourth Plan:

> On the positive side the plan was shown to have made major advances in the definition of the economy's problems and of government objectives, although its omission of a strategy to reduce regional disparities is a major blemish ... Subject to qualifications to be mentioned in a moment the plan achieves an impressive degree of internal consistency in its policies and important advances in the adequacy of the policies. The major qualifications relate to an apparent inconsistency with respect to the urban-rural terms of trade and weaknesses in its treatment of the balance of payments. A rather strong and systematic tendency to over-optimism in its growth targets has been identified as an additional weakness, reducing the plan's claim to provide a superior data base for making investment and other decisions concerning the future. Its main defect, however, is its apparent inflexibility in a political-economy environment which is very prone to changes unforeseen when the plan was being prepared.

Actual developments were indeed very different. International terms of trade deteriorated because of higher oil prices and lower coffee prices. Unrest in neighbouring countries and recession in the industrialised world caused a decrease in demand for Kenyan products. Agricultural growth was negative in 1979 and 1980, leading to overall GDP growth rates of 4.2 and 3.3 per cent. The changes in circumstances were acknowledged by the Government in 1980, when it scaled down growth targets and development projects. As the 1983 World Bank country economic report indicates:

PLANNING FOR BASIC NEEDS

The effort to bring the fiscal and balance of payment situation under control, while quite successful, has had the inevitable adverse consequences for growth of incomes and employment since 1980. In addition, because of the preoccupation of policy-makers and administrative personnel with crisis management, growth and revitalising of agriculture, in order to ensure future growth with reasonable external balance, has been slow. (World Bank, 1983, p. 3.)

The Fifth Plan (1984-88) is therefore less optimistic, something which is already reflected in its main theme: "mobilising domestic resources for equitable development". The Plan recognises the slow increase in the resource base over the past years and sets as one of its main objectives a reduction of the debt-service/export ratio in order to maintain a constant level of imports in the future.

Kenya is a very open economy. In 1976, exports of goods and services equalled 32 per cent of GDP, while imports equalled 36 per cent. Although these ratios vary from year to year, mainly because of fluctuating prices on the world market of Kenya's major export products, the situation at the end of the 1970s was not much different from that in the early days of independence. In the decade 1960-70, exports of goods and non-factor services formed 30.9 per cent of total GDP and imports 30 per cent, while in the period 1970-77, the percentages were slightly higher, namely 32.1 and 34 per cent (World Bank, 1980a). Average figures for 1981-82 are 29 per cent and 36.5 per cent, reflecting the increasing trade deficit. The period 1983-84 saw a decrease in the import content of GDP. Average figures for exports and imports were 29.9 and 31.6 per cent respectively.

The structure of imports changed somewhat, however. Consumer goods (including food) dropped from 20 per cent of total imports in 1970 to 12 per cent in 1979 and 10 per cent in 1982, making room for an increase in fuels and lubricants (up from 9.4 per cent to 23.7 per cent, and 40.1 per cent in 1982 in value terms) and in machinery and other capital equipment (up from 14.7 to 20.2 per cent in 1979, but down to 16.7 per cent in 1982). These trends reflect partly a deliberate attempt to produce more goods locally and partly the increased receipts from refined oil exported to East African regions, as well as the large increase in imports of high priced energy.

Kenyan exports consist mainly of three products, coffee, tea and refined oil from the Mombasa refinery. The prices of the first two are subject to heavy fluctuations on the world market, while the value-added on the third product is fairly small. The structure of exports in value terms has not changed much over time.

The structure of its imports and exports makes Kenya's position rather vulnerable. Although imports of consumer goods have diminished because of import substitution, this has resulted in a greater dependence on inputs for the import substitution process, such as fuels, small machinery, etc. Kenya's exports, on the other hand, are still goods with a high price elasticity of demand (coffee and tea), from which the proceeds will be low as long as the world recession continues.

3.2 Income distribution and basic needs
    in Kenya's development process

Kenya ranks among the countries with the highest level of income inequality, with a Gini ratio in the range of 0.55 to 0.60. The poorest 40 per cent of the population receive only 9 per cent of the national income, while 60 per cent of the national income accrues to the richest 20 per cent, based on 1976 data. This degree of income inequality is similar in all provinces and most sectors. Within the rural sector, however, it appears that the inequality among smallholders is significantly less than among other rural households including large farmers, intermediate farmers, landless persons and pastoralists (Vandemoortele and van der Hoeven, 1982).

Although quite a lot of research has been carried out on changes in income inequality, the results are far from being unequivocal. The Government of Kenya, in its Fourth Development Plan, claims a relative decrease in inequality, stating that the share in the national income of the 25 per cent poorest increased from 4.1 per cent in 1969 to 7.2 per cent in 1976 (Republic of Kenya, 1979a, p. 5). An ILO study, however, rejects the conclusion of a decrease in income inequality, and suggests on the basis of some regional studies an increase in income inequality especially between urban and rural areas (Ghai et al., 1979). A World Bank study (Collier and Lal, 1980) is also inconclusive about changes in overall income inequality; it argues that while the urban-rural gap has declined, inequality within the rural areas has increased.

Jamal (1982) comes to the conclusion that in 1976 inequality was increasing; this is based upon a careful consideration of inequalities both between rural and urban areas and within urban and rural areas. He shows that an often used index, namely that of the ratio of per capita peasant income to per capita wage income, had decreased, partly because of falling real wages, but that inequality between smallholders and large farmers and between wage

43

earners and non-wage earners had increased, leading to an overall increase in income inequality. This tendency has probably continued since 1976: real wages have been decreasing since the end of the 1960s, with a noticeable drop between 1971 and 1975, followed by some increase in 1976, but not sufficient to bring wages up to the 1970 level. Real wages then remained fairly stable up to 1981, after which they dropped quite drastically to reach a 1984 level of 75 per cent of the 1970 level (Republic of Kenya, CBS, Economic Survey, various issues). Together with the non-exporting small-scale farmers, wage earners have been the group hardest hit during the last decade.

Recently, it has been argued that poverty has decreased substantially for the middle peasantry, not so much because of efficient allocation on rural factor markets but because of the complex interaction between rural factor markets and urban labour market participation which provided the middle peasantry with risk capital to undertake more innovative farming methods (Collier and Lal, 1984).

Indicators to measure progress in satisfying basic needs are difficult to obtain. In some instances, a national average would provide an insight, but in many cases national averages conceal the important issue of who exactly has benefited.

Table 3.1 provides some national indicators of basic needs in 1960, 1978 and 1982.

Below we give a short overview of progress made in some basic needs areas.

Nutrition: Based upon partial studies Ghai et al. (1979) have produced a profile of the nutritional problems of the most affected groups, which are food crop producers with an average household income below K.£50 per annum (1975 prices) and virtually no cash sales; the landless poor; cash crop producers with an average income below K.£125; the urban unemployed and underemployed, and the pastoralists. More information on regional disparities can be gained from a study by Crawford and Thorbecke (1978). Based upon a general poverty line of K.£110 and a food poverty line of K.£85 for the average household, they found, using 1976 data that 38.5 per cent of smallholders were below the poverty line and 35.8 per cent of those households below the food poverty line. There are, however, large provincial differentials, with the latter figure ranging from 14.5 per cent in Central Province to 42.3 per cent in Nyanza. Studies differ in opinion regarding urban poverty. Collier and Lal, for example, state that it has never been a serious problem (Collier and Lal, 1984). However, assuming a simple diet of maize and beans, Vandemoortele and van der Hoeven (1982) arrive at a figure of 15 per cent for urban poverty.

Table 3.1. Some indicators of basic needs: Kenya, 1960-82

	1960	1978	1982
Life expectancy at birth (years)	47	53	57
Child death rate (per cent)	25	14	13
Crude birth rate per thousand	55	55	55
Crude death rate per thousand	24	14	12
Population per physician	10 560	11 950	7 890[1]
Population per nursing person	2 230	1 120	550[1]
Number enrolled in primary school as % of age group	47	99	104[1]
Number enrolled in secondary school as % of age group	2	17	19
Adult literacy rate	20	40	n.a.
Per cent of population with access to safe drinking water	n.a.	17	n.a.
Per cent of labour force in agriculture	86	79	78

[1] 1981 figure. See note 2 at end of chapter.

n.a. = not available.

Source. World Bank: World Development Report, 1985 and previous years (Washington, DC).

Health: Information on health is hampered by the lack of any meaningful trends, apart from in-patient/out-patient ratios in some selected health institutions. A study by Anker and Knowles (1980) observed that life expectancy at birth is significantly lower in areas where disease is more prevalent, particularly Nyanza, Western Province and Central Province. The difficulties in collecting health statistics make it necessary to gain some impression by means of so-called "input" indicators, such as the number of health centres, dispensaries, doctors, nurses, midwives, etc. All of these show increases over the period 1969-79, but the distribution of health facilities remains regionally inequitable.

Vandemoortele (1983) calculated the variation coefficients of the distribution of hospital beds per province in 1970 and 1980 and concluded that the additional investments in health infrastructure had lowered the inter-provincial disparities but not dramatically or even significantly. Differences between health services in Nairobi and the rural areas remain high, while attention is still given predominantly to curative rather than preventive services, despite the dominance of environment-related diseases.

Education: Kenya has undoubtedly been successful in expanding the numbers enrolled in basic education. Primary school enrolment increased from 1 million in 1964 to over 3 million in 1979. However, there are considerable regional differences, both in quality of education and in access. Overall enrolment in 1977 was 86 per cent of children of primary school age,[2] but this rate varied from 102 per cent for Central and Western Provinces to 57 per cent for Coast and only 11 per cent for North-Eastern Province. Adult literacy programmes are still small-scale. The Integrated Rural Survey found that provinces with an advantage in primary school provision also scored well on adult literacy rates.

In his survey of basic needs performance, Vandemoortele (1983) shows that, regarding primary education, government policy is to decentralise financial responsibility to the local communities. This, however, prevented poor households and communities from benefiting equally.

Housing: Despite low rural housing standards housing appears to be more of an urban problem. The 1979–83 Development Plan admits that "approximately 35 per cent of all urban households exist in squatter settlements and slums". The main problem is the low income of tenants. According to actual income levels, 25 per cent of the urban population will not be able to afford even a serviced plot of acceptable standard. However, as shown by Vandemoortele (1983), housing programmes have rarely reached the poorer groups. Even the low-cost side and service schemes often turn into medium- and even high-cost housing schemes.

The Fourth Development Plan (1979–83) focuses on the alleviation of poverty and satisfaction of basic needs, stating that:

The objective of alleviating poverty will be pursued on four fronts: (1) the creation of income-earning opportunities; (2) the improvement of expenditure patterns; (3) the provision of other basic needs such as nutrition, health care, basic education, water and housing; and (4) institution building. (Republic of Kenya, 1979c, p. 11).

The Plan also contains a list of basic needs targets for the end of the planning period. This list is reproduced in table 3.2. Unfortunately, there is as yet little statistical material available to assess to what extent basic needs targets have been met.

The Fifth Development Plan (1984-88) is consequently less candid about future basic needs programmes. It stresses more the importance of the private sector in providing basic needs:

> The continuing rate of the extended family system has already been noted. Voluntary agencies and Harambe efforts provide significant supplementary services in health, education and training, family planning, etc. ... During this period of continuing financial austerity in the public sector, a greater share of the responsibility for providing basic needs to the people must be borne by the private sector and those who benefit from the services available. (Republic of Kenya, 1983, pp. 57-58.)

As basic needs targets are treated less explicitly, a table stating precise basic needs targets at the end of the planning period similar to the one in the Fourth Plan is lacking in the Fifth Plan.

Notes

[1] As will be discussed in Chapter 5 even this high population growth rate appears to be an underestimation. The Fifth Development Plan (1984-88) reports a population growth rate of 3.8 per cent per annum for the intercensal period and uses this growth rate for projections in the Plan.

[2] This figure differs from the figure given in table 3.1 because of different definition of the relevant age groups. Furthermore, since children older than the relevant age group attend primary school, enrolment figures can exceed 100 per cent.

Table 3.2. Basic needs targets, Fourth Development Plan (1979–83)

Target	1976	1983	Measurement
GDP at market prices	1 429	2 194	K.£ million 1976 6.3% growth rate.
GDP per capita	103.9	125.6	K.£ 1976
Inflation	16	6.8%	Annual rate, GDP
Population	13 752 000	17 470 000	Based on a 3.5% growth rate.
Population growth rate (%)	3.5	3.5	This may be slightly higher.
Crude birth rate	49.0	46.5	Births/1,000 population
Employment			
Modern sector	915 000	1 250 000	
Rural	4 045 000	5 140 000	
Urban informal	125 000	195 000	
Employment as percentage of labour force	5 085 000	6 585 000	
	90.6	92.2	
Education (1978–84)			
Rural literacy, 15+ population	65%M 31%F	100%M 100%F	Ability to read in any language.
Primary	3 135 000	3 825 000	Total enrolment.
Secondary (government aided)	133 000	157 000	Form I to VI includes vocational, agricultural, commercial.
Harambee Institute of Technology	1 007	3 859	
Harambee other than Institutes of Technology	190 799	233 000	Assisted and aided including church and private
Technical	6 480	8 424	
Polytechnic	3 282	4 185	
Special education	3 619	9 629	
University	6 250	8 900	
Health care			
Hospitals	64	70	Government hospitals – province and district.
Health institutions	761	806	Government hospitals, health centres and sub-centres, dispensaries.
Doctor density	10.3	11.9	Number per 100,000 population.
Registered and enrolled nurses density	95	110	
Access to health centres, rural (%)	11.0	12.0	Household less than 2 km distant.
Malaria	250 000	150 000	Number of cases.

Water[2]			
Rural holdings (per cent)	44	60	Holdings with water.
Rural access to water (per cent)	11	8	Over 2 km to water service.
Housing			
Rural[2] No. perm structure (%)	27.0	30.0	Dwellings with corrugated roof.
Dwellings with more than two rooms (%)	48.0	52.0	
Houses with electricity (%)	1.0	1.2	
Urban			
Number of units planned		13.6	Thousands per annum.
Number of plots serviced		5.6	Thousands per annum.
Food[3]			
Calories per capita	2 070	2 220	Per capita/day.
Protein grams	57	65.5	Per capita/day.
Mildly malnourished	30	22	Children aged 1-4 years.
Severely malnourished (%)	5	2.5	Children aged 1-4 years.
Rural impoverished (%)	40	33	Household income less than K.£120 (1975) per year.
Infrastructure			
Rural access to (%):			
Co-op store	18.0	21.0	Less than 2 km.
Market	38.0	47.0	Less than 2 km.
Duka	64.0	70.0	Less than 2 km.
Bus	46.0	51.0	Less than 2 km to public bus route.
Matatu	61.0	67.0	Less than 2 km.
School: primary	68.0	72.0	Less than 8 km.
secondary	54.0	60.0	Less than 8 km.
Telephone	(1978) 1.01	1.52	Per thousand population.
Security			
National Social Security Fund	1 028 000	1 333 000	Number employees registered.

1 This is a selection of targets and is not meant to be exhaustive.

2 Based on IRSII 1976-77 data. This survey covered rural smallholders and rural non-agricultural population which are estimed at 11.7 million or about 80 per cent of the total population.

3 Based on IRSI 1974-75. This survey covered rural smallholders and represents a population of about 10 million. Parts of the Rift Valley were somewhat underrepresented.

Source. Reprint of table 3.15 of Republic of Kenya: Development Plan 1979-1983, Part I, pp. 104-105.

PART II
DETAILED DESCRIPTION
OF THE MODEL

4 The basic needs subsystem

We start the discussion of the various parts of the model with a discussion of the basic needs subsystem in the model.

The basic needs subsystem performs various functions. It calculates first how much is spent on each of the basic needs categories and how much each of the socio-economic groups is benefiting from expenditure on basic needs. These are the so-called input indicators. Then, based upon the various input indicators, it calculates to what extent the basic needs of the various socio-economic groups, as well as of the country as a whole, are being met. This is done through the so-called output indicators of basic needs.[1] The major linkages within the basic needs and demographic subsystem as well as of these systems with the other subsystems in the model are indicated in figure 4.1.

The effects of the basic needs subsystem and the demographic subsystem (see Chapter 5) on the other parts of the model are discussed in Chapter 6.

In the model we distinguish between five basic needs categories, namely primary education, secondary education, health, other publicly provided basic needs and nutrition. The first four categories are mainly, but, as we will discuss, not exclusively, provided through public services while the latter is provided through private consumption.

53

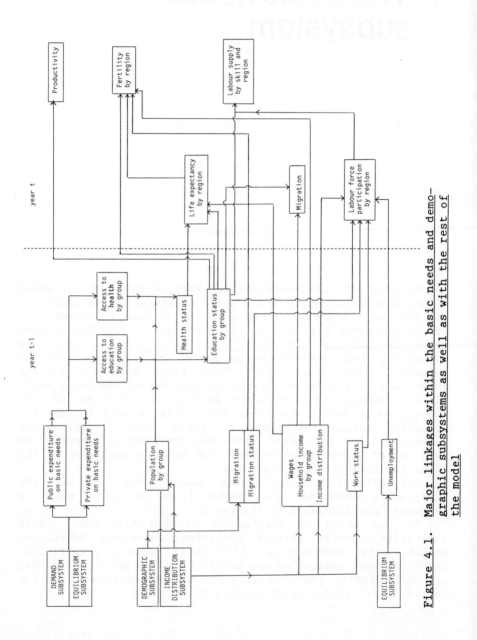

Figure 4.1. Major linkages within the basic needs and demographic subsystems as well as with the rest of the model

4.1 Input indicators

Publicly provided basic needs

In the model, as we have seen, we distinguish between four different basic needs public expenditure categories: primary education, secondary education, health and other basic needs (water and housing). Since the economic system of the model has two categories of government expenditure – namely government expenditure on education and health and other government expenditure – we have first to relate the four basic needs expenditure categories to the two government expenditure categories of the economic system (see section 8.3 on "Government expenditure and revenue"). This takes place through fixed proportions, which are based upon actual base year (1976) expenditure shares but which can (and will) be changed as part of policy scenarios.

For the year 1976 and for the base run values we have:

$$GCBN(1) = 0.504 \ GC(13) \qquad GIBN(1) = 0.01 \ GI(13) \qquad [1]$$
$$GCBN(2) = 0.113 \ GC(13) \qquad GIBN(2) = 0.17 \ GI(13) \qquad [2]$$
$$GCBN(3) = 0.219 \ GC(13) \qquad GIBN(3) = 0.62 \ GI(13) \qquad [3]$$
$$GCBN(4) = 0.050 \ GC(12) \qquad GIBN(4) = 0.05 \ GI(12) \qquad [4]$$

where

GCBN(1)	=	recurrent expenditure on primary education
GIBN(1)	=	capital expenditure on primary education
GCBN(2)	=	recurrent expenditure on secondary education
GIBN(2)	=	capital expenditure on secondary education
GCBN(3)	=	recurrent expenditure on health
GIBN(3)	=	capital expenditure on health
GCBN(4)	=	recurrent expenditure on other basic needs
GIBN(4)	=	capital expenditure on other basic needs
GC(13)	=	public recurrent expenditure on health and education
GC(12)	=	public recurrent expenditure on general government services
GI(13)	=	public investment expenditure on health and education
GI(12)	=	public investment expenditure on general government services

Public expenditure on primary education, secondary education and health form part of government expenditure in model sector 13 (public expenditure on health and education). Since this sector comprises more expenditure items than the three basic needs items, the coefficients do not add up to 1.

Public expenditure on other basic needs categories forms part of government expenditure in model sector 12 (other government expenditure). Since public expenditure on housing is limited we have restricted ourselves to including only expenditure on water under this category.

However, not all socio-economic groups profit equally from publicly provided services. Jimenez (1986) even argues:

> The public sector in developing countries has traditionally played an important role in the financing of educational and health services. This review finds, however, that the share of public subsidies in these two sectors is not progressive, that is, proportionally higher for individuals in the higher socio-economic groups. (p. 127)

Reasons for a regressive delivery pattern are often the heavy subsidy on secondary and tertiary education, which often benefits higher income groups disproportionally and the large allocations to curative health systems in urban areas to the detriment of much cheaper preventive health systems in rural areas. In Chapter 3 we showed that such was indeed the case in Kenya.

We thus have to model explicitly the fact that access to basic needs items is not proportional for each socio-economic group. We introduce, therefore, a matrix $B(g,h)$, which distributes government expenditure on basic needs item h to group g:

$$GCBN(g,h) = B(g,h) \; GCBN \, (h) \qquad\qquad [5]$$
$$h = 1,\ldots,4$$
$$GIBN(g,h) = B(g,h) \; GIBN \, (h) \qquad g = 1,\ldots,8 \qquad [6]$$

$$[B] = [P]*[G] \qquad\qquad [7]$$

The matrix B is a policy variable, consisting of a multiplication of two matrices P(t) and G. The matrix P(t) represents the relevant population share of each socio-economic group in year t, while the matrix G represents bias in allocation of basic needs expenditure.[2] For health and other basic needs (basic needs sectors 3 and 4) the columns of the matrix P represent population shares for all ages, while for primary and secondary education (basic needs sectors 1 and 2) school age population is taken. When policies are completely egalitarian G should be set at unit value. However, for socio-economic groups which receive a proportionally lower share of basic needs expenditure g, the element $B(g,h)$ has a value lower than 1, while for a group receiving a disproportionally high share the value is above 1. The matrix G for the base year 1976, representing inequality coefficients by socio-economic group and by expenditure category, is presented in table 4.1.

As can be seen from table 4.1, peasant farmers (group 1) and unskilled agricultural workers (group 3) receive less than their proportional share of all basic needs items, while within the urban areas informal sector and unskilled formal sector workers (groups 5 and 7) have a lower allocation than other urban groups.

Privately provided basic needs

Basic needs are not, however, satisfied through public expenditure alone. Private expenditure and consumption also contribute to basic needs satisfaction. Nutrition is exclusively a matter of private expenditure, but households also spend money on other basic needs categories.

Private consumption influences calorie intake. Calorie intake could be reflected in the model through a relation between household income and calorie consumption. However, as Crawford and Thorbecke (1981), and Greer and Thorbecke (1986), among others, have shown, it is rather difficult to establish a proper relationship between household expenditure and calorie intake as diets among groups with the same income level differ considerably, both because of different tastes and because different food products are available. It is even questionable whether such a relationship is well behaved. Households in higher income brackets may even consume food products with a lower nutritional level, as these goods provide more status (Kaplinsky, 1980b).

For the above reasons the Kenya basic needs model adopts another approach, based upon a normative assumption about food expenditure and calorie intake. The cost of obtaining a nutritionally adequate diet is assessed, for urban and rural households. These values then determine the required basic needs food expenditure levels. Making use of food expenditure shares one can then calculate so-called basic needs expenditure levels and basic needs income levels required to satisfy the basic food intake level. Knowing the expenditure and income distribution between as well as within socio-economic groups, one can assess the percentage shortfall in basic needs expenditure for each group as well as for the country as a whole (and indirectly also the amount of food deficits). (These mechanisms and the base year values are discussed in section 11.6 on the "Determination of poverty".)

Another private expenditure item that weighs heavily on the household budget is education, and to a lesser extent health.

Table 4.1. Inequality coefficient of public basic needs expenditure on socio-economic groups, 1976

Socio-economic group	Basic needs sector			
	Primary education	Secondary education	Health	Other basic needs
1. Peasant farmer	0.86	0.66	0.15	0.29
2. Agricultural workers, skilled	1.06	1.18	0.76	0.52
3. Agricultural workers, unskilled	0.94	0.88	0.58	0.32
4. Agricultural employers and professionals	1.60	1.64	0.97	0.67
5. Informal sector workers	0.97	0.83	0.63	0.48
6. Non-agricultural workers, skilled	1.29	2.19	1.68	1.52
7. Non-agricultural workers, unskilled	1.00	1.00	1.00	1.00
8. Non-agricultural employers and professionals	1.29	3.03	2.30	1.52

Note. Inequality coefficients are for each year normed so that the sum of the product of the coefficient and the relevant population share of each socio-economic group adds up to 1.

58

Since enrolment rates for secondary education were very low in the early 1970s, the Government has actively supported the so-called "Harambee" movements which aim to provide secondary schools through the financial participation of the community, with some government support to cover the costs of teachers' salaries. The Social Accounting Matrix of 1976 reports a total of K.£10.065 million for private expenditure on education. We still have to determine how much of this amount is allocated to primary and how much to secondary education. In the model we have assumed that there is no private expenditure on primary education, although this is not strictly true, since parents often make considerable contributions to school maintenance funds, etc. The costs are small, however, compared with costs for secondary education. A study of education expenses (World Bank, 1985) indicates that in unaided secondary education 80 per cent of the recurrent costs are borne by the parents. Furthermore, it states that 57 per cent of pupils attending secondary school go to an unaided school. With a recurrent cost of K.£74 per student per year and a total enrolment rate of 283,777 pupils in 1976, this would amount to a total of K.£9.575 million for private expenditure on secondary education. Although this is lower than total private expenditure on education in the national accounts, it does not leave much room for expenditure on other education categories. Given the enormous expenditure on secondary education we have used for the base year value of private secondary education expenditure the estimate of K.£9.575 million.

As to expenditure on health, the national accounts and the input-output table report a total of K.£5.160 million for private expenditure on health in 1976, which has been retained in the model.

Private expenditure on other basic needs, restricted, as mentioned above, to expenditure on water amenities, is neither reported in budget surveys nor in national accounts. For the purpose of this model we have assumed an annual cost for users in urban and rural areas of 25 per cent of the recurrent cost of the water schemes, which amounts to K.£4.642 million for the country as a whole.

Consumption surveys give us some indication as to how private expenditure on basic needs is distributed over the socio-economic groups. Table 8.1 in Chapter 8 gives expenditure by the various socio-economic groups on products and services from the various sectors. Government services are split into education and health (sector 13) and other government services (sector 12). According to this table total private expenditure on education and health consisted of K.£15.15 million in 1976, of which, as calculated above,

K.£9.575 million is attributed to secondary education – 63 per cent of this expenditure category. Private expenditure on health, totalling K.£5.160 million, constituted about 34 per cent. Private expenditure on water supply, totalling K.£1.160 million, as explained above, represents 25 per cent of private expenditure on services other than education and health.

$$PCBN(g,1) = 0.0 \qquad [8]$$

$$PCBN(g,2) = 0.63 \; PC_{13,g} \qquad [9]$$

$$PCBN(g,3) = 0.34 \; PC_{13,g} \qquad [10]$$

$$PCBN(g,4) = 0.25 \; PC_{12,g} \qquad [11]$$

with

$$PCBN(1) = 0 \qquad [12]$$

$$PCBN(h) = \sum_{g=1}^{8} PCBN(g,h) \qquad h = 2,4 \qquad [13]$$

where

$PCBN(g,h)$	=	private expenditure of socio-economic group g on basic needs item h
$PCBN(1)$	=	total private expenditure on primary education
$PCBN(2)$	=	total private expenditure on secondary education
$PCBN(3)$	=	total private expenditure on health
$PCBN(4)$	=	total private expenditure on water
$PC_{13,g}$	=	expenditure of socio-economic group g on education and health
$PC_{12,g}$	=	expenditure of socio-economic group g on other public services

4.2 Output indicators

The previous section discussed government and private expenditure on basic needs (and the distribution of the former among the various socio-economic groups). Indicators reflecting expenditure on basic needs were labelled input indicators. In this section we discuss how the input indicators affect the so-called output indicators of basic needs (as discussed in section 1.4) and the shortfall of each socio-economic group in relation to these indicators.

Shortfalls in basic needs satisfaction for the four groups of basic needs variables in the model – primary education, secondary education, health and water supply (as indicated above, the fifth basic needs category, nutrition, is treated differently) - are calculated as follows.

For each basic needs category a so-called unit cost is calculated indicating the amount needed to provide one person (or one student) with adequate services. For each socio-economic group the total amounts for government expenditure and for private expenditure are already determined. Dividing this amount by the unit cost gives the total number of persons (or pupils) being covered.

$$COV(g,h) = \min \left(\frac{GCBN(g,h) + PCBN(g,h)}{UNC(h)}, \frac{GIBN(g,h)}{UNI(h)} \right) \qquad [14]$$

$$COVPER(g,h) = COV(g,h)/POPBN(g,h) \qquad [15]$$

where

$COV(g,h)$ = number of persons (pupils) in group g covered by basic needs category h

$GCBN(g,h)$ = government expenditure on basic needs category h "received" by group g

$PCBN(g,h)$ = private expenditure on basic needs category h by group g

$UNC(h)$ = unit cost of recurrent expenditure for basic needs category h

$UNI(h)$ = unit cost of capital expenditure for basic needs category h

$COVPER(g,h)$ = percentage relevant population in group g covered by basic needs category h

$POPBN(g,h)$ = relevant population for basic needs category h in socio-economic group g
for h = 1 (primary education) children aged 6-12
h = 2 (secondary education) children aged 12-18
h = 3,4, total population

Unit costs of basic needs are indicated in table 4.2. The way they have been derived is described in Appendix 6.

The last element needed in the calibration is the percentage of the population (or relevant age group in the case of education) covered by the provision of basic needs.[3] For primary and secondary education the enrolment rates provided by the Ministry of Education have been taken. For health and other basic needs (water supply) information is taken from the basic needs targets table for 1976, as reported in the Fourth Development Plan (1979-83) (our table 3.2). National coverage of health is based upon an 11 per cent coverage in rural areas (defined as having access to a health unit within 2 kilometres' distance) and an 80 per cent coverage in urban areas. This results in a national average of 22.85 per cent. Rural access to decent water sources, according to table 3.2 is also estimated at 11 per cent, while that in urban areas is estimated at 80 per cent. This again gives a national average of 22.85 per cent.

Table 4.2. Unit costs and coverage of basic needs, 1976 (K.£ per person)

	Recurrent costs	Capital costs	% population satisfied[1]
Primary education	16.00	0.10	85
Secondary education	84.00	29.00	20
Health	2.08	0.22	23
Water	1.45	0.07	23

[1] For education percentage of relevant age group.

Constructed in this way, the system allows for experiments with various themes from the basic needs debate. First, we can include experiments reflecting "efficiency in basic needs expenditure". Many authors, including Streeten (1981), have argued that when targeted rightly expenditure for basic needs can be made more efficient (a shift from curative to preventive medicine, for example). Furthermore, certain elements of government provided services could well be undertaken by the community itself, in order to relax pressure on the central government budget. Ghai (1980) quotes various examples. By lowering the unit costs for basic needs expenditure categories such policies can be simulated in the model.

Another issue is quality improvement in the provision of basic needs. The system is based on actual expenditure patterns; this may - and actually does hide - substandard performance, especially in primary education and in health care. We might, therefore, experiment with the inclusion of desired rather than actual spending figures. This would imply an increase in unit cost.

Increases in unit cost can also be caused by inefficiency in delivery. When public programmes are expanded rapidly, without explicit targeting, access to services may not increase proportionally. This can be reflected in the model by an increase in the unit costs of basic needs. (For further details see section 13.6, where an experiment of this kind will be described.)

4.3 Education

In the previous section we discussed access to primary and secondary education (or primary and secondary school enrolment). Although this is an important source of information on the satisfaction of basic needs in the field of education, we need to know not only how many children in the relevant school age can go to school but also the education level of the population. Many of these education stock variables determine other relations in the model.

We need first to translate enrolment ratios (the percentage of the school age population in school) into age-specific completion ratios (the percentage of persons of a certain age who have completed various levels of education).

From the previous section we have for each socio-economic group the enrolment ratios in primary and secondary education. Weighting these with the relevant school population share we construct rural and urban primary and secondary school enrolment ratios.

$$\text{COVPERRU}(h) = \frac{\displaystyle\sum_{g=1}^{4} \text{POPBN}(g,h) * \text{COVPER}(g,h)}{\displaystyle\sum_{g=1}^{4} \text{POPBN}(g,h)} \qquad h = 1,2 \qquad [16]$$

$$\text{COVPERUB}(h) = \frac{\displaystyle\sum_{g=5}^{8} \text{POPBN}(g,h) * \text{COVPER}(g,h)}{\displaystyle\sum_{g=5}^{8} \text{POPBN}(g,h)} \qquad h = 1,2 \qquad [17]$$

where

COVPERRU(h) = rural enrolment rate: h = 1, primary education
                                     h = 2, secondary education
COVPERUB(h) = urban enrolment rate: h = 1, primary education
                                     h = 2, secondary education
Other variables are defined above in formulae [14] and [15].

For the urban and rural completion rates we then have the following relations. The enrolment rate at year 14 determines the completion rate for primary education of that age cohort and the enrolment rate at year 18 determines the completion rate for secondary education[4] of that age cohort, taking into account, however, a certain level of drop-out.

$$CR1R(k)^t = CR1R(k-1)^{t-1} \qquad \text{for } k > 14 \qquad [18]$$

$$CR1R(14)^t = COVPERRU(1)* (1 - DROPOUT(1)) \qquad [19]$$

$$CR1U(k)^t = CR1U(k-1)^{t-1} \qquad \text{for } k > 14 \qquad [20]$$

$$CR1U(14)^t = COVPERUB(1)*(1 - DROPOUT(1)) \qquad [21]$$

$$CR2R(k)^t = CR2R(k-1)^{t-1} \qquad \text{for } k > 18 \qquad [22]$$

$$CR2R(18)^t = COVPERRU(2)* (1 - DROPOUT(2)) \qquad [23]$$

$$CR2U(k)^t = CR2U(k-1)^{t-1} \qquad \text{for } k > 18 \qquad [24]$$

$$CR2U(18) = COVPERUB(2)*(1 - DROPOUT(2)) \qquad [25]$$

where

$CR1R(k)^t$ = completion rate for primary education of a person aged k at year t in rural areas

$CR1U(k)^t$ = completion rate for primary education of a person aged k at year t in urban areas

$CR2R(k)^t$ = completion rate for secondary education of a person aged k at year t in rural areas

$CR2U(k)^t$ = completion rate for secondary education of a person aged k at year t in urban areas

DROPOUT(1) = drop out rate for primary education

DROPOUT(2) = drop out rate for secondary education

According to World Bank (1985), the drop-out rate in primary and secondary education in 1976 amounted to 26 per cent and 10 per cent respectively.

In order for the system to be initialised we need to have completion rates of the population in the base year, which are given in table 4.3.

For the rest of the model we still have to define some more concepts. First, in order to calculate labour force participation rates we must subtract from the population the number of persons enrolled in school, as the labour force participation rates relate to the population not in school. For that we define age- and sex-specific enrolment rates as follows.

$$ENROLR(1,k) = FEPR*COVPERRU(1) * \frac{\sum_s RP2(s,k)}{RP2(1,k)} \qquad [26]$$

$$\text{for} \qquad k \lessgtr 13$$

$$FESR*COVPERRU(2) * \frac{\sum_s RP2(s,k)}{RP2(1,k)} \qquad [27]$$

$$\text{for } 14 \lessgtr k < 18$$

$$ENROLR(2,k) = (1-FEPR)*COVPERRU(1) * \frac{\sum_s RP2(s,k)}{RP2(2,k)} \qquad [28]$$

$$\text{for} \qquad k \lessgtr 13$$

$$(1-FESR)*COVPERRU(2) * \frac{\sum_s RP2(s,k)}{RP2(2,k)} \qquad [29]$$

$$\text{for } 14 \lessgtr k < 18$$

$$ENROLU(1,k) = FEPU*COVPERUB(1) * \frac{\sum_s UP2(s,k)}{UP2(1,k)} \qquad [30]$$

$$\text{for} \qquad k \lessgtr 13$$

$$FESU*COVPERUB(2) * \frac{\sum_s UP2(s,k)}{UP2(1,k)} \qquad [31]$$

$$\text{for } 14 \lessgtr k < 18$$

$$ENROLU(2,k) = (1-FEPU)*COVPERUB(1) * \frac{\sum_s UP2(s,k)}{UP2(2,k)} \qquad [32]$$

$$\text{for} \qquad k \lessgtr 13$$

$$(1-FESU)*COVPERUB(2) * \frac{\sum_s UP2(s,k)}{UP2(2,k)} \qquad [33]$$

$$\text{for } 14 \lessgtr k < 18$$

where

$ENROLR(1,k)$ = female school enrolment rate at age k in rural areas

$ENROLR(2,k)$ = male school enrolment rate at age k in rural areas

$ENROLU(1,k)$ = female school enrolment rate at age k in urban areas

$ENROLU(2,k)$ = male school enrolment rate at age k in urban areas

FEPR   =   share of females in primary school enrolment in
               rural areas in base year
FESR   =   share of females in secondary school enrolment
               in rural areas in base year
FEPU   =   share of females in primary school enrolment in
               urban areas in base year
FESU   =   share of females in secondary school enrolment
               in urban areas in base year
RP2(s,k)   =   rural population by gender and age
UP2(s,k)   =   urban population by gender and age

For the base year (and for the rest of the simulations),
we have the following values for the share of female enrolment.

FEPR = 0.460
FESR = 0.369
FEPU = 0.482
FESU = 0.378

These are taken from Educational trends 1973-77 (Republic of
Kenya, CBS, n.d., c 1979).

Table 4.3.   Completion rates for primary and secondary
             education, 1976

Age group	All country		Urban		Rural	
	Primary	Secondary	Primary	Secondary	Primary	Secondary
12–14	0.85	...	0.99	...	0.83	...
15–19	0.81	0.21	0.94	0.32	0.79	0.19
20–24	0.70	0.27	0.81	0.41	0.68	0.25
25–29	0.63	0.20	0.73	0.30	0.61	0.19
30–34	0.55	0.14	0.64	0.21	0.54	0.13
35–39	0.45	0.08	0.52	0.12	0.44	0.07
40–44	0.39	0.06	0.45	0.09	0.38	0.06
45–59	0.33	0.04	0.38	0.06	0.32	0.09
50–54	0.25	0.02	0.29	0.03	0.24	0.02
55+	0.15	0.01	0.17	0.02	0.14	0.01

Source. Population Census 1979, as reported in Statistical
         Abstract for total country. Urban/rural split calcu-
         lated according to information from the 1969 census.

In the demographic section we will use a further refinement of the educational system (as will be seen in the behavioural equations), namely the percentage of population with Standard 5 and with Form 4 completed. The former is not exactly equal to primary school enrolment since primary school goes up to Standard 7. Although this would have only a slight impact, it is important for initialisation purposes; in order to introduce completion rates for Standard 5 we have to correct completion rates for primary school in the following way. For the population who had already completed primary education in 1976 we have multiplied the completion rate with different factors for rural and urban males and females, based upon the population census of 1979, in order to arrive at a Standard 5 completion rate. For projections with the model, we have used the drop-out rate from Standard 5 to Standard 7 in order to adapt the Standard 7 completion rate to a completion rate for Standard 5. According to World Bank (1985), the average drop-out rate between Standard 5 and Standard 7 was 15 per cent.

This gives the following variables:

$$ED2R = \frac{\sum\limits_{s} \sum\limits_{k=15}^{66} (CROR(k) - CR2R(k)) * RP2(s,k)}{\sum\limits_{s} \sum\limits_{k=15}^{66} RP2(s,k)} \qquad [34]$$

$$ED3R = \frac{\sum\limits_{s} \sum\limits_{k=15}^{66} CR2R(k) * RP2(s,k)}{\sum\limits_{s} \sum\limits_{k=15}^{66} RP2(s,k)} \qquad [35]$$

where

$ED2R$ = proportion of rural persons aged 15 and above having passed Standard 5 but not Form 4

$ED3R$ = proportion of rural persons aged 15 and above having passed Form 4

$CROR(k)$ = age-specific completion rate Standard 5, rural areas

$CR2R(k)$ = age-specific completion rate secondary education, rural areas

$RP2(s,k)$ = rural population by gender and age

Similar formulae as [34] and [35] are developed to calculate:

EDW2R = proportion of rural women aged 15–49 with
education higher than Standard 5 but lower
than Form 4   [36]

EDW3R = proportion of rural women aged 15–49 with
education higher than Form 4   [37]

EDW2U = proportion of urban women aged 15–49 with
education higher than Standard 5 but lower
than Form 4   [38]

EDW3U = proportion of urban women aged 15–49 with
education higher than Form 4   [39]

EDUCR = population in rural areas aged between 15
and 65 with education higher than Standard 7   [40]

EDUCU = population in urban areas aged between 15
and 65 with education higher than Standard 7   [41]

4.4 Health

The health-related output indicators, namely female life
expectancy and crude birth rate, are discussed in the next
chapter, on the demographic subsystem.

Notes

[1] For a discussion on input and output indicators see
Hopkins and van der Hoeven (1983).

[2] In the base run of the model, the matrix G is calibrated
in such a way that the matrix B represents actual
expenditure shares on basic needs for each socio-economic
group. These expenditure shares have been derived from
various micro-studies as well as from a study on public
expenditure patterns (Vandemoortele, 1983).

[3] In calibrating base year values the calculated shortfall
patterns are checked against actual indicators of
shortfalls, as reported in various social services for
the base year. If discrepancies exist the model adjusts
in the base year the cost figures UNC(h) automatically to
arrive at the actual shortfall levels.

[4] In defining completed secondary education we have taken

68

the cut-off point to be Form 4. Although secondary education is provided up to Form 6, a large number of pupils terminate education at Form 4 level. In 1979, of the 20-24 year age group, 336,000 persons had completed Form 4 while only 28,000 had completed Form 6. It thus seems justified to take the cut-off point to be at Form 4 level.

5 The demographic subsystem

Anker and Knowles have published a detailed analysis of demographic developments in Kenya based upon an extended household survey carried out in 1974 and a cross-section analysis with district-level data based upon 1969 figures supplemented by other data (Anker and Knowles, 1982, 1983). Because of marked differences both between households and between districts, the variation in the data appeared to be great enough to identify the necessary elements of structural changes. Some experiments with their findings proved satisfactory for the purposes of the Kenya basic needs model. Hence the parameters of the equations for fertility, life expectancy at birth, migration and labour force participation have been derived from their data set. This procedure is judged to be better than parameter estimation from cross-section analysis of international data, which is often applied in long-term simulation models in order to pick up structural changes (e.g. Rodgers et al., 1978).

As indicated in the previous chapter, strong links exist between the basic needs subsystem and the demographic subsystem (see figure 4.1). Using some of the variables determined in the basic needs subsystem, the demographic subsystem generates – among other things – estimates of life expectancy which are among the major output indicators for basic needs performance.

71

PLANNING FOR BASIC NEEDS

5.1 Fertility

Determinants of fertility are complex, and no single factor can be held responsible for a decline in fertility. Lewis (1981) lists eight factors which are most often associated with falling fertility rates:

1. status of women and female labour force participation rate;
2. education;
3. income;
4. economic value of children;
5. health care;
6. family planning;
7. biological phenomena; and
8. urbanisation.

Where infant mortality is high, fertility is generally high as well. Improvements in health practices raise the chances of survival of mother and child. Analysis over the last decade has indicated the importance of women's education and labour force participation (Standing, 1978).

Kenya is a country with an extremely high fertility rate. It became apparent that the figures given in the 1979 Population Census, which reported a population growth rate of 3.4 per cent, were still underestimating the real population growth rate in Kenya, which approaches a level of almost 4 per cent. One important factor is that fertility among urban educated women is not decreasing, despite many observations that education tends to lower fertility over the long run.

The model calculates different urban and rural fertility rates.

The equations for the crude birth rate estimated by Anker and Knowles (1983, p. 458) are:

Rural:

$$NB = -9.5706 + 0.6301 \text{ AGE} - 0.00659 \text{ AGE}^2 - 0.4446 \text{ EDW2} \qquad [42]$$
$$(14.59) \qquad (9.62) \qquad (3.32)$$

$$- 1.8783 \text{ EDW3} + 0.0794 \text{ EDH} + 0.0118 \text{ LAND} + 0.9805 \text{ DEATH}$$
$$(3.06) \qquad (4.52) \qquad (4.47) \qquad (5.96)$$

(t statistics in brackets) $\qquad R^2 = 0.51 \quad N = 1587$

Urban:

$$NB = -12.6339 + 0.6882 \ AGE - 0.007795 \ AGE^2 + 0.3017 \ EDW2 \quad [43]$$
$$(0.85) \qquad (4.71) \qquad\qquad (1.19)$$

$$- \ 0.3338 \ EDW3 + 0.002 \ EDH + 0.7988 \ MIGRANT + 2.3516 \ DEATH$$
$$(0.76) \qquad\quad (0.01) \qquad (3.01) \qquad\qquad (3.35)$$

(t statistics in brackets) $\qquad R^2 = 0.51 \quad N = 274$

where

NB   = number of live births
AGE   = woman's age in years
EDW2   = whether woman has achieved at least Standard 5 and less than Form 4 in secondary school
EDW3   = whether woman has achieved Form 4 in secondary school
EDH   = number of grades of school completed by husband
LAND   = number of climate adjusted acres of land owned by rural households
DEATH   = inverse of the survival rate among the woman's own live birth
MIGRANT = whether woman is a rural-urban migrant

    Several transformations have to take place before this equation can be used in the Kenya basic needs model.

    First, as Anker and Knowles indicate, the above equations exclude primary sterility. According to more detailed district level data on fertility (which is not used for simulation purposes), a decline in the primary sterility rate of 1 per cent causes an increase in total fertility of 0.0758. Based upon the data file for districts, the sterility pattern was determined as follows (Anker and Knowles, 1983, p. 460):

$$STERILE = 12.5091 - 0.3659 \ (EDW2 + EDW3) + 0.1810 \ URBAN \quad [44]$$
$$(3.80) \qquad\qquad\qquad (4.23)$$

(t statistics in brackets) $\qquad R^2 = 0.35 \quad N = 41$

where

STERILE = percentage of ever-married women aged 40-49 without a birth
URBAN   = percentage of district's population in an urban area

For EDW2 and EDW3 see under formulae [42] and [43].

The variables EDW2 and EDW3 are believed to proxy cultural variables, since a bias against education exists in areas of high sterility, and the coefficient is, for simulation purposes, therefore divided by three in order to reflect a more realistic influence over time.

As to the effect of sterility on fertility, another point needs to be taken into account. It was indicated above that a 1 per cent decline in sterility increases total fertility by 0.0758 per cent. But in equations [42] and [43] we do not estimate total fertility which is a measure of completed fertility (i.e. the expected number of children a woman at the age of 49 will have had in her life) but the average number of live births of all women in the fertile age group. Average fertility was, according to the district-level equation, 7.6, and the average number of live births in rural and urban areas was 4.25 and 3.18 respectively. The coefficient for sterility was therefore divided by two in order to be incorporated into the equation for number of births.

For the rural fertility equation the effects of husband's education and ownership of land have been interpreted as proxies for permanent income, and translated into a relation between fertility and household income per adult equivalent in order for the effects to be included in the model. Elasticities have been calculated at sample means, and the sum of these two elasticities has been taken to represent an elasticity between income and fertility. The elasticity so determined is converted back into a coefficient for income per adult using sample mean values of income per adult and fertility (Anker and Knowles, 1983, p. 454). For urban areas the coefficient of husband's education was deemed to be insignificant and the effect of sample mean was put into the constant term.

Furthermore, since age is a control and not a behavioural variable, both in urban and rural areas, and since the model requires a fertility function for the total age group of women aged 15-49, the influence of age has been ignored.

This gives the following equations used for model purposes:

Rural:

$$BRR(t) = C_1 - 0.4446 \; EDW2R(t-1) - 1.8783 \; EDW3R(t-1) \qquad [45]$$

$$+ \; 0.3302 \; YAPAE(t-1) + 0.9805 \; \frac{1}{(SR3R(t))}$$

$$- \; 0.0379 \; STERILE(t)$$

$$STERILE(t) = C_2 - 0.1220 \; (EDW2R(t-1) + EDW3R(t-1)) \qquad [46]$$

Urban:

$$BRU(t) = C_3 + 0.3017 \ EDW2U(t-1) - 0.338 \ EDW3U(t-1) \qquad [47]$$

$$+ \ 2.3516 \ \frac{1}{(SR3U(t))} + 0.7988 \ WMIGR(t-1)$$

$$- \ 0.0379 \ STERILE(t)$$

$$STERILE(t) = C_4 - 0.1220 \ (EDW2U(t-1) + EDW3U(t-1)) \qquad [48]$$

where

BRR	=	behavioural estimate of fertility in rural areas
BRU	=	behavioural estimate of fertility in urban areas
EDW2R	=	proportion of rural women aged 15-49 with education higher than Standard 5 but lower than Form 4
EDW2U	=	proportion of urban women aged 15-49 with education higher than Standard 5 but lower than Form 4
EDW3R	=	proportion of rural women aged 15-49 with education higher than Form 4
EDW3U	=	proportion of urban women aged 15-49 with education higher than Form 4
YAPAE	=	household income per adult equivalent in rural areas (in thousands K.sh.)
SR3R	=	proportion of births surviving to age three in rural areas
SR3U	=	proportion of births surviving to age three in urban areas
STERILE	=	proportion of ever-married women aged 40-49 without any birth
WMIGR	=	proportion of urban women aged 15-49 who are immigrants
C	=	constant term (see below)

This transformed equation forms the basis of the fertility equations. As the equations are linear and not in double-log form the coefficients do not represent elasticities and have to be adapted for simulation purposes. This has been done according to the following procedure.

Both BRR and BRU for model year 1 were calibrated by adjusting the constant term so that with the initial value of the independent variables the value of BRR and BRU were equal to sample means (4.25 and 3.28 births, respectively; Anker and Knowles, 1982, p. 195).

It was then assumed that proportional changes in the behavioural estimate of fertility cause similar proportional changes in the crude birth rate which is used in population accounting.

Thus

$$CBR(t) = (\frac{CBR(1)}{BRR(1)})\ BRR(t) \qquad [49]$$

$$CBU(t) = (\frac{CBU(1)}{BRU(1)})\ BRU(t) \qquad [50]$$

where

CBR	=	crude birth rate, rural
CBU	=	crude birth rate, urban
BRR	=	behavioural estimate fertility, rural
BRU	=	behavioural estimate fertility, urban
BRR(1)	=	4.25
BRU(1)	=	3.28
CBR(1)	=	53.74
CBU(1)	=	47.52

The values of CBR(1) and CBU(1) have been determined from the national fertility survey as reported in the 1979 issue of the Economic Survey (Republic of Kenya, CBS).

5.2 Mortality

Major indicators of mortality are infant mortality and child mortality. Model life tables can then translate child mortality into female life expectancy at birth, which in turn can provide survival rates for all age groups from which crude death rates can be calculated.

Life expectancy differs greatly between countries. As Lewis (1981) reports, the major variable explaining life expectancy appears to be the literacy rate. She found a correlation coefficient of 0.81 based upon 29 developing countries, and cited the unpublished works of Grosse and Perry (1979), Berg (1982) and Hicks (1979),[1] who found even higher correlations, between 0.81 and 0.96. Apart from literacy, Lewis mentions fertility and nutrition and environment as determinants of life expectancy.

Life expectancy at birth has been increasing steadily in Kenya from 47 years in 1960 to 57 years in 1982. The latter figure is not only above the average for low-income countries (excluding the Sahel) in Africa (49 years), but also above the average for middle-income African countries (50 years) (World Bank, 1984).

Since in household surveys life expectancy at birth is difficult to measure, the behavioural relations for mortality in urban and rural areas are based upon survival rates for three-year-olds (which can then be translated into figures for

life expectancy).
The following equations were chosen from those developed by Anker and Knowles (1983, p. 477):

$$\text{SURVIVE3} = \underset{(2.17)}{0.0010} \text{ YEAR} - \underset{(1.67)}{0.0096} \text{ MALE} - \underset{(6.94)}{0.0494} \text{ MALARIA} \qquad [51]$$

$$+ \underset{(3.61)}{0.0286} \text{ ED2} + \underset{(3.01)}{0.0118} \text{ INCOME}$$

$$- \underset{(1.98)}{0.00072} \text{ (INCOME)}^2$$

(t statistics in brackets) $R^2 = 0.014$ $N = 6305$

where

SURVIVE3 = probability indicating whether child survived to age three
MALE = binary variable indicating whether child is male
MALARIA = binary variable indicating prevalence of malaria
ED2 = whether mother has passed Standard 5 or not
INCOME = household income per adult equivalent (in thousands K.sh.)
YEAR = year of birth

Several adaptations have to be made for the behavioural equation for mortality to be used in the model.
First, the effect of the binary variable MALE is ignored, as this effect is already incorporated in the model life tables. Second, the variable MALARIA measuring the incidence of malaria, is taken to indicate the effects of improved sanitation and improved access to health facilities. Third, the variable YEAR is taken to measure improvements in general health facilities. In trial runs the effect of YEAR over the full period proved too strong. It improved survival rates by 0.025, which is roughly equal to adding 5.47 years to life expectancy at birth. The coefficient of the variable was therefore divided by two.
The effect of improved sanitation and access to health facilities is captured by the effect of the variable MALARIA in the following way.
As a result of successful health campaigns and improved access to health facilities, malaria will be eliminated over a period of 25 years. A health campaign is deemed to be successful if the access rate for the urban or rural population has passed the 80 per cent mark.

PLANNING FOR BASIC NEEDS

The coefficient is determined as follows. The sample mean value of MALARIA is 0.21, indicating that 21 per cent of the population was still living in malarious areas. If malaria was eliminated in 25 years this would add an amount of $0.0494 * 0.21 = 0.01037$ to the survival rate at age three or an annual amount of $0.01037 / 25 = 0.000415$.

After these transformations we arrive at the following model specification:

$$SR3U(t) = C_1 + 0.02860 \ (EDW2U(t-1) + EDW3U(t-1)) \qquad [52]$$

$$+ 0.0118 \ (YNAPAE(t-1)) - 0.00072 \ (YNAPAE(t-1))^2$$

$$+ 0.0005 \ NYEAR + 0.000415 \ \sum_1^t HFU$$

$$SR3R(t) = C_1 + 0.02860 \ (EDW2R(t-1) + EDW3R(t-1)) \qquad [53]$$

$$+ 0.0118 \ (YAPAE(t-1)) - 0.00072 \ (YAPAE(t-1))^2$$

$$+ 0.0005 \ NYEAR + 0.000415 \ \sum_1^t HFR$$

where

SR3U   = survival probability at age three, urban
SR3R   = survival probability at age three, rural
EDW2U = proportion of urban women (aged 15–49) with education higher than Standard 5 but lower than Form 4
EDW3U = proportion of urban women (aged 15–49) with education higher than Form 4
EDW2R = proportion of rural women (aged 15–49) with education higher than Standard 5 but lower than Form 4
EDW3R = proportion of rural women (aged 15–49) with education higher than Form 4
YNAPAE = average household income per adult equivalent in urban areas (in thousands K.sh.)
YAPAE = average household income per adult equivalent in rural areas (in thousands K.sh.)
NYEAR = model year
HFU   = binary variable indicating whether in each year access to health in urban areas is equal to or greater than 80 per cent
HFR   = binary variable indicating whether in each year access to health in rural areas is equal to or greater than 80 per cent

C_1 = constant term (see below)
C_2 = constant term (see below)

The values of the constant term are determined by initialising in the base year the survival rate in urban and rural areas:

$$SR3U(1) = 0.914$$
$$SR3R(1) = 0.871$$

These rates, according to Coale-Demeny Model Life tables, correspond to a female life expectancy in urban and rural areas (FLEOU, FLEOR) of 61.7 and 54.8 years respectively, and an average female life expectancy of 55.7 years, as reported in the fertility survey for the year 1977 (Republic of Kenya, CBS, Economic Survey, 1979).
During the simulation the model calculates first the survival probability at age three, translates this through the Coale-Demeny Model Life tables into female life expectancy at birth and into age- and gender-specific survival rates.

$$FLEOR(t) = f(CDMLT, SR3R(t))$$

$$SR(s,k)(t) = f(CDMLT, FLEOR(t)) \quad (rural) \qquad [54]$$

$$FLEOU(t) = f(CDMLT, SR3U(t))$$

$$SU(s,k)(t) = f(CDMLT, FLEOU(t)) \quad (urban) \qquad [55]$$

where

CDMLT   = Coale-Demeny Model Life tables
FLEOR   = female life expectancy at birth in rural areas
FLEOU   = female life expectancy at birth in urban areas
$SR(s,k)$ = gender (s) and age (k) specific survival rate, rural areas
$SU(s,k)$ = gender (s) and age (k) specific survival rate, urban areas

5.3 Migration

The literature on rural-urban migration has expanded greatly during the last decade. The main conclusion reached has been that rural-urban migration cannot be explained purely in terms of the difference between urban and rural incomes and the rural migrant's expectation of a job in an urban area (the so-called Harris-Todaro models) (Harris and Todaro, 1970). These factors are certainly important, but their influence often depends on broader structural factors, such as the system of land tenure, changes in technology, distribution of government services, levels of education and the nature of the urban labour market – some of which are, however, difficult to quantify.

The following equation for migration was chosen from district-level data developed by Anker and Knowles (1983, pp. 490–491):

$$\ln(\text{MUR}/\text{POP}) = -0.3562 \ln (\text{DN}) - 0.4240 \ln (\text{DM}) \qquad [56]$$
$$\phantom{\ln(\text{MUR}/\text{POP}) =} (1.76) \qquad\qquad (2.06)$$

$$+ 0.7378 \ln (\text{DK}) - 0.0620 \ln (\text{DR})$$
$$(3.00) \qquad\qquad (0.24)$$

$$+ 0.7242 \ln (\text{LIT}) + 0.0684 \ln (\text{URB})$$
$$(3.39) \qquad\qquad (3.18)$$

$$- 0.1900 \ln (\text{LAND}) - 0.2391 \ln (\text{XWI})$$
$$(1.51) \qquad\qquad (1.16)$$

$$+ 0.4426 \ln (\text{XWR}) - 6.6676$$
$$(2.20)$$

(t statistics in brackets) $\bar{R}^2$ adj = 0.57;   N = 37

where

MUR = number of lifetime out-migrants from origin district observed to be residing in an urban area when population censuses are carried out
POP = population of origin district in 1969
DN   = distance from origin district to Nairobi
DM   = distance from origin district to Mombasa
DK   = distance from origin district to Nakuru
DR   = distance to nearest town outside district other than above
LIT = percentage of adults with five years or more education
URB = percentage of origin district population residing in towns of 2,000 or more persons
LAND = number of hectares per person active in agriculture
WI   = non-agricultural modern sector earning in district
WR   = non-agricultural modern sector earning in nearest town
EI   = non-agricultural sector employment rate in district of origin
ER   = non-agricultural sector employment rate in nearest town
XWI = EI * WI
XWR = ER * WR

Several transformations have to be made in order for this equation to be included in the model. First, the equation has to be reformulated in terms of the variables of the model. Second, the dependent variable MUR/POP, which represents the stock of migrants, has to be transformed into a flow concept in which we distinguish the differing migratory propensities of males and females and of different age groups. Third, the equation may be simplified by incorporating the effects of the distance variables and the variable URB (the percentage of origin district population living in an urban area) in the constant, as these variables are regarded as permanent factors. Fourth, the variable LAND indicates the relative pressure on agricultural resources; in our model it is replaced by the ratio of rural to urban income.

This gives the following equation for use in the model.

$$\ln(MIG(t)) = C + 0.724 \ln(ED2R(t-1) + ED3R(t-1)) \qquad [57]$$

$$- 0.1900 \ln(YAPAE(t-1)/YNAPAE(t-1))$$

$$- 0.239 \ln(ERGR_2(t-1))$$

$$+ 0.4425 \ln(ERGR_6(t-1))$$

where

MIG	=	behavioural estimate of rural–urban migration
ED2R	=	proportion of rural persons aged 15 and over having passed Standard 5 but not passed Form 4
ED3R	=	proportion of rural persons aged 15 and over having passed Form 4
YAPAE	=	average household income, rural areas, per adult equivalent
YNAPAE	=	average household income, urban areas, per adult equivalent
$ERGR_2$	=	average wage, skilled workers, rural areas
$ERGR_6$	=	average wage, skilled workers, urban areas

Further, we assume that changes in the behavioural rate of migration have a proportional effect on rural–urban migration as a percentage of rural population.

$$RUM(t) = \frac{RUM(1)}{MIG(1)} MIG(t) \qquad [58]$$

Taking logarithms we get

$$\ln(RUM(t)) = \ln\left(\frac{RUM(1)}{MIG(1)}\right) + \ln(MIG(t)) \qquad [59]$$

PLANNING FOR BASIC NEEDS

Since the model equation is in double logarithmic form we can replace ln(MIG(t)) in equation [57] by ln(RUM(t)) while adding ln(RUM(1)/MIG(1)) to the constant term and adjusting the new constant term in such a way that for the base year the equation gives the value of rural-urban migration as a percentage of rural population; according to the 1979 census, this was 0.54 per cent.

Intensity of migration depends on gender, age and education. The latter effect is already incorporated in the behavioural equation for migration given above [57]. Our model therefore distingushes migration propensities according to gender and age, the age groups being younger than 15 years, between 15 and 49 years, and older than 49 years.

In order to initialise the age-specific migration rates we used the following equation from Anker and Knowles (1983, p. 498):

$$RMG = -0.0880 + 0.0074 \text{ MALE} + 0.0392 \text{ ED2} + 0.0917 \text{ ED3} \qquad [60]$$
$$\qquad\quad (1.56) \qquad\qquad (7.35) \qquad\quad (4.78)$$

$$+ 0.0105 \text{ AGE} - 0.0002693 \text{ (AGE)}^2$$
$$\quad (7.10) \qquad\qquad (6.49)$$

$$+ 0.000001908 \text{ (AGE)}^3 + 0.0482 \text{ MED3}$$
$$\quad (5.58) \qquad\qquad\qquad (2.22)$$

(t statistics in brackets); $\bar{R}^2$ adj = 0.035; N = 8448

where

RMG = rural-urban migration, 1963-74
MALE = binary variable
ED2 = proportion of population aged 15 years and above with education higher than Standard 5 but lower than Form 4
ED3 = proportion of population aged 15 years and above with education higher than Form 4
AGE = age
MED3 = interactive term between MALE and ED3

In order to determine age-specific migration rates the terms dealing with education (ED2, ED3, MED3) were all added to the constant, as the influence of education is already incorporated in the migration rate for the whole population.

Furthermore, when weighted by rural population share the age- and gender-specific migration rates should add up to the behaviourally determined total rural-urban migration rate.

$$RUM = \sum_s \sum_k RUMS(s,k) * POPSHARE(s,k) \qquad [61]$$

82

Applying equation [60] and proportionally adjusting the age- and gender-specific rates to satisfy [61] resulted in the following rates:

Female   Male

RUMS[1,k] = 0.3213	RUMS[2,k] = 0.4680	$k \leqslant 15$
RUMS[1,k] = 0.7080	RUMS[2,k] = 0.8584	$15 < k < 45$ [62]
RUMS[1,k] = 0.0397	RUMS[2,k] = 0.1864	$k \geqslant 45$

These rates apply only in the base year, however, since the model adjusts the age-specific rates proportionally every year in order to satisfy equation [61].

In two relations in the model a stock concept of migrants is used. First we have the proportion of urban women aged 15-49 who are immigrants (WMIGR) in the urban fertility equation (equation [47]). Second, we have the proportion of male rural-urban migrants aged between 20 and 59 as a proportion of the total rural population (MIGR) in the rural labour force participation rate (equation [70]). These stock variables are generated as follows.

$$STOCKW2(k) = [STOCKW(k-1) + RUMS(1,k) * RP(1,k)] * SU(1,k) \quad [63]$$

$$WMIGR = \sum_{k=15}^{49} STOCKW2 / \sum_{k=15}^{49} UP2(1,k) \quad [64]$$

$$STOCK2(k) = [STOCK(k-1) + RUMS(2,k) * RP(2,k)] * SU(2,k) \quad [65]$$

$$MIGR = \sum_{20}^{59} STOCK2(k) / RPOP \quad [66]$$

where

STOCKW2(k)	=	number of women of age k living in an urban area at year t who are immigrants
STOCKW(k)	=	number of women of age k living in an urban area at year t-1 who are immigrants
STOCK2(k)	=	number of males of age k living in an urban area at year t who are immigrants
STOCK(k)	=	number of males of age k living in an urban area at year t-1 who are immigrants
RUMS(1,k)	=	age-specific female migration rate
RUMS(2,k)	=	age-specific male migration rate
RP (1,k)	=	female rural population by age
UP (1,k)	=	female urban population by age

SU (1,k)   = age-specific urban female survival rates
SU (2,k)   = age-specific urban male survival rates
RPOP   = rural population

In order to initialise the two variables WMIGR and MIGR we have to determine their base year values. These were computed from values used in Anker and Knowles (1983) for 1969 and by applying actual migration, birth and survival rates for 1969-76. This resulted in the following figures:

WMIGR (1976) = 0.681
MIGR (1976) = 0.189

5.4 Labour force participation

The issue of labour force participation in economic development is complex. As Standing (1978) has noted, labour force participation rates vary widely between countries, and the definition and consequent measurement of the labour force greatly influence the level of the unemployment rate. This is especially true in countries where the majority of the labour force is self-employed and/or engaged in production for own consumption. The gender division of labour is particularly important here. While male labour force participation rates do not seem to vary widely, female labour force participation rates do.

Standing and Sheehan (1979) report that in explaining labour force participation the following explanatory factors are often used: age, marital status, education, presence of children, wage, family income, health, and migrant status. There are also the macro variables, unemployment, urbanisation, type of employment, and agricultural employment.

In Kenya, labour force participation rates for females differ considerably between urban and rural areas (see table 5.1). Different behavioural relations were therefore introduced. For female labour force participation rates in urban and rural areas the following relation was chosen from the household survey cited earlier (Anker and Knowles, 1983, p. 519):

LF12 = + 0.0930 EDW2 + 0.4088 EDW3 + 0.0191 INCOME   [67]
           (2.04)   (4.77)   (1.73)

        - 0.0034 UNEMP + 0.0269 SERVWAGE + 0.0031 SERVICE - 0.0691
          (1.20)   (1.26)   (1.99)

(t statistics in brackets) R^2 = 0.17; N = 352; F = 8.76

$$LWT = 0.3350 \text{ FARM} - 0.0012 \text{ LAND} - 0.0191 \text{ INCOME} \qquad [68]$$
$$(12.29) \qquad (2.02) \qquad (2.50)$$

$$+ 0.1317 \text{ HUSAWAY} + 0.4924$$
$$(3.24)$$

(t statistics in brackets) $R^2 = 0.12$; $N = 1209$; $F = 42.98$

where

LF12	=	binary variable indicating labour force participation in last 12 months (urban)
LWT	=	weighted labour force participation rate since marriage
EDW2	=	binary variable, indicating whether woman has completed Standard 5 but not Form 4
EDW3	=	binary variable, indicating whether woman has completed Form 4
INCOME	=	household income per adult equivalent
UNEMP	=	unemployment rate proxy: percentage of adult population not employed in modern sector
SERVWAGE	=	wages in service sector
SERVICE	=	percentage urban population in service employment
FARM	=	binary variable indicating land ownership
LAND	=	amount of land owned
HUSAWAY	=	binary variable indicating absence of husband

In order to use these behavioural equations for female labour force participation rates several adaptations had to be made.

For simulation purposes the positive effect of income was excluded, as this is thought to be a permanent aspect of the Kenyan urban labour market where women of well-to-do families are working. Increased average urban income over time would therefore not result in increased female labour force participation rates.

In rural areas the effect of land ownership, being an indicator for accumulated wealth, was combined with that of income by calculating the elasticity between LAND and LWT at sample means, adding this elasticity to that between INCOME and LWT and finally reconverting the combined elasticities back into an income effect at sample means (Anker and Knowles, 1983, p. 519). Second, HUSAWAY was proxied by the ratio of rural-urban male migrants aged 20-59 years living in urban areas to rural households. The coefficient is set so that at sample means it has the same elasticity as estimated for HUSAWAY (Anker and Knowles, 1983, p. 520), which resulted in a value of 0.0277. Since we want the independent variable to be related to population rather than household size, which is implied by HUSAWAY, and since the mean household size in the sample was 5.9, the coefficient was divided by the average household size and became 0.1634. Since the model does not generate land ownership its effect was included in the constant term.

This gives the following behavioural equations for labour force participation:

$$FLPUB(t) = C_1 + 0.0930 \ EDW2U(t-1) + 0.4088 \ EDW3U(t-1) \qquad [69]$$

$$- 0.0034 \ UNEMP(t-1) + 0.0269 \ SERVWAGE(t-1)$$

$$+ 0.0031 \ SERVICE(t-1)$$

$$FLPRU(t) = C_2 - 0.0367 \ YAPAE(t-1) + 0.1634 \ MIGR(t) \qquad [70]$$

where

FLPUB	=	behavioural variable indicating female labour force participation in urban areas
EDW2U	=	proportion of urban women aged 15–49 with education higher than Standard 5 but lower than Form 4
EDW3U	=	proportion of urban women aged 15–49 with education higher than Form 4
UNEMP	=	unemployment rate in urban areas
SERVWAGE	=	average wage in services
SERVICE	=	percentage of urban workers employed in modern sector services
FLPRU	=	female labour force participation rate in rural areas
YAPAE	=	rural household income per adult equivalent
MIGR	=	male rural-urban migrants aged 20–59 years as a proportion of the rural population

All independent variables in the equation are explained in equations in other parts of the model except for the variables relating to the service industry, which are defined as follows.

$$SERVICE = \frac{WORKS_{11} + WORKU_{11}}{\displaystyle\sum_{5}^{8} EAP_g} \qquad [71]$$

$$\text{SERVWAGE} \quad = \quad \frac{W_{11}}{\text{WORKS}_{11} + \text{WORKU}_{11}} \qquad [72]$$

where

WORKS_{11} = number of skilled workers in modern services
WORKU_{11} = number of unskilled workers in modern services
EAP_g = economic active population in socio-economic group g
W_{11} = wage bill in modern service sector

Since we use age-specific labour force participation rates in the model we still need to provide a link between these and the behavioural relation indicated above.

Based upon the female labour force participation rates and the age distribution and fractions of persons aged up to 18 not in school, the female labour force participation rate for urban and rural areas is determined.

$$\text{FLPRU} \quad = \quad \sum_{k=10}^{66} \text{ARRU}(1,k) * \text{RPOPS}(1,k) \qquad [73]$$

$$\text{FLPUB} \quad = \quad \sum_{k=10}^{66} \text{ARUB}(1,k) * \text{UPOPS}(1,k) \qquad [74]$$

$$\text{RPOPS}(1,k) \quad = \quad (1-\text{ENROLR}(1,k)) * \text{RP}(1,k) \qquad [75]$$

$$\text{UPOPS}(1,k) \quad = \quad (1-\text{ENROLU}(1,k)) * \text{RP}(1,k) \qquad [76]$$

where

FLPRU = total rural female labour force participation rate
FLPUB = total urban female labour force participation rate
$\text{ARRU}(1,k)$ = age-specific rural female labour force participation rate
$\text{ARUB}(1,k)$ = age-specific urban female labour force participation rate
$\text{RPOPS}(1,k)$ = age-specific rural female population not in school
$\text{UPOPS}(1,k)$ = age-specific urban female population not in school
$\text{ENROLU}(1,k)$ = urban female school enrolment rate at age k (see formulae [30] and [31])

ENROLR(1,k) = rural female school enrolment rate at age k
(see formulae [26] and [27])
UP(1,k)   = urban female population at age k
RP(1,k)   = rural female population at age k

The base year values for FLPRU and FLPUR (FLPRU(1) = 0.55 and FLPUR(1) = 0.18) were used to determine the constant terms C_1 and C_2 in equations [69] and [70].

During the simulation, changes in the behavioural total female labour force participation rates in urban and rural areas cause proportional changes in the age-specific female labour force participation rates.

Age-specific male labour force participation rates in both rural and urban areas remain constant over time.

$$ARRU^t(1,k) = [ARRU^t(1,k)/FLPRU(1)] * FLPRU(t) \qquad [77]$$

$$ARUB^t(1,k) = [ARUB^t(1,k)/FLPUB(1)] * FLPUB(t) \qquad [78]$$

$$ARRU(2,k) = constant \qquad [79]$$

$$ARUB(2,k) = constant \qquad [80]$$

where

ARRU(2,k) = rural male labour force participation rate
ARUB(2,k) = urban male labour force participation rate

Other variables are defined in formulae [73] and [74].

Male and female labour force participation rates being determined, the urban and rural labour force can be determined, based upon population not in school, according to formulae [73] and [74]. Chapters 6 and 7 describe in more detail how urban and rural labour force by skill level is determined.

Various surveys have found that labour force participation rates are very high in Kenya (Anker and Knowles, 1983; Bigsten, 1982). The reason for this high rate is that in the absence of any social or basic security no household head can afford to be idle and not looking for work. This is confirmed by a recently published worldwide estimate of economically active population (ILO, 1986, pp. 36, 37, 38).

Initial values for age-specific labour force participation rates based upon population not in school are given in table 5.1.

Table 5.1. Labour force participation rates, 1976

Age	Male labour force participation (urban + rural) ARUB(2,k) ARRU(2,k)	Female labour force participation	
		Urban ARUB(1,k)	Rural ARRU(1,k)
11-14	32.2	2.2	6.6
15-19	78.9	19.4	58.2
20-24	95.8	21.5	64.4
25-29	98.3	24.6	73.5
30-39	98.3	25.9	77.7
40-49	98.3	26.7	80.1
50-59	96.5	26.1	78.2
60-65	86.4	17.1	51.4
65+	86.4	17.1	51.4

Source. Bigsten (1980), p. 190.

5.5 Population projections

Since the model treats population by age group, population accounting is fairly simple in the model. It consists mainly of cohorts shifting from one year to the other, taking into account survival rates and migration rates. The population is split into three groups: age = 0, which gives the number of births (model age 1); ages 1-65; age 66 and above (model age 66).

Age 0

For each year the model has determined the urban and rural crude birth rate (see formulae [49] and [50]). A fixed gender ratio of 1.04 is assumed, based upon the findings of the 1969 Population Census, indicating that more males than females are born.

$$RBORN = CBR * \sum_{s=1}^{2} \sum_{k=1}^{66} RP(s,k) \qquad [81]$$

$$RP2(1,1) = \frac{1}{2.04} \; RBORN \qquad\qquad [82]$$

$$RP2(2,1) = \frac{1.04}{2.04} \; RBORN \qquad\qquad [83]$$

$$UBORN = CBU * \sum_{s=1}^{2} \sum_{k=1}^{66} UP(s,k) \qquad\qquad [84]$$

$$UP2(1,1) = \frac{1}{2.04} \; UBORN \qquad\qquad [85]$$

$$UP2(2,1) = \frac{1.04}{2.04} \; UBORN \qquad\qquad [86]$$

where

RBORN	=	rural births in year t
UBORN	=	urban births in year t
CBR	=	crude birth rate, rural
CBU	=	crude birth rate, urban
RP(s,k)	=	rural population by gender and age in year t-1
UP(s,k)	=	urban population by gender and age in year t-1
RP2(s,k)	=	rural population by gender and age in year t
UP2(s,k)	=	urban population by gender and age in year t
s	=	gender (1 = female; 2 = male)
k	=	model age (1, 66)

Ages 1-65

Here we have to take into account migration and survival probabilities.

$$RP2(s,k) = RP(s,k-1) * [1-RUMS(s,k-1)] * SR(s,k-1) \qquad [87]$$

$$UP2(s,k) = [UP(s,k-1)$$

$$+ RUMS(s,k-1) * RP(s,k-1)] * SU(s,k-1) \qquad [88]$$

where

RUMS(s,k)	=	age- and gender-specific migration rates
SR(s,k)	=	survival probability, rural
SU(s,K)	=	survival probability, urban

Age 65 and over

In this group no cohort movement takes place, so population accounting must be treated differently (k=66).

$$RP2(s,k) = RP(s,k-1) * [1-RUMS(s,k-1)] * SR(s,k-1) \qquad [89]$$

$$+ RP(s,k) * [1-RUMS(s,k)] * SR(s,k)$$

$$UP2(s,k) = [UP(s,k-1) \qquad [90]$$

$$+ RUMS(s,k-1) * RP(s,k-1)] * SU(s,k-1)$$

$$+ [UP(s,k) + RUMS(s,k) * RP(s,k)] * SU(s,k)$$

Total population

Total population is calculated by summing population by age and gender.

$$RPOP = \sum_s \sum_k RP2(s,k) \qquad [91]$$

$$UPOP = \sum_s \sum_k UP2(s,k) \qquad [92]$$

where

RPOP = total rural population in year t
UPOP = total urban population in year t

Since population accounting in the model operates through cohorts we need to provide the population by age, gender and location for the year 1976. In order to arrive at this, the following procedure has been applied. Male and female population distribution in urban and rural areas according to the 1969 census has been taken and projected until 1976, making use of known values for fertility rates, mortality rates from the 1977 Baseline Demographic Survey, and migration rates from the 1979 census, by running the demographic part of the model independently.

This resulted in the population distribution shown in table 5.2.

It is difficult to test whether this population distribution represents the "real" population distribution, since this is not published or given anywhere for 1976. All

Table 5.2. Population distribution: Kenya, 1976

Year	Rural population				Urban population			
	Female		Male		Female		Male	
	No.	%	No.	%	No.	%	No.	%
0	302 095	5.01	314 179	5.34	35 086	4.90	36 490	4.09
1-4	937 847	15.57	954 674	16.24	113 756	15.88	115 797	12.98
5-9	938 831	15.58	949 633	16.151	107 888	15.06	112 506	12.61
10-14	769 538	12.77	790 252	13.44	79 385	11.08	78 092	8.75
15-19	631 726	10.49	646 111	10.99	68 794	9.60	68 100	7.63
20-24	503 408	8.36	510 782	8.69	71 785	10.02	74 310	8.33
25-29	401 155	6.66	383 365	6.52	71 741	10.01	95 305	10.68
30-34	330 858	5.49	296 915	5.05	56 844	7.94	92 415	10.36
35-39	280 350	4.65	243 122	4.13	36 268	5.06	71 468	8.01
40-44	231 967	3.85	198 299	3.37	24 975	3.49	54 138	6.07
45-49	189 210	3.14	163 250	2.78	17 034	2.38	36 258	4.13
50-54	150 741	2.50	128 955	2.19	12 382	1.73	26 258	2.94
55-59	118 352	1.96	103 440	1.76	7 752	1.08	12 943	1.45
60-64	88 581	1.47	76 315	1.30	5 190	0.72	7 172	0.80
65+	149 386	2.48	120 932	2.06	7 473	1.04	10 309	1.16
Total	6 024 916	100.00	5 880 224	100.00	716 353	100.00	892 182	100.00

Source. See text.

we can do is to test whether the model prediction for 1979 matches the population figures for 1979, as found by the census (see table 5.3).

Table 5.3. <u>A comparison of population in 1979 by age according to 1979 census and to base run model results</u>

Age group	Population according to 1979 census		Population according to base run results	
	No. (thousands)	%	No. (thousands)	%
0-4	2 843.4	18.6	3 204.6	19.1
5-9	2 491.8	16.3	2 427.8	16.0
10-14	2 704.8	13.5	1 911.7	12.6
15-19	1 741.8	11.4	1 574.1	10.4
20-24	1 327.4	8.7	1 290.3	8.5
25-29	1 055.7	6.9	1 290.3	8.5
30-34	818.1	5.3	862.4	6.9
35-39	615.6	4.0	700.5	4.6
40-44	535.2	3.5	560.0	3.7
45-49	440.9	2.9	450.8	3.0
50-54	373.9	2.4	353.1	2.3
55-59	275.3	1.8	268.8	1.8
60+	733.1	4.8	508.1	3.4
Total	15 330.0	100.0	15 170.0	100.0

The total population figures for the simulation exercise compare surprisingly well with the results of the 1979 census, although the model outcomes are somewhat more biased towards younger children and the census towards teenagers. However, while the population growth rate according to the census amounts to 3.4 per cent, results of the earlier cited 1977 Baseline Fertility Survey and other information suggest a rate of 3.9-4.0 per cent, which is the figure currently used in international circles and in the United Nations <u>World population prospects</u> (New York, 1985). Since the model starts with a population growth of 3.93 per cent in the base run, the "overestimation" of the 0-4 year old group may be more realistic than the actual 1979 census data.

Note

[1] Later published as Hicks (1982), where Hicks qualifies his correlation results. By applying other methodologies, however, he still finds strong linkages between education and life expectancy (p. 494).

6 Effects of basic needs and demographic variables on the other parts of the model

In the previous two chapters we described how the values for major basic needs and demographic variables are determined. In this chapter we take a closer look at how these variables affect other parts of the model. We will also refer to some discussion in the literature, discussed in Chapter 1.

It might at this point be useful to recall some of the equations from the demographic section, to illustrate how the effects of various basic needs variables on other variables can reinforce each other. Education level and life expectancy, for example, were major determinants of crude birth rate, while life expectancy at birth depended amongst other things on society's educational attainment and on health-related expenditures (sections 5.1 and 5.2). But the basic needs and demographic variables also have various linkage effects in the model outside these subsystems.

We will list the other major effects first and then discuss them one at a time.

- skill composition of the labour force;
- labour productivity;
- value added share in gross output;
- changing patterns of consumption.

6.1 Skill composition of the labour force

The basic needs and demographic subsystems generate the

95

active population as well as their education level. However, for the supply subsystem we need a distinction between skilled and unskilled labour as separate factors of production.

An elegant method has been proposed by Tinbergen (1975), who argues for the construction of a production function into which both the required and the actual schooling of the labour force are incorporated. With levels of actual schooling ranging from i=1...v and levels of required schooling ranging from j=1...s one arrives in principle[1] at s*v categories of labour. The production function would be of the form $Y = f(l_{11},...,l_{sv},$ other factors). One can then achieve a detailed mapping between educational achievement and skill requirements.

In the basic needs model the assumption is made that low-skill jobs would be occupied mainly by workers with a low education level, while high-skill jobs would be performed by those with a high education level. In its most extreme form, this assumption would imply, for v=s, that $l_{ij} = 0$ for $i \neq j$. The Urban Food Purchasing Survey (Republic of Kenya, CBS, 1977) allowed a first and tentative check of this assumption. The households in the sample were mapped on a 3 x 3 matrix consisting of three education and three skill levels:

- low education : up to Standard 7
- high education : above Standard 7
- high skill : professional, technical and clerical
- low skill : others
- and two groups of non-stated and unemployed (see table 6.1).

Almost all low-skill jobs were in fact held by those with a low education level. With regard to high-skill occupations, the ratio of those with a high level of education to those with a low level was 3:2. However, of those educated to a high level, 75 per cent were engaged in high-skill occupations. As education becomes more accessible, those with more education are likely to push out those with less education, which would reinforce the strong correlation between education and skill level groups. Moreover, if we leave aside the residual group, both the skilled/unskilled split and the less educated/more educated split lead to a similar picture in terms of expenditure patterns, thus reinforcing our assumption that we are dealing with two distinct groups. For the highly educated group per capita expenditure is K.sh.3,698 and food consumption is 32 per cent of total consumption, while for the skilled group per capita expenditure is K.sh.3,350 and food consumption is again 32 per cent. For the less educated group

Table 6.1. The relation between skill level and education level in urban areas

Occupation	Education				Household size	Household income per capita (K.sh.)	Total expenditure per capita (K.sh.)	% expenditure on food
	Low	High	Not stated	Total				
Not stated	4	0	0	4	7.00	1 446	1 120	50
High-skill	62	91	0	153	5.80	3 322	3 350	32
Low-skill	270	33	11	314	5.51	2 004	2 233	39
Total	336	124	11	471	5.62	2 427	2 587	36
Household size	5.78	5.31	5.63	5.62				
Household income per capita (K.sh.)	1 972	3 770	1 218	2 427				
Total expenditure per capita	2 210	3 698	1 549	2 587				
% expenditure on food	39	32	44	36				

Source. Based on the Urban Food Purchasing Survey (Republic of Kenya, CBS, 1977).

per capita expenditure is K.sh.2,210 and food consumption is 39 per cent while, for the low-skill group per capita expenditure is K.sh.2,233 and food consumption is again 39 per cent.

The procedure of mapping education groups on to skill groups thus seems to be acceptable, at least as regards urban areas in Kenya.

Based upon figures from the Urban Food Purchasing Survey a matrix was constructed to map educational attainment on to skill levels. However, although the mapping is justified in the base year, it was found in trial runs that a considerable excess supply of skilled labour would be generated for projections over 15 years and longer because of the rapidly increasing educational attainment of the population. In reality this will mean that jobs previously occupied by workers with a low education level will be occupied in the future by more educated workers, so that educational requirements for jobs will be increased. In order to allow for this phenomenon a weighting procedure was applied so that the skill content of the rural and urban labour force is partly determined by the education level in year t and partly by the skilled/unskilled ratio in the base year.

A second consideration is that in the base run of the model we assume a fixed ratio between skilled and unskilled wages. As Tinbergen has argued when discussing allegations that there is an excess of university graduates in industrial countries, there is no pre-ordained wage ratio between skilled and unskilled workers (Tinbergen, 1975, p. 105). In some policy experiments we have allowed for changes in the wage ratio between skilled and unskilled workers and consequent substitution effects in the production functions (as explained in Chapter 9, section 4, and Chapter 11, section 2).

$$\text{SKCFU(t)} = (1-a) \ [\frac{\text{SKCFU(0)}}{\text{EDUCU(0)}} \ast \text{EDUCU(t)}] + a \ \text{SKCFU (0)} \qquad [93]$$

$$\text{SKCFR(t)} = (1-b) \ [\frac{\text{SKCFR(0)}}{\text{EDUCR(0)}} \ast \text{EDUCR(t)}] + b \ \text{SKCFR (0)} \qquad [94]$$

where

SKCFU(t)	=	skill coefficient, urban areas, in year t
SKCFR(t)	=	skill coefficient, rural areas, in year t
EDUCU(t)	=	population in urban areas aged 15–65 with education higher than Standard 7 in year t
EDUCR(t)	=	population in rural areas aged 15–65 with education higher than Standard 7 in year t
a	=	weighting factor in urban areas (a = 0.75)
b	=	weighting factor in rural areas (b = 0.55)

6.2 Labour productivity

As discussed in Chapter 1, the impact of basic needs satisfaction on labour productivity is an important factor when it comes to justifying a basic needs approach. Although macro-studies have often shown econometric relations between growth and the provision of basic needs, the direction of the causation could not always be clearly determined. Furthermore, while micro-studies mostly suggested that increased provision of basic needs had positive effects on labour productivity, results could be inconclusive at the macro level since the success of one group might have been at the expense of another group.

The question of micro and macro effects also proved difficult when it came to estimating the parameters for the Kenya basic needs model. Based upon available international data, it would be possible to build in a relation between growth in total output and increases in basic needs satisfaction (or more than average increases in basic needs satisfaction). But as the model is disaggregated by economic sectors and by different socio-economic groups, the linkages become much more complicated. Unlike the studies discussed earlier, the model would have to specify to what extent increased satisfaction of basic needs of group g influences production factor p of the production function in sector j. In Kenya data are lacking to answer such questions fully. For agriculture we were, however, able to find survey data which allowed us to incorporate educational attainment in the production functions both for small- and for large-scale agricultural production. Results are given in Appendix 5.[2] For urban areas such information was not available. In urban areas, however, education changes the skill composition of the labour force, with skilled labour having a higher marginal productivity in the production function than unskilled labour. Furthermore, the model allows experiments with increased non-factor productivity in non-agricultural production functions due to increased basic needs satisfaction.

6.3 Value added share in gross output

It can be argued that basic needs policies may change the production process and that this might change the technical coefficients of the input-output table and the share of value added in gross output. This question was investigated by Skolka (1984), who carried out a comparative analysis for 37 countries for which a standardised input-output table was available comprising eight sectors. In only one sector (agriculture) did Skolka find a highly significant decrease in the share of value added. For agro-food, energy, basic products, light industry and services a small but still significant decrease was found, while for the capital goods and construction sectors no significant correlation was obtained. In order to test for the influence of increased basic needs satisfaction, countries were divided into above and below average performers, after regressing literacy and life expectancy rates on GDP per capita. Investigating patterns of change in the share of value added for the eight sectors in the two different subsectors did not, however, give any significant results. The hypothesis that basic needs policies influence the share of value added (and consequently technical coefficients of the input-output tables) had to be rejected. The present version of the Kenya basic needs model still makes use, therefore, of constant value added shares in gross output.

6.4 Changes in patterns of consumption

Increased expenditure on basic needs by public authorities may change the consumption patterns of households, partly because expenditure on privately bought basic needs items may decrease and partly because tastes and habits may change. This question has not, however, been dealt with in the literature, and preliminary research on an international data set proved inconclusive. The effect of the changed budget constraint can be handled in the model by varying the share of average household expenditure on government services (average for all groups 2.2 per cent) and the share on private trade and services (14.2 per cent), although this is not done in the present study.

Notes

[1] Tinbergen does, however, assume a shortage of educated manpower and poses the restriction v $\leqslant$ s. As we will show later, in an expanding economy the definition of required schooling will have to change in order for this inequality to hold.

[2] An original formulation of the influence of basic needs which related production not only to education but also to health centres and education gave insignificant results.

$$\text{RDPR} = \frac{\text{LSURU} + \text{LSSRU}}{\text{RPOP}} \qquad [101]$$

$$\text{UDPR} = \frac{\text{LSUUB} + \text{LSSUB}}{\text{UPOP}} \qquad [102]$$

where

RDPR = rural dependency ratio
UDPR = urban dependency ratio
RPOP = total rural population
UPOP = total urban population

We have now derived labour supply in rural and urban areas, but we still need to make one more correction in order to take account of the fact that non-agricultural activities do take place in rural areas. It has been estimated that in 1976, 231,849 persons working in rural areas belonged to the non-agricultural labour force. This group represents 5 per cent of the rural labour force (Crawford and Thorbecke, 1978). We have to add this supply of non-agricultural rural labour to that in urban areas in order to obtain the supply of labour in non-agricultural activities.

$$\begin{array}{lll}
\text{MOLABS} = \text{LSSUB} + \text{a LSSRU} & \text{where a} = 0.05 & [103] \\
\text{MOLABU} = \text{LSUUB} + \text{a LSURU} & \text{where a} = 0.05 & [104]
\end{array}$$

$$\begin{array}{ll}
\text{AGLABS} = (1-\text{a}) \text{ LSSRU} & [105] \\
\text{AGLABU} = (1-\text{a}) \text{ LSURU} & [106]
\end{array}$$

where

MOLABS = non-agricultural skilled labour supply
MOLABU = non-agricultural unskilled labour supply
AGLABS = agricultural skilled labour supply
AGLABU = agricultural unskilled labour supply

For the functioning of the model we need to determine the supply of labour among the different sectors, as labour supply by sector and available capital by sector are used in the production functions in order to calculate supply on the product market. Total employment is then calculated according to how the labour market adjusts after convergence between supply and demand on the product market has taken place; this is described in Chapter 9.

We assume that growth in sectoral value added in year t-1 determines the amount of additional skilled labour (LDS_j) needed in each sector,

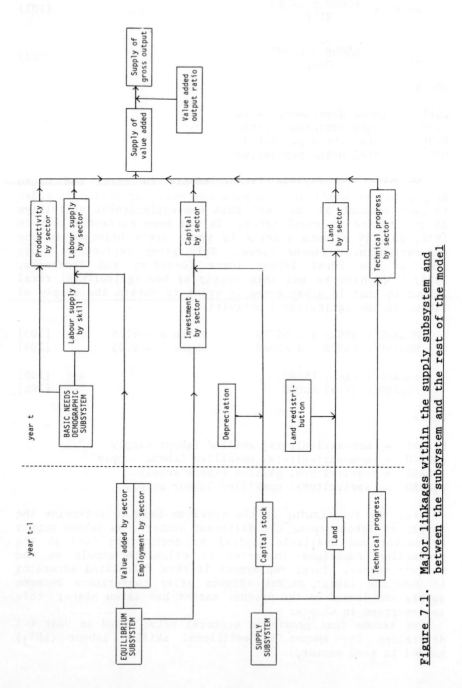

Figure 7.1. Major linkages within the supply subsystem and between the subsystem and the rest of the model

104

$$LDS_j = a_j^s * \Delta VA_j (t-1) \qquad [107]$$

where

$$a_j^s = \frac{LS_j(t-1)}{VA_j(t-1)} \qquad [108]$$

where $LS_j(t-1)$ indicates last year's skilled employment in sector j.

Two cases may arise:

(i) when $\sum_{j=1}^{2} (LDS_j(t) + LS_j(t-1)) > AGLABS$ [109]

or $\sum_{j=3}^{14} (LDS_j(t) + LS_j(t-1)) > MOLABS$

there is excess demand and all labour requirements are reduced proportionally in order to meet the labour supply condition.

(ii) when $\sum_{j=1}^{2} (LDS_j(t) + LS_j(t-1)) < AGLABS$ [110]

or $\sum_{j=3}^{14} (LDS_j(t) + LS_j(t-1)) < MOLABS$

there is excess supply but no upward adjustment of demand takes place. Even with the economy functioning at full capacity there could be unemployment.

The same mechanism is applied for supply of unskilled labour per sector (LDU_i).

$$LDU_i = a_j^u * \Delta VA_j(t-1) \qquad [111]$$

7.2 Supply of capital

$$K_i(t) = K_i(t-1) + NIV_i \qquad [112]$$

$$NIV_i = I_i + IG_i - D_i \qquad [113]$$

$$D_i = d_i K_i \qquad [114]$$

where

K_i = capital in sector i
I_i = gross private investment in sector i
IG_i = government investment
NIV_i = net (new) investment in sector i
D_i = depreciation of capital in sector i

Values for the depreciation rate d_i and for the amount of capital in the base year are given in table 7.1 and table 7.2 respectively. How the values for I_i and IG_i in year t are determined is described in Chapter 9 where also base year figures are given.

7.3 Determination of potential value added

(a) Agriculture

The model distinguishes throughout between small-scale agriculture (sector 1) and large-scale agriculture (sector 2). For small-scale agriculture three different categories are distinguished based upon farm size in 1976, namely:

$$j = 1, \quad 0\text{--}1 \text{ hectares}$$
$$j = 2, \quad 1\text{--}4 \text{ hectares}$$
$$j = 3, \quad 4\text{--}8 \text{ hectares}$$

and for each category productivity per hectare is calculated. Distribution of the production factors over the three categories is given by the parameters b_j, l_j and k_j below.

Land is distributed between small-scale and large-scale agriculture according to a fixed parameter (which can be changed in policy experiments).

$$LANDL = (1-a) \, LAND \qquad [115]$$

$$LANDS = a \, LAND \qquad [116]$$

$$LANDS_j = b_j \, LANDS \qquad [117]$$

where

LAND = total available arable land
LANDL = land used for large-scale agriculture
LANDS = land used for small-scale agriculture
$LANDS_j$ = land used for small-scale agriculture, sector j

$$VAS_1 = \sum_{j=1}^{3} VASS_j * LANDS_{1,j} \qquad [118]$$

$$VASS_j = A_{1,j} L_{1,j}^{a1,j} K_{1,j}^{b1,j} d_{i,j}^{c1,j} e^{t1,j} \qquad [119]$$

$$L_{1,j} = \frac{l_j(LDU_1 + LDS_1)}{LANDS_j} \qquad \sum_{j=1}^{3} l_j = 1 \qquad [120]$$

$$K_{1,j} = \frac{k_j K_1}{LAND_j} \qquad \sum_{j=1}^{3} k_j = 1 \qquad [121]$$

where

VAS_1 = total value added in small-scale agriculture
$VASS_j$ = value added per hectare in small-scale agriculture for size j
$L_{1,j}$ = labour used per hectare (for determination of LDU_1 and LDS_1 see section on labour supply, formulae [107]-[111])
$K_{1,j}$ = capital stock per hectare in small-scale agriculture for size j
$LANDS_j$ = land available in small-scale agriculture for size j
$d_{1,j}$ = percentage of persons with more than elementary education
$t1,j$ = technical progress
e = mathematical constant (base of natural logarithm)

Value added in large-scale agriculture (VAS_2) is calculated according to a slightly different relation:

$$VAS_2 = VAL_2 * LANDL \qquad [122]$$

$$VAL_2 = A_2 \left(\frac{LDU_2 + LDS_2}{LANDL}\right)^{b2} \left(\frac{K_2}{LANDL}\right)^{c2} e^{t2} \qquad [123]$$

where

VAL_2 = value added per hectare in large-scale agriculture
LDU_2 = unskilled labour available for large-scale agriculture
LDS_2 = skilled labour available for large-scale agriculture
K_2 = capital stock in large-scale agriculture

LANDL = area available for large-scale agriculture
t_2 = technical progress in large-scale agriculture
e = mathematical constant

The parameters of the production function are given in table 7.1, which is based upon the regression results reported in Appendix 5, section 6.

The base year values are given in table 7.2 for large-scale and small-scale agriculture, and are based upon Appendix 1 for value added, employment and capital, and Appendix 5 for the differentiation between the three small-scale farming sectors. Estimations for arable land have been derived from Chibber and Shah (1983).

(b) Non-agriculture

For all other sectors, except for sectors 12, 13 and 14 (government services, education and health, and ownership of dwellings) a normal Cobb-Douglas production function is used to determine value added. (For further discussion of this, see Appendix 4.)

$$VAS_j = A_j (LDU_j)^{a_j} (LDS_j)^{b_j} K_j^{c_j} e^{t_j} \qquad [124]$$

where

K_j = capital in sector j
LDU_j = unskilled labour in sector j
LDS_j = skilled labour in sector j
t_j = technical progress in sector j

while

$$VAS_{14} = (COR_{14})^{-1} K_{14} e^{t_{14}} \qquad [125]$$

in which

COR_{14} = capital-output ratio for ownership of dwelling.

For sectors 12 and 13 value added depends on demand factors, as will be explained in Chapter 9.

After $VAS_{(j)}$ has been calculated for each sector, total supply of gross output (XS_j) is calculated by means of value added coefficients expressing the value added/gross output ratios.

$$VAC_j = 1 - \sum_i a_{i,j} - \sum_i am_{i,j} \qquad [126]$$

and

$$XS_j = VAC_j^{-1} VAS_j \qquad [127]$$

where $a_{i,j}$ are the elements of the domestic input-output matrix and $am_{i,j}$ the elements of the matrix of imported intermediate inputs (see Appendix 3).

The parameters of the sectoral production functions are reported in table 7.1, which is based upon the regression results for non-agriculture reported in Appendix 4, section 4, and for agriculture in Appendix 5, section 6.

The structure of production is given in table 7.2, which is based on Appendix 1 and Appendix 5.

PLANNING FOR BASIC NEEDS

Table 7.1. Production functions (parameters)

1. Industry and services

	Coefficient capital	Coefficient skilled labour	Coefficient unskilled labour	Depre- ciation	Technical progress
3. Mining	0.206	0.580	0.214	0.05	0.005
4. Food manufacturing	0.486	0.396	0.118	0.05	0.005
5. Non-food manufac- turing	0.264	0.567	0.169	0.05	0.005
6. Modern building and construction	0.131	0.730	0.139	0.07	0.005
7. Traditional building and construction	0.131	-	0.869	0.07	0.005
8. Transport and communications	0.200	0.640	0.160	0.07	0.005
9. Modern trade	0.566	0.210	0.224	0.05	0.005
10. Traditional trade and services	0.200	-	0.800	0.02	0.005
11. Modern services	0.484	0.403	0.113	0.02	0.005
12. General government services	-	-	-	0.02	0.005
13. Government services relating to edu- cation and health	-	-	-	0.04	0.005
14. Ownership of dwellings	1.0	-	-	0.02	0.005

2. Agriculture

	Coefficient labour	Coefficient capital	Technical progress	Depreciation	Education dummy
Small-scale agriculture					
Group 1	0.97	0.06	0.005	0.04	0.05
Group 2	0.70	0.10	0.005	0.04	0.19
Group 3	0.70	0.10	0.005	0.04	0.19
Large-scale agriculture	0.499	0.473	0.01	0.04	

110

Table 7.2. Structure of production (1976 values)

1. Industry and services

	Capital (K.£ million)	Unskilled labour (thousands)	Skilled labour (thousands)	Value added (K.£ mill.)
3. Mining	32.27	2.8	2.0	3.25
4. Food manufacturing	207.88	19.7	13.5	94.57
5. Non-food manufacturing	368.51	58.7	41.1	168.71
6. Modern building and construction	114.00	26.6	21.4	46.52
7. Traditional building and construction	24.69	-	-	19.45
8. Transport and communications	285.00	19.9	29.6	65.10
9. Modern trade	179.67	31.5	37.3	109.07
10. Traditional trade and services	39.82	135.4	-	49.83
11. Modern services	74.48	31.5	30.4	89.61
12. General government services	294.72	81.6	21.8	82.47
13. Government services relating to education and health	126.30	24.8	99.5	98.56
14. Ownership of dwellings	293.94	-	-	75.12

2. Agriculture

	Land (million hectares)	Labour (millions)			Capital (K.£ million)	Value added (K.£ million)
		All	Unskilled	Skillled		
Small-scale						
Group 1	0.801	2.5141			62.30	200.64
Group 2	1.413	1.2871			49.37	109.96
Group 3	1.243	0.3750			22.23	59.52
Total small-scale	3.457	4.1769			133.90	370.12
Total large-scale	2.689		0.1899	0.0072	105.31	134.77

8 Demand on the product market

Final demand is calculated according to the normal accounting identity

$$FD_i = PC_i + INV_i + GC_i + GI_i + EXP_i \qquad [128]$$

where

FD_i	=	final demand for product i
PC_i	=	private consumption of product i
INV_i	=	private investment demand for product i
GC_i	=	government consumption of product i
GI_i	=	government investment demand for product i
EXP_i	=	export of product i

The major linkages within the demand subsystem and with other subsystems over time are indicated in figure 8.1.

8.1 Consumption by socio-economic group

The Social Accounting Matrix (Republic of Kenya, CBS, 1981) provides final consumer demand for the products of each sector by urban and rural income classes. For the purposes of the model this has been reworked into consumer demand by the eight socio-economic groups and by the 14 sectors in the model, arriving at an 8 x 14 matrix. Table 8.1 provides the thus derived expenditure (1976) figures, while the average budget shares are given in table 8.2 both for total consumer

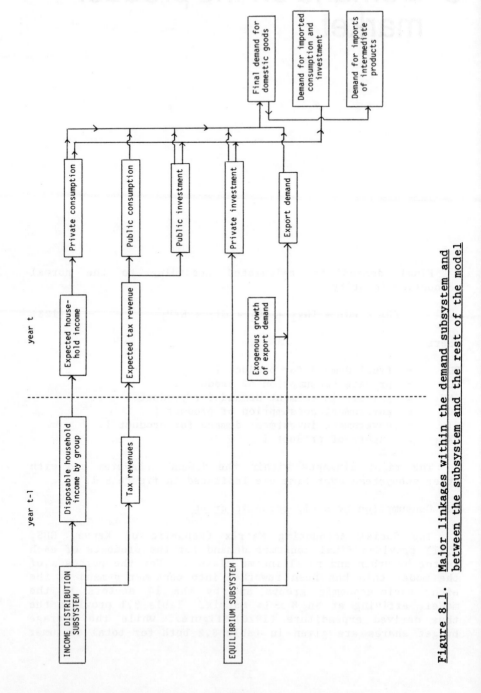

Figure 8.1. <u>Major linkages within the demand subsystem and between the subsystem and the rest of the model</u>

Table 8.1. Consumption expenditure by socio-economic group and by economic sector, Kenya, 1976 (K.£ million)

Group	Sector AGTRAD	AGRMOD	MINING	MANFOOD	MANNONF	BUCOMOD	BUCOTRAD	TRANSP	TRAMOD	TRASETRA	SERMOD	GOVPUADM	GOVEDHE	OWNSDWEL	TOTAL
1. Peasant farmers	164.96	0.0	0.0	57.47	34.53	0.0	0.0	10.68	16.57	4.01	3.74	1.35	0.83	0.0	294.14
2. Agricultural workers, skilled	4.39	0.0	0.0	1.60	0.77	0.0	0.0	0.26	0.29	0.23	0.29	0.09	0.06	0.0	7.98
3. Agricultural workers, unskilled	16.90	0.0	0.0	6.16	3.07	0.0	0.0	1.10	1.10	0.80	1.10	0.22	0.33	0.33	30.78
4. Agricultural employers/ professionals	11.08	0.0	0.0	4.85 (1.0)	8.50 (4.1)	0.0	0.0	2.57 (1.0)	4.25 (0.76)	1.28	2.13	0.14	1.44 (0.74)	6.50	42.74 (7.60)
5. Non-agricultural informal sector workers	7.70	2.50	0.0	15.34	9.67	0.0	0.0	4.00	2.50	1.80	1.00	0.30	0.20	6.10	51.12
6. Non-agricultural workers, skilled	45.17	21.93	0.0	63.90 (2.9)	62.89 (29.5)	0.0	0.0	19.06 (6.54)	18.60 (2.0)	37.93	10.32	1.50	7.65 (3.12)	44.83	333.18 (44.06)
7. Non-agricultural workers, unskilled	10.70	3.50	0.0	23.20	7.25	0.0	0.0	5.80	2.40	3.57	2.09	0.40	1.80	11.80	72.51
8. Non-agricultural employers/ professionals	2.20	5.80 (2.28)	0.0	12.15 (7.89)	21.62 (16.39)	0.0	0.0	11.53 (7.52)	4.67 (2.30)	3.00	5.64 (1.38)	0.61	2.84 (2.34)	8.40	78.46 (40.10)
TOTAL	263.10	33.73	0.0	184.07	148.30	0.0	0.0	55.00	50.38	52.62	26.31	4.61	15.15	77.63	910.89
of which imported expenditure goods	(0.0)	(2.28)	(0.0)	(11.79)	(49.99)	(0.0)	(0.0)	(15.06)	(5.06)	(0.0)	(1.38)	(0.0)	(6.20)	(0.0)	(91.76)

Figures in brackets = value of imported goods.

Source. Data base Kenya basic needs model and Social Accounting Matrix (Republic of Kenya, CBS, 1981).

115

Table 8.2. Average budget shares of the eight socio-economic groups (percentages)

Group	Sector							
	Agriculture	Food manu-facturing	Non-food manufacturing	Transport	Trade and services	Government services	Housing (inc. imputed rent)	Total
1. Peasant farmers	56.08	19.54	11.74	3.63	8.27	0.74	0.0	100.00
2. Agricultural workers, skilled	54.96	20.01	9.65	3.34	10.17	1.86	0.0	100.00
3. Agricultural workers, unskilled	54.92	20.01	9.99	3.57	9.74	1.78	0.0	100.00
4. Agricultural employers/professionals	25.93	11.35 (1.71)	19.89 (8.74)	6.00 (3.43)	17.90 (1.30)	3.70 (2.50)	15.21	100.00 (17.69)
5. Non-agricultural informal sector workers	19.95	30.03	18.92	7.82	10.37	0.98	11.93	100.00
6. Non-agricultural workers, skilled	20.14	19.00 (0.87)	18.90 (8.76)	5.76 (1.81)	20.06 (0.60)	2.75 (0.72)	13.45	100.00 (12.76)
7. Non-agricultural workers, unskilled	19.58	32.00	10.00	8.00	11.12	3.03	16.27	100.00
8. Non-agricultural employers/professionals	10.20 (2.90)	15.49 (10.06)	27.56 (19.99)	14.70 (8.95)	16.96 (4.69)	4.40 (2.98)	10.71	100.00 (49.57)
9. Average for all groups	32.59	20.21	16.28	6.04	14.20	2.17	8.52	100.00

Figures in brackets = budget share of imported goods.

Source. As table 8.1.

Table 8.3. Expenditure elasticities, own price elasticities and food cross-price elasticities by socio-economic group and by economic sector

Group	Sector										
	AGTRAD	AGRMOD	MANFOOD	MANNONF	TRANSP	TRAMOD	TRASETRA	SERMOD	GOVPUADM	GOVEDHE	OWNSDWEL
1. Peasant farmers	0.68	0.56	0.56	0.58	0.86	0.73	0.73	0.73	0.73	0.73	—
	-0.35	-0.29	-0.29	-0.15	-0.20	-0.18	-0.18	-0.18	-0.18	-0.18	
	—	—	—	-0.41	-0.57	-0.48	-0.48	-0.48	-0.48	-0.48	
2. Agricultural workers, skilled	0.24	1.39	1.39	2.01	2.92	1.21	1.21	1.21	1.21	1.21	—
	-0.23	-0.88	-0.88	-0.33	-0.38	-0.22	-0.22	-0.22	-0.22	-0.22	
	—	—	—	-1.75	-2.35	-0.97	-0.97	-0.97	-0.97	-0.97	
3. Agricultural workers, unskilled	0.24	0.72	0.72	1.95	2.15	1.02	1.02	1.02	1.02	1.02	—
	-0.23	-0.74	-0.74	-1.30	-1.51	-0.78	-0.78	-0.78	-0.78	-0.78	
	—	—	—	-0.74	-0.82	-0.39	-0.39	-0.39	-0.39	-0.39	
4. Agricultural employers/ professionals	0.24	1.39	1.39	2.01	2.92	1.21	1.21	1.21	1.21	1.21	1.15
	-0.23	-0.88	-0.88	-0.38	-0.22	-0.22	-0.22	-0.22	-0.22	-0.22	-0.48
	—	—	—	-1.75	-2.35	-0.97	-0.97	-0.97	-0.97	-0.97	-0.37
5. Non-agricultural informal sector workers	0.51	0.51	0.51	0.95	1.15	2.73	2.73	2.73	2.73	1.14	0.86
	-0.47	-0.47	-0.47	-0.64	-0.71	-1.55	-1.55	-1.55	-1.55	-0.72	-0.55
	—	—	—	0.32	-0.37	-0.40	-0.26	-0.26	-0.26	-0.49	-0.37
6. Non-agricultural workers, unskilled	0.51	0.51	0.51	0.95	1.15	2.73	2.73	2.73	2.73	1.14	0.86
	-0.47	-0.47	-0.47	-0.64	-0.71	-1.55	-1.55	-1.55	-1.55	-0.72	-0.55
	—	—	—	-0.32	-0.37	-0.88	-0.88	-0.88	-0.88	-0.37	-0.37
7. Non-agricultural workers, unskilled	0.51	0.51	0.51	0.95	1.15	2.73	2.73	2.73	2.73	1.14	0.86
	-0.47	-0.47	-0.47	-0.64	-0.71	-1.55	-1.55	-1.55	-1.55	-0.72	-0.55
	—	—	—	-0.32	-0.37	-0.88	-0.88	-0.88	-0.88	-0.37	-0.28
8. Non-agricultural employers/ professionals	0.71	0.71	0.71	1.71	0.35	0.78	0.78	0.78	0.78	1.03	0.13
	-0.43	-0.43	-0.43	-0.70	-0.16	-0.36	-0.36	-0.36	-0.36	-0.40	-0.05
	—	—	—	-0.43	-0.09	-0.19	-0.19	-0.19	-0.19	-0.26	-0.03

Source. As table 8.1.

117

goods and for imported goods. The usual picture emerges: high budget shares for agricultural and manufactured food products among the poor groups in both agricultural and non-agricultural sectors. The large budget share for imported goods among non-agricultural employers and professionals is striking: half of their consumption expenditure is on imported consumer goods. Their consumption of imported goods accounts for almost half of all imported consumer goods and consists mainly of manufactured products and transport. Also noticeable is the high share of housing in the consumption expenditure of (especially the poorer) non-agricultural groups.

In order to gauge the future consumption patterns of the socio-economic groups we have calculated for each group, using an extended linear expenditure system (ELES) (Vandemoortele and van der Hoeven, 1982), the expenditure elasticities, own price elasticities and food cross-price elasticities (table 8.3).

Based upon this information, the following consumption relations have been applied in the Kenya basic needs model:

$$\ln PC_{ig} = A_{ig} + B_{ig} \ln INC_g + C_{ig} \ln P_i + D_{ig} \ln FP \qquad [129]$$

with $\quad PC_i = \sum_g PC_{ig}$

where

PC_i = total consumption of product i
PC_{ig} = consumption of product i by a household in group g
INC_g = total expected income of a household in group g
P_i = price of product i
FP = price of food
A_{ig} = constant (depending on consumption patterns in the base year)
B_{ig} = expenditure elasticity)
C_{ig} = own price elasticity) for good i in household
D_{ig} = food price elasticity) belonging to group g

The expected income of socio-economic group g in year t depends on income in year t-1 times the growth factor of income experienced in year t-1.

$$INC_g(t) = DISP_g(t-1) * \frac{DISP_g(t-1)}{DISP_g(t-2)} \qquad [130]$$

where

118

$DISP_g(t)$ = disposable income of group g in year t. See formula [257] in Chapter 11.

Since the model is expressed in constant prices, P_i and FP are set to zero; the price elasticities C and D are consequently not used in the present version of the model.

8.2 Investment

Private demand for investment goods is determined as follows:

$$INV_i = b_i \sum_j I_j \qquad [131]$$

Public demand for investment goods as explained in the next section (formula [136]) is determined as follows.

$$GI_i = d_i \, GI$$

where

INV_i = private investment demand for sector i goods
$\sum_j I_j$ = total private gross investment
GI_i = public investment demand for sector i goods
GI = total public investment

Values for b_i and d_i are given in table 8.4.
These figures have been derived with minor adjustments from the 1976 input-output table (see also Appendix 3).

Table 8.4.   Coefficients of public and private
demand for investment goods

$b_2 = 0.01990$	$d_2 = 0.02184$
$b_5 = 0.45471$	$d_5 = 0.49894$
$b_6 = 0.40456$	$d_6 = 0.44433$
$b_7 = 0.08865$	$d_7 = 0.0$
$b_9 = 0.03180$	$d_9 = 0.03489$

Source.   Appendix 3.

Base year values of GI_i and INV_i are given in table 8.6.

8.3 Government expenditure and revenue

The value of government expenditure for 1976 is given in table 8.6. Government expenditure is split into expenditure on health and education (GOVEDHE) and expenditure on public administration (GOVPVADM); as regards the former category a further distinction is made between expenditure on primary education, secondary education, health and other basic needs as described in Chapter 4. Total government expenditure (GE) is made up of recurrent expenditure and investment (GC and GI) respectively. The split between recurrent expenditure and investment expenditure is based upon initial 1976 conditions.

$$GE = GOVREV(t-1) * \frac{VA(t-1)}{VA(t-2)} \qquad [132]$$

$$GC = a\ GE \qquad [133]$$

$$GI = b\ GE \qquad \text{with } a+b = 1 \qquad [134]$$

$$GC_i = c_i\ GC \qquad [135]$$

$$GI_i = d_i\ GI \qquad [136]$$

where

GE	=	total government expenditure
GC_i	=	recurrent public expenditure demand for sector i
GI_i	=	public investment demand for sector i
VA	=	total GDP
GOVREV	=	government revenue

Total government revenue is determined by tax revenues and by internal borrowing.

$$GOVREV = TD + TDI + TIND + TIMP + TEXP + BINT \qquad [137]$$

Sources of government revenue are:

1. <u>Direct taxes</u> as a percentage of income in each socio-economic group (TD) as well as a percentage of profits in each sector (TDI).

2. <u>Indirect taxes</u> as a percentage of gross value added in each sector (TIND).

3. <u>Import/export taxes</u> levied on imports and exports for each sector (TIMP and TEXP).

4. <u>Borrowing</u>. We assume that part of the savings of the private sector and of industry can be used by the Government (BINT).
This gives the following equation:

(1) $\quad TD \quad = \sum_g a_g Y_g$ [138]

$\quad TDI \quad = \sum_i b_i PROFIT_i$ [139]

(2) $\quad TIND \quad = \sum_i c_i VA_i$ [140]

(3) $\quad TIMP \quad = \sum_i d_i M_i$ [141]

$\quad TEXP \quad = \sum_i e_i EXP_i$ [142]

(4) $\quad BINT \quad = f \sum_g SAGR_g + g \sum_i PROFSAV_i$ [143]

where

Y_g = income per socio-economic group
$PROFIT_i$ = profits in sector i
VA_i = value added of good i
M_i = imports of good i
EXP_i = exports of good i
$SAGR_g$ = saving by socio-economic group g
$PROFSAV_i$ = retained profits by sector i

Values for the tax coefficients in the base run are based upon the 1976 situation but can be changed as part of the scenario experiments. Base run values are indicated in table 8.5.

Table 8.5. Government revenue (base run parameters)

Parameters for direct taxation on personal income				Parameters for borrowing
a_1 = 0.0165	a_5 = 0.0429			f = 0.0
a_2 = 0.0533	a_6 = 0.0571			g = 0.0
a_3 = 0.0740	a_7 = 0.0399			
a_4 = 0.2359	a_8 = 0.2682			

Parameter for direct taxation on profits	Parameters for indirect taxation	Parameters for import taxes	Parameters for export taxes
b_1 = 0.183	c_1 = 0.0	d_1 = 0.0	e_1 = 0.0
b_2 = 0.217	c_2 = 0.021	d_2 = 0.037	e_2 = 0.0
b_3 = 0.205	c_c = 0.039	d_3 = 0.165	e_3 = 0.0
b_4 = 0.200	c_4 = 0.449	d_4 = 0.192	e_4 = 0.0
b_5 = 0.200	c_5 = 0.291	d_5 = 0.145	e_5 = 0.0
b_6 = 0.201	c_6 = 0.009	d_6 = 0.0	e_6 = 0.0
b_7 = 0.0	c_7 = 0.0	d_7 = 0.0	e_7 = 0.0
b_8 = 0.199	c_8 = 0.014	d_8 = 0.0	e_8 = 0.0
b_9 = 0.200	c_9 = 0.023	d_9 = 0.0	e_9 = 0.0
b_{10} = 0.0	c_{10} = 0.0	d_{10} = 0.0	e_{10} = 0.0
b_{11} = 0.199	c_{11} = 0.052	d_{11} = 0.0	e_{11} = 0.0
b_{12} = 0.0	c_{12} = 0.0	d_{12} = 0.0	e_{12} = 0.0
b_{13} = 0.0	c_{13} = 0.0	d_{13} = 0.0	e_{13} = 0.0
b_{14} = 0.192	c_{14} = 0.088	d_{14} = 0.0	e_{14} = 0.0

8.4 Imports

Imports play an important role in the Kenyan economy. The model distinguishes between three different import categories: imports of final consumer goods (M^1), of investment goods (M^2), and of intermediate goods (M^3). The following relations hold in the model:

$$M_i^1 = \sum_g m_{ig}^1 PC_{ig} \qquad\qquad [145]$$

$$M_i^2 = m_i^2(INV_i + GI_i) \qquad\qquad [146]$$

$$M_i^3 = \sum_j am_{ij} [FD_j - M_j^1 - M_j^2] \qquad\qquad [147]$$

where

m_{ig}^1 = coefficient of matrix of imported consumption of product i by group g

PC_{ig} = consumption of product i by group g

m_i^2 = import coefficient of capital goods i

INV_i = private investment demand for good i

GI_i = government investment demand for good i

am_{ij} = coefficient of matrix of imported intermediate goods

Import of consumer goods of a particular category depends not only on total consumption expenditure but also on the expenditure patterns on that particular item by the various socio-economic groups (which have quite different expenditure and import propensities, as reported in table 8.2). Imported consumer goods amounted to 9.9 per cent of the total supply of consumer goods.

Imports of intermediate goods are determined with the help of the matrix of coefficients of intermediate inputs. Appendix 3 describes how the matrix for total intermediate inputs, domestic intermediate inputs and imported intermediate inputs was constructed. Imported intermediate goods amounted in 1976 to 24.5 per cent of total intermediate deliveries.

The imports of intermediate goods also contain the (indirect) imports of government services. According to standard national accounts practices, as applied in the input-output tables for Kenya, direct import by the Government is nil (see table A3.6), and consequently government imports form part of deliveries from sectors to government services.

123

Imports of capital goods per sector depend on total investment demand by sector. The importing of capital goods takes place almost entirely through the non-food manufacturing sector, where imports have a share of 65 per cent in investment demand. The only other sector which imports capital goods is modern building and construction, where imports have a share of 0.82 per cent. All other elements of m_i^2 are zero (see table 8.2). Import of capital goods in 1976 amounted to 27.3 per cent of total investment demand.

Total imports per sector are:

$$M_i = M_i^1 + M_i^2 + M_i^3 \qquad\qquad [148]$$

Imports can be constrained by foreign exchange availability. (Chapter 10 describes how total foreign exchange is determined.) If the foreign exchange constraint does exist, imports of consumer goods are scaled downwards proportionally in order to satisfy the constraint (FE).

$$M_i^{1*} = [\frac{M_i^1 - (M - FE)}{M^1}] M_i^1 \qquad \text{if FE} < M \qquad [149]$$

The scaling down of imports creates an increased demand for domestic production. This demand pull is taken into account in the convergency mechanism of the product market (see Chapter 9, equation [157]). Since convergency takes place partly through quantity adjustment, imports and exports can be adjusted upwards or downwards (Chapter 9, equations [157]-[174]). Because of this the final determination of imported consumer goods and imported intermediate goods in a particular year takes place after the convergency mechanism of the product market has determined value added and final demand for each sector.

Restrictions on imports of consumer goods do not only push up demand for import substitutes in a given year; they also affect consumption patterns over time. Between 1972 and 1976 consumer goods imports declined from 22.5 per cent to 18 per cent of all imports (Republic of Kenya, Statistical Abstract, various issues).

This tendency to increased import substitution of consumption goods is captured in the model by changing the coefficient for imported consumer goods each year.

$$m_{i,g}^{1*} = m_{i,g}^{1} \left[1-a \left(\frac{M_i^1 - M_i^{1*}}{M_i^1} \right) \right] \quad \text{if } M_i^{1*} < M_i^1 \quad [150]$$

where

$m_{i,g}^{1*}$ = adjusted matrix of import coefficients of consumer goods

a = parameter reflecting the relative change in the import coefficients of consumer goods.

The parameter a in formula [150] has been set for model experiments at 0.1. In consequence imported consumer goods as a percentage of total consumer goods supply declined during the 25-year period of the base run from 9.9 to 4.8 per cent, and as a percentage of total imports from 18.2 to 9.4 per cent (see Chapter 12).

8.5 Exports

The growth of demand for exports in each sector is determined exogenously and can be changed as part of a scenario. The growth factors of export demand in the base run are given in table 8.7, while the base year values are given in table 8.6. The assumptions underlying the growth factor for exports are further discussed in Chapter 12, where we discuss some parameters for the base run in more detail.

However, as will be discussed in Chapter 9, initial demand for exports in year t can be adjusted upwards or downwards in order to arrive at convergency on the product market (see especially formulae [161]-[169]). As a consequence, two assumptions can be made for export growth. Either foreign demand is not accommodating and export demand in year t+1 follows the trend before adjustment in year t [151] or foreign demand is accommodating and the growth factor applies to the adjusted value of exports [152]. The latter formulation has been retained for the base run. The former formulation has been included in some scenarios.

$$EXP_i(t) = EXP_i(t-1) * EG_i(t) \quad [151]$$

or

$$EXP_i(t) = EXP_i^1(t-1) * EG_i(t) \quad [152]$$

where

PLANNING FOR BASIC NEEDS

$EXP_i(t)$ = unadjusted exports of sector i in year t

$EXP_i^1(t)$ = adjusted exports of sector i in year t

$EG_i(t)$ = growth factor of exports in sector i in year t

Table 8.6. Values of final demand by sector, 1976 (K.£ million)

Sector	PC	GC	GI	INV	EXP	MPC	MPI	MPIP	MPT
	Final demand in 1976								
1. Small-scale agriculture	263.10	0.00	0.00	0.00	77.06	0.00	0.00	0.00	0.00
2. Large-scale agriculture	33.73	0.00	1.74	4.26	64.98	2.22	0.00	9.13	11.34
3. Mining	0.00	0.00	0.00	0.00	2.54	0.00	0.00	113.02	113.02
4. Food manufacturing	184.07	0.00	0.00	0.00	33.48	11.78	0.00	8.94	20.72
5. Non-food manufacturing	148.30	0.00	39.71	97.30	110.13	48.70	89.94	163.25	301.90
6. Modern building and construction	0.00	0.00	0.00	86.57	0.00	0.00	1.00	0.01	1.01
7. Traditional building and construction	0.00	0.00	0.00	18.97	0.00	0.00	0.00	0.00	0.00
8. Transport and communications	55.00	0.00	0.00	0.00	73.09	14.98	0.00	9.77	24.75
9. Modern trade	50.38	0.00	2.78	6.80	68.12	1.85	0.00	0.01	1.87
10. Traditional trade and services	52.62	0.00	0.00	0.00	0.00	0.00	0.00	0.00	0.00
11. Modern services	26.32	0.00	0.00	0.00	19.45	4.48	0.00	18.35	22.83
12. General government services	4.61	138.72	0.00	0.00	0.00	0.00	0.00	0.00	0.00
13. Government services relating to education and health	15.15	114.71	0.00	0.00	0.00	6.15	0.00	0.00	6.15
14. Ownership of dwellings	77.63	0.00	0.00	0.00	2.72	0.50	0.00	0.00	0.50
TOTAL	910.89	253.43	79.59	213.90	451.55	90.61	90.94	322.47	504.08

PC   = private consumption
GC   = government consumption
GI   = government investment
INV = private investment
EXP = exports

MPC = imported consumer goods
MPI = imported investment goods
MPIP = imported intermediate goods
MPT = total imports

Table 8.7. Import content of demand for capital goods and growth factor of demand for exports by sector

Sector	Imports as a fraction of demand for capital goods in sector i	Growth factor of demand for exports by five-year period				
		1976-80	1981-85	1986-90	1991-95	1996-2000
1. Small-scale agriculture	0.0	0.032	0.032	0.045	0.045	0.045
2. Large-scale agriculture	0.0	0.032	0.032	0.045	0.045	0.045
3. Mining	0.0	0.035	0.011	0.011	0.011	0.011
4. Food manufacturing	0.0	0.010	0.010	0.040	0.040	0.040
5. Non-food manufacturing	0.6564	0.010	0.010	0.040	0.040	0.040
6. Modern building and construction	0.0082	0.000	0.000	0.000	0.000	0.000
7. Traditional building and construction	0.0	0.000	0.000	0.000	0.000	0.000
8. Transport and communications	0.0	0.020	0.023	0.040	0.040	0.040
9. Modern trade	0.0	0.020	0.023	0.040	0.040	0.040
10. Traditional trade and services	0.0	0.000	0.000	0.000	0.000	0.000
11. Modern services	0.0	0.020	0.023	0.040	0.040	0.040
12. General government services	0.0	0.000	0.000	0.000	0.000	0.000
13. Government services relating to education and health	0.0	0.000	0.000	0.000	0.000	0.000
14. Ownership of dwellings	0.0	0.000	0.000	0.000	0.000	0.000

9 Convergency mechanisms

9.1 Introduction

Rather than assume an exogenous supply constraint as other
simulation models have done (e.g. Rodgers et al., 1978),[1]
the Kenya basic needs model develops the demand side and the
supply side fully for both the product and the factor markets.
The advantage of this approach is easy to understand. As
indicated earlier the basic needs subsystem affects both the
composition of the labour force and labour productivity in the
various sectors where there could be an output (or, better,
capacity) augmenting effect. With output constrained
exogenously, this would lead, among other things, to lower
utilisation of the production factor of labour and could lead
to other inconsistencies in the model. Although lower
utilisation of labour should not be excluded from the model it
should not be forced upon it. Hence our decision to treat
demand and supply aspects separately.

Treating demand and supply separately does, however, force
us to describe the mechanism which equilibrates demand and
supply in order for the macro accounting identities to hold.
Unfortunately, an equilibrating mechanism is difficult to
design (and hence often partly avoided in simulation models);
one could even wonder why one needs to pay attention to demand
and supply interactions, since the simulations cover a long
time span. However, such interactions could only be ignored
if we were convinced that a (temporary) disequilibrium between
supply and demand did not affect the growth path of the
economy.

129

PLANNING FOR BASIC NEEDS

This might be the case if the economy could grow unconstrained by supply of factor inputs or foreign exchange. For a developing economy like Kenya, however, this is certainly not the situation. Certain elements in the development process will be scarce. Consequently we may have (and do have, as will be shown in the discussion of the results) a binding constraint in one of the markets (capital market or foreign exchange market). Such binding constraints will affect the growth pattern of the economy. And the reaction or adaptation induced by these constraints will affect not only the rate of growth but also the distribution of income between various groups (Taylor and Lysy, 1979).

Having explicitly made the case for the development of both the demand and the supply side of the model, we now have to decide how the convergence between demand and supply should take place[2] in order to satisfy the accounting identities. Recall that (initial) disequilibrium may occur on four different markets:

(a) the foreign exchange market;
(b) the product market;
(c) the labour market;
(d) the capital market.

The "standard" theoretical solution is to attach prices to labour, capital products and foreign exchange and assume that a Walrasian auctioneer fixes prices in such a way that all markets clear. Although it has been shown that such a process, under certain assumptions, will lead to a unique solution (Dorfman et al., 1958, Chapter 13; Dervis et al., 1982, section 5.3), it is only recently that models have been developed which incorporate these aspects: the so-called general equilibrium models (for a good description see Dervis et al., 1982; for some (self-)critique, Taylor, 1979).

In practice, however, most general equilibrium models deal with simulations ranging from five to ten years, mainly because of the complicated solution algorithms needed to determine prices on factor and product markets. In the basic needs model we are interested in longer term issues and have therefore not incorporated all the elements of the general equilibrium school. As we will show later, we have nevertheless taken into account some aspects of the general equilibrium models, notably the sequence of solutions in the various markets and the notion of convergency within one time period and the consequences of this for the behaviour of economic and social variables in another time period (Dervis et al., 1982, Chapters 5 and 6).

A second and perhaps equally important reason for

130

diverging from the general equilibrium model is that in a developing economy such as that of Kenya, many markets are imperfect and often do not clear through prices. Non-clearance through prices can have several causes. Markets may be too thin on information to arrive at an equilibrium. Prices may be controlled by the State (either for motives of social justice or through the influence of powerful socio-economic groups). As a consequence the model uses mainly quantity adjustment in clearing markets. As will become clear from the ensuing description, quantity adjustment as applied here does not result in a complete absence of "price"-influenced effects. Adjusted quantities affect behaviour of consumption and investment (but less so on the labour market) in the next period, capturing effects which normally come about through prices.

We will first discuss the working of the convergency mechanism and then the expected consequences of the convergency rules for the behaviour of the model. In discussing the convergency mechanism it is important to take into account the sequence of the various mechanisms (see figure 9.1).

9.2 Convergence on the foreign exchange market

The demand side of the model not only provides the domestic demand structure of the model but also foreign demand, thus giving an indication of the foreign exchange gap. As was indicated earlier, imports are split into three categories: imports of consumer goods, imports of capital goods and imports of intermediate goods. If the excess of imports over exports cannot be covered by sufficient external borrowing (which itself forms part of the scenario analysis, see Chapters 12 and 14), imports are reduced in order to satisfy the foreign exchange constraint (see formula [149], Chapter 8). In the first instance, imports of consumer goods are reduced, but when imports of consumer goods reach a minimum level, capital goods and intermediate goods imports can also be reduced.

9.3 Convergence on the product market

After the final demand outcomes have been checked against possible constraints on the foreign exchange market, convergence takes place on the product market. In most sectors the market is determined by its short side; thus in the case of excess supply the demand structure determines the outcome of the market, while in the case of excess demand the supply side is the determining factor.

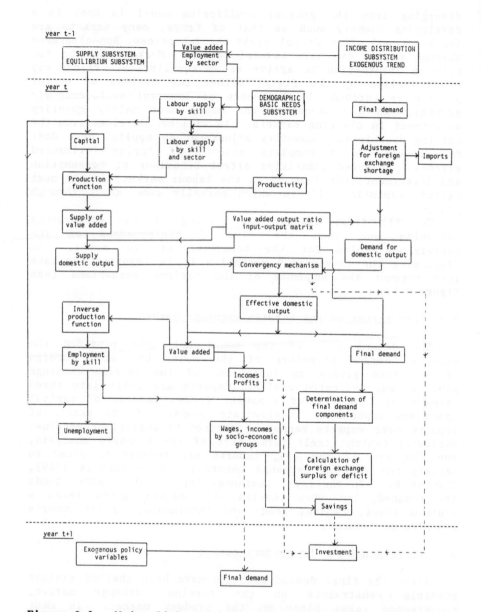

year t-1

| SUPPLY SUBSYSTEM EQUILIBRIUM SUBSYSTEM | Value added Employment by sector | INCOME DISTRIBUTION SUBSYSTEM EXOGENOUS TREND |

year t

DEMOGRAPHIC BASIC NEEDS SUBSYSTEM

Labour supply by skill

Final demand

Capital

Labour supply by skill and sector

Adjustment for foreign exchange shortage — Imports

Production function — Productivity

Supply of value added

Value added output ratio input-output matrix

Supply domestic output

Demand for domestic output

Convergency mechanism

Effective domestic output

Inverse production function

Value added

Final demand

Employment by skill

Incomes Profits

Determination of final demand components

Unemployment

Wages, incomes by socio-economic groups

Calculation of foreign exchange surplus or deficit

Savings

year t+1

Exogenous policy variables

Investment

Final demand

Figure 9.1. Major linkages indicating the various convergency mechanisms

There are, however, notable exceptions to this rule. For small-scale agricultural production, the market is always dominated by the supply side since demand can adjust easily, consisting as it does of exports and of consumption of own produce; the latter forms a large proportion of the demand of peasant farmers. In large-scale agriculture, too, the market is mainly dominated by the supply side, since a considerable part of final demand consists of exports. For the public services market output is determined by the demand side which is almost, following standard national account practices, totally dominated by public expenditure (which itself is already constrained by tax receipts and public borrowing regulations). Another exception is the non-agricultural sectors producing tradeables (food and non-food manufacturing, and to a lesser extent services). Here, however, disequilibrium is only partly solved through increased imports or exports.

If excess demand exists in a certain sector, the final demand aspirations of the market parties have to adjust to the new situation. Private consumption and government consumption are adjusted downwards and imports adjusted upwards (provided the sector is an importing sector and provided the foreign exchange constraint is not binding).

The formal framework is as follows.

All sectors have to satisfy the following balance equation, written in matrix notation:

$$FD = [I-A] \ X + (M^{1*} + M^2) \tag{153}$$

where

FD = vector of final domestic demand
A   = matrix of domestic input-output coefficients
M^{1*} = vector of adjusted imports of consumer goods
M^2 = vector of imports of capital goods
X   = vector of gross output

Gross output is determined by:

$$X = b^{-1} \ VAS \tag{154}$$

where

VAS = vector of value added
b   = vector of value added/gross output ratio (defined in formula [126] as VAC]

This means that for each sector the following relation needs to hold:

$$PC_i + GC_i + INV_i + GI_i + E_i - M_i^{1*} - M_i^2 \qquad [155]$$

$$= b_i^{-1} VAS_i - \sum_j a_{ij} b_j^{-1} VAS_j$$

The left-hand side of equation [155] represents the demand side and the right-hand side the supply side, as determined in Chapter 7 and Chapter 8 respectively.
This we label for short:

$$Z_i = Q_i \qquad [156]$$

However, as the demand side and the supply side are determined independently, except for government services and education and health (sectors 12 and 13) which are demand determined, we have no guarantee that the equation holds for any other sector and we have a situation where we have either

(1) Excess supply: $Z_i - Q_i < 0$

or

(2) Excess demand: $Z_i - Q_i > 0$

In the case of excess demand, final demand, with the exception of government and private investments, is adjusted downwards, while in the case of importing sectors (mainly food and non-food manufacturing and, to a lesser extent, trade, transport and food manufacturing) imports of consumer goods and capital goods are allowed to adjust upwards.
The following formulae apply:

$$(IMP_i)^1 = (1+a)(IMP_i) \quad \text{with} \quad a = \frac{Z_i - Q_i}{PC_i + GC_i + EXP_i} \qquad [157]$$

where

$$IMP_i = M_i^{1*} + M_i^2 \qquad [158]$$

$(IMP_i)^1$ and IMP stand for the adjusted and unadjusted sum of imports of final consumer goods and of capital goods (see Chapter 8, formulae [145]-[149]).

$$PC_i^1 = (1-b_i) PC_i \qquad [159]$$

134

$$GC_i^1 = (1-b_i) \, GC_i \quad \text{where} - b_i = \frac{Z_i - Q_i + (IMP_i^1 - IMP_i)}{PC_i + GC_i + EXP_i} \qquad [160]$$

$$EXP_i^1 = (1-b_i) \, EXP_i \qquad [161]$$

and where the variable with a prime $(^1)$ indicates the adjusted value.

In the case of excess supply $(Z_i - Q_i < 0)$ convergency is more complex.

For small-scale agriculture (sector 1), as explained above, demand consists purely of private consumption and exports; both adjust completely to supply, and the following rule applies.

$$PC_1^1 = (1-b_1) \, PC_1 \quad \text{where} - b_1 = \frac{Z_1 - Q_1}{PC_1 + EXP_1} \qquad [162]$$

$$EXP_1^1 = (1-b_1) \, PC_1 \qquad [163]$$

For large-scale agriculture the excess supply can also be exported. However, since some of Kenya's exports are restricted by quota, we have assumed that only 75 per cent of the excess supply can be exported and we have:

$$EXP_2^1 = (1-b_2) \, EXP_2 \quad \text{where} - b_2 = 0.75 \, \frac{Z_2 - Q_2}{EXP_2} \qquad [164]$$

$$PC_2^1 = PC_2 \qquad [165]$$

For the non-agricultural sectors the short side dominancy rules of the market apply, and excess supply is allowed to exist. The final demand components are consequently not adjusted.

$$(M_i^{1*} + M_i^2)^1 = M_i^{1*} + M_i^2 \qquad [166]$$

$$PC_i^1 = PC_i \qquad [167]$$

$$GC_i^1 = GC_i \qquad [168]$$

$$EXP_i^1 = EXP_i \qquad [169]$$

After the adjustment on the product market the adjusted value added for each sector is calculated (in matrix notation):

$$X^1 = [1-A]^{-1} (FD^1 - (M^{1*} + M^2)^1) \qquad [170]$$

$$VA = b \ X^1 \qquad [171]$$

where

FD^1	=	vector of adjusted final demand
[A]	=	matrix of domestic input-output coefficients
b	=	vector of value added/gross output ratios
X^1	=	vector of gross output, adjusted
$(M^{1*} + M^2)^1$	=	vector of imported final consumer and capital goods, adjusted

For small-scale agriculture total value added is distributed among the three different farm categories, according to their original share when supply of gross output and value added was determined.

$$VASA \ (i) = [\frac{VASS(i)}{\Sigma \, VASS(i)}] \ VA \ (1) \qquad i = 1,...,3 \qquad [172]$$

where

VASA(i) = value added in small-scale agriculture by farm-size group i after convergency
VASS(i) = supply of value added in small-scale agriculture by farm-size group i before convergency (see equation [119])

After the adjustment an index of excess supply (or excess demand if excess supply is negative) for each sector is calculated.

$$EXSUP_i = VAS_i - VA_i \qquad [173]$$

Since gross output and value added are determined we are

also able to calculate the adjusted intermediate imports (in matrix notation)

$$(M_i^3)^1 = [AM] (FD^1 - (M^{1*} + M^2)^1)$$ [174]

where

$(M_i^3)^1$ = vector of adjusted import of intermediate imports

AM = matrix of intermediate imports

FD^1 = vector of adjusted final demand

$(M^{1*} + M^2)^1$ = vector of adjusted imported final consumer and capital goods

9.4 Convergence on the labour market

Chapter 7 described the determination of the capital stock and of labour supply by skill as well as the number of workers who would be able to find employment if past economic performance continued. This allowed the total productive capacity of the economy to be calculated. After equilibrium on the product market and the determination of value added and gross output a mechanism is needed to determine the size of the labour force which can effectively be engaged in the production process – apart from small-scale agriculture where value added is determined by the supply of output and where consequently employment is determined according to Chapter 7.

In order to determine labour demand in the other sectors we use the production function as discussed earlier.

$$VA_j = A_j (LU_j)^{aj} (LD_j)^{bj} K_j^{cj} e^{tj}$$ [175]

This is the same formulation as formula [124] in Chapter 7 for the supply side. However, in the present formula value added (VA) is given rather than being the dependent variable (VAS), as in formula [124]. Furthermore, the capital stock (K) and technical progress (t) are already determined – which leaves us to determine skilled and unskilled labour (LU and LS). Since we need to determine two variables (LU) and (LS) we need another condition. We write equation [175] as a nested Cobb-Douglas function.

$$VA_j = A_j (L_j)^{1-cj} K^{cj} e^{tj}$$ [176]

with

$$L_j = LU_j^{\frac{aj}{1-cj}} \; LS_J^{\frac{bj}{1-cj}} \hspace{3cm} [177]$$

However, since $aj + bj + cj = 1$, we may write

$$L_j = LU_j^{pj} \; LS_j^{1-pj} \hspace{2cm} \text{with } pj = \frac{aj}{1-cj}$$

From equation [176] we can now determine L_j, since all other variables are determined. However, applying formula [176] directly to determine L_j would imply that we were allocating all technical progress (tj) to improving factor payments rather than factor inputs. In order to avoid this, part of the technical progress is therefore used to engage more workers rather than to pay workers higher salaries. As discussed in Chapter 3, real wages have not increased in Kenya during the 1970s, increases in the wage bill being used to expand employment. In the model, therefore, 25 per cent of technical progress is used to increase wages and 75 per cent to increase employment.

Consequently, labour demand is determined as follows:

$$L_j = [\; VA_j \; A_j^{-1} \; K^{-cj} \; e^{-taj}]^{\frac{1}{1-cj}} \hspace{2cm} [178]$$

where $taj = 0.25 \; t_j$

Having determined total labour demand we still need to determine how demand for labour is split between demand for skilled and for unskilled labour. This is determined by the ratio of unskilled wages (wu_j) to skilled wages (ws_j), which, as we will discuss in Chapter 11, is a policy parameter in the model.

$$LS_j = \frac{pj}{(1-pj)} \; \frac{wu_j}{ws_j} \; LU_j \hspace{2cm} [179]$$

$$LU_j = L_j - LS_j \hspace{3cm} [180]$$

For all sectors, unemployment for skilled and unskilled workers is then determined as a residual.

$$USAG = AGLABS - \sum_{j=1}^{2} LS_j \qquad [181]$$

$$UUAG = AGLABU - \sum_{j=1}^{2} LU_j \qquad [182]$$

$$USMO = MOLABS - \sum_{j=3}^{14} LS_j \qquad [183]$$

$$UUMO = MOLABU - \sum_{j=3}^{14} LU_j \qquad [184]$$

where

USAG   = unemployment, skilled labour, agricultural sector
UUAG   = unemployment, unskilled labour, agricultural sector
USMO   = unemployment, skilled labour, non-agricultural sector
UUMO   = unemployment, unskilled labour, non-agricultural sector
AGLABS = labour supply, skilled agricultural sector; see equation [105]
AGLABU = labour supply, unskilled agricultural sector; see equation [106]
MOLABS = labour supply, skilled non-agricultural sector; see equation [103]
MOLABU = labour supply, unskilled non-agricultural sector; see equation [104]

Unemployment rates (UNEMPA and UNEMPM) are calculated by dividing the number of unemployed by the total labour supply in the respective categories for the agricultural and non-agricultural sectors.

9.5 Convergence on the capital market: Determination of investment

The last part of the convergency mechanism is the determination of the savings investment gap in year t. This gap follows directly from the determination of the value added by sector and the final demand vector (section 9.3) and from the determination of income and expenditure of socio-economic groups and enterprises as discussed in Chapter 11.

The savings gap is consequently defined as follows.

$$\text{SAVGAP} = \sum_i \text{INV}_i + \sum_i \text{GI}_i - \sum_h \text{SAGR}_h - \sum_i \text{PROFSAV}_i - (\text{GE} - \sum_i \text{GC}_i) \quad [185]$$

where

SAVGAP	=	savings gap
$\sum_i \text{INV}_i$	=	total private investment demand
$\sum_i \text{GI}_i$	=	total government investment
$\sum_h \text{SAGR}_h$	=	total private savings of all socio-economic groups (see formula [260]
$\sum_i \text{PROFSAV}_i$	=	total business savings of all sectors (see formula [246]
GE	=	government expenditure
$\sum_i \text{GC}_i$	=	total recurrent government expenditure (see formulae [135] and [168]

Since the model applies standard national account definitions the savings gap generated according to formula [185] is equal to the foreign exchange gap (GAP) calculated according to formula [212].

As indicated in the description of the model, the behaviour of economic variables in year t determines investment behaviour in the year t+1.

Investment in each sector in period t+1 is determined by the actual growth in value added in year t, by excess demand for the products of that sector in year t, and by the expected investible funds in the year t+1 which depend on savings behaviour in year t.

This gives the following equations:

$$\text{IEXA}_i(t+1) = [a_i \ (\text{VA}_i(t) - \text{VA}_i(t-1)) \ ] * \text{PRES}_i(t) \qquad [186]$$

$$\text{PRES}_i(t) = 1 - b_i \ \text{EXSUP}_i(t) \qquad \text{if } \text{EXSUP}_i < 0 \qquad [187]$$

$$= 1 \qquad \text{if } \text{EXSUP}_i \geqslant 0$$

where

$\text{IEXA}_i(t+1)$	=	investment intention in sector i for year t+1
$\text{VA}_i(t)$	=	value added in year t
PRES_i	=	effect of excess demand in sector i on investment
EXSUP_i	=	excess supply in sector i in year (t)

where the "accelerator" a_i equals the capital-output ratio of sector i and the "excess demand pressure coefficient" b_i

140

also equals the capital-output ratio but can be changed in order to present more optimistic investment behaviour.

Having determined investment intentions in each sector, the combined investment intentions as indicated have to be checked against available investible funds and a mechanism has to be applied to match investment and savings.

Basically three mechanisms to close the gap have been applied in recent models (Taylor, 1979, 1983; Dervis et al., 1982). The first mechanism is that of neo-classical closure, where total investment equals available savings from households, government, institutions and foreign sources. Through interest rate policies and credit allocation, this amount of savings is then distributed to the various sectors which ask for investible funds (the higher their expected profit rates, and the higher their expected increase in output, the more willing investors in a particular sector are to pay for investible funds).

In the second investment savings mechanism it is no longer assumed that aggregate savings are determined solely as the sum of behaviourally determined savings of individual market parties. It is also assumed that the government is able, through monetary and fiscal policies, to determine a target national savings rate in order to respond to investment demand.

A third mechanism, in the Kaldorian or neo-Keynesian fashion, also assumes that the amount of savings required by investors is always met. But the principal mechanism to make savings equal to investment is in this case a change in the real incomes of social groups (in particular workers and entrepreneurs) through inflation (caused by excess investment demand). As these groups are assumed to have different savings rates, incomes will have to change sufficiently to ensure that savings will match investment.

From this description alone, it is clear that these three different investment-savings closure mechanisms will each have a different impact on sectoral income distribution and consequently on sectoral growth. Taylor and Lysy (1979) and Taylor (1979) have demonstrated, using a general equilibrium model for Brazil, that model outcomes differ substantially according to the closure mechanisms chosen.

In the Kenya basic needs model we have not followed, strictly, any of the three alternatives; instead we have tried to develop a mechanism which is as close as possible to the situation in Kenya.

One feature of the capital market in the poorer developing countries like Kenya is fragmentation, which means that investible funds do not move smoothly from one sector to another. The capital market is characterised by structural rigidities. Nor has the economy reached such an advanced industrial level that Kaldorian or neo-Keynesian mechanisms can work properly.

As a consequence we have dealt with investible resources in two ways in the model. First, the capital market is split between retained savings of enterprises in each sector, on the one hand, and savings by households and foreign savings, on the other.

In a first step, investment intentions are checked against expected retained savings in each sector. If investment is lower than 50 per cent of expected retained savings, we assume that because of rigidities in the capital market that 50 per cent is kept in the sector and only 50 per cent of investible funds is moving out of the sector.[3] Hence actual investment can be larger than initial investment because of rigidities in the market.

If investment is larger than the amount of immobile expected retained savings the additional amount needed is financed from household savings or from external savings. Thus for each sector we have:

if $\quad$ $IEXA_i(t+1) \leqslant 0.5\ EXPRFSAV_i(t+1)$ $\qquad$ [188]

then $\quad$ $IEXA_i(t+1) = 0.5\ EXPRFSAV_i(t+1)$ $\qquad$ [189]

and $\quad$ $IB_i(t+1) = 0.0$ $\qquad$ [190]

if $\quad$ $IEXA_i(t+1) > 0.5\ EXPRFSAV_i(t+1)$ $\qquad$ [191]

then $\quad$ $IB_i(t+1) = IEXA_i(t+1) - 0.5\ EXPRFSAV_i(t+1)$ $\qquad$ [192]

with $\quad$ $EXPRFSAV_i(t+1) = PROFSAV_i(t) * (VA_i(t)/VA_i(t-1))$ $\quad$ [193]

where

$EXPRFSAV_i(t+1)$ = expected retained savings in sector i

$PROFSAV_i(t)$ $\quad$ = retained savings in sector i (see formula [246])

$IB_i(t)$ $\qquad$ = demand for investment financed outside retained savings by sector i

Expected investible funds is given by

$$INVFUND(t+1) = \sum_i 0.5\ EXPRSAV_i(t+1) \qquad [194]$$

$$+ \sum_g SAGR_g(t) * (Y_g(t)/Y_g(t-1))$$

$$+ GAP(t) * (VA(t)/VA(t-1))$$

where

INVFUND(t+1)	=	expected investible funds in year t+1
EXPRSAV(t+1)	=	expected retained savings in sector i
$SAGR_g(t)$	=	savings by socio-economic group g (see formula [260])
$Y_g(t)$	=	total income of socio-economic group g (see formula [255])
GAP(t)	=	foreign exchange gap (see formula [212])
VA(t)	=	total GDP

In case demand for investible funds is larger than the expected investible funds each sector's share is rationed as follows:[4]

$$if \quad \sum_i IB_i(t+1) > INVFUND(t+1) \tag{195}$$

$$we\ have \quad I_i(t+1) = c_i(INVFUND(t+1)) + 0.5\ EXPRSAV_i \tag{196}$$

$$with \quad c_i = \frac{IB_i(t+1)}{\Sigma IB_i(t+1)}$$

however

$$if \quad \sum_i IB_i(t+1) \leqslant INVFUND(t+1) \tag{197}$$

$$we\ have \quad I_i(t+1) = IB_i(t+1) + 0.5\ EXPRSAV_i \tag{198}$$

Investment in each sector in the base year is given in table 9.1.

Total government investment (GI) in year t+1 depends on the public funds available for investment, as discussed in section 8.3 on government expenditure and revenue; its determination does not belong to the convergency mechanism. Government investment in each sector i is determined by a policy parameter b_i:

$$IG(t+1)_i = b_i \ GI(t+1) \tag{199}$$

where

$IG(t+1)_i$	=	government investment in sector i
GI(t+1)	=	total amount of government investment (see formula [134])

The value of b_i is determined by the distribution of government investment among the sectors of the economy in 1976, as indicated in table 9.1.

PLANNING FOR BASIC NEEDS

Table 9.1. Public and private investment in each sector
(base year only) (K.£ million)

Sector	Gross private investment	Gross public investment
1. Small-scale agriculture	17.91	–
2. Large-scale agriculture	23.67	1.23
3. Mining	1.67	–
4. Food manufacturing	27.18	1.83
5. Non-food manufacturing	26.31	24.83
6. Modern building and construction	9.76	0.37
7. Traditional building and construction	23.52	–
8. Transport and communications	39.30	12.70
9. Modern trade	15.03	6.50
10. Traditional trade and services	1.52	–
11. Modern services	13.03	1.18
12. General government services	–	13.18
13. Government services relating to education and health	–	12.85
14. Ownership of dwellings	15.18	4.92
TOTAL	213.90	79.59

Governments can, however, reallocate private investment to particular sectors (by means of credit and interest policies which are not themselves modelled).

In the present model we distinguish between five basic needs elements, namely food, primary education, secondary education, health and water. The last four categories are served by the public sector (sectors 12 and 13 in the model). The private sector providing basic needs in the model is agriculture.

Thus, if IG_i is the element of the investment vector according to the above procedure, then government can influence this by:

$$\sum_{i=1}^{nl} IG_i = (1+a) \sum_{i=1}^{nl} IG_i \qquad [200]$$

$$i = 1,\ldots,nl; \quad \text{basic needs sectors}$$
$$n_1 = 2$$

$$\sum_{i=nl}^{n} IG_i = (1-b) \sum_{i=nl}^{n} IG_i \qquad [201]$$

where a and b are determined so that total investment remains constant.

$$i = nl,\ldots,n \text{ non-basic needs sectors}$$
$$n = 14, \text{ excluding } 12 \text{ and } 13$$

The implications of varying the allocation coefficients is not studied in the scenarios of the present study.

9.6 Stability of the convergency mechanism

One important question in large-scale modelling is that of stability. Does the system described above behave in a stable fashion? The proof of the pudding is, of course, in the eating, and we will discuss in Chapters 12 to 14 the stability of the base run and the scenario experiments. But it might also be useful to compare the stability of the model with other findings in the literature.

Convergency and stability (or instability) resulting from convergency can perhaps best be illustrated by examining how the two gaps in the macro-economic accounting framework, the savings gap and the foreign exchange gap, are made equal. The existence of these two gaps was extensively discussed in the literature some years ago, particularly with reference to designing appropriate investment strategies in order to arrive at higher growth. Gunning (1983) has recently shown that this two-gap literature dealt incompletely with reasonable properties of a fixed price equilibrium mechanism. Taylor (1979) also argues that two-gap "models" often pose the problem of whether the savings gap or the foreign exchange gap is binding, but rarely give an explicit account of how "the gap between the gaps" (in Taylor's terminology) is closed.

In the Kenya basic needs model an attempt is made through the convergency mechanisms on the various markets to provide a realistic picture of how the two gaps are made equal. In order to show how this occurs, we give a simple formulation following Taylor (1979), with a simplified notation of the two-gap problem.

The balance of payments restriction can be summarised as:

$$m_1(PC + GC) + m_2(INV + GI) \qquad [202]$$

$$+ m_3 (PC + GC + INV + GI + EXP) - F - EXP \leqslant 0$$

where

m_1 = import coefficient of consumption

m_2 = import coefficient of capital

m_3 = intermediate imports

F = autonomous capital inflow

The other variables are defined in Chapter 8, equation [128], and are the usual components of final demand.

In order to ease the exposition we write the above equation in a simple form (in which the letters used to indicate the variables do not necessarily correspond to the variables in the model and are thus only relevant to this section).

$$a_1 \, C + a_2 \, I + a_3 \, E - F - E \leqslant 0 \qquad\qquad [203]$$

where

a_1 = $m_1 + m_3$

a_2 = $m_2 + m_3$

a_3 = m_3

I = INV + GI

C = PC + GC

E = EXP

For the base year we have approximately the following values:

a_1 = 0.34

a_2 = 0.56

a_3 = 0.26

The saving restriction is as follows:

$$I - F - s \, (C + E) \leqslant 0 \qquad\qquad [204]$$

where s represents savings rate as a percentage of domestic consumption and exports, which is about 15 per cent.

In figure 9.2, equations [203] and [204] are plotted for given values of C and E and with the equality sign pertaining. Thus, I is related to F according to [203] in line I and according to [204] in line II.

The situation of the economy in the base run is characterised for most years by the point X where the foreign

146

exchange gap is binding., i.e. for given F* the inequality I (203) < I (204) holds. To bridge the gap, and in order to increase or keep up investment, imports of consumer goods are reduced and consequently the parameter (a_1) decreases. This makes line I (203) move to the left north corner, so freeing some imports for investment and achieving a higher level of investment with a given amount of autonomous capital F*. However, as imports of consumer goods decrease and supply of domestic goods cannot increase, savings go up. The parameter (s) in [204] consequently increases, shifting line I (204) upwards, thus allowing for higher investments. These higher investments require, in turn, higher imports, necessitating an additional reduction of a_1, and so on. This process could make the model unstable if the increased savings effect resulting in higher capital imports is greater than the import reducing effect of decreased consumer imports. Below we will show that such is not the case.

At the equilibrium point X the following indentity holds:

$$\frac{1}{a_2} [F + (1-a_3) E - a_1 C] = F + s (C + E) \qquad [205]$$

and, after rearranging

$$F = \frac{a_3 + a_2(s-1)}{1 - a_2} E + \frac{a_1 + a_2 s}{1 - a_2} C \qquad [206]$$

A decrease in the import coefficient of consumption (da_1) decreases the need for autonomous external capital flows (dF) by

$$d F = \frac{1}{1 - a_2} C da_1 \qquad [207]$$

An increase in the savings ratio (ds) increases the need for autonomous external capital flows (dF) by

$$d F = \frac{a_2}{1 - a_2} (C+E) ds \qquad [208]$$

However, since we know how much imports of consumer goods have decreased we also know how much savings ((C+E)ds) will increase:

Increase in savings $= C da_1$

147

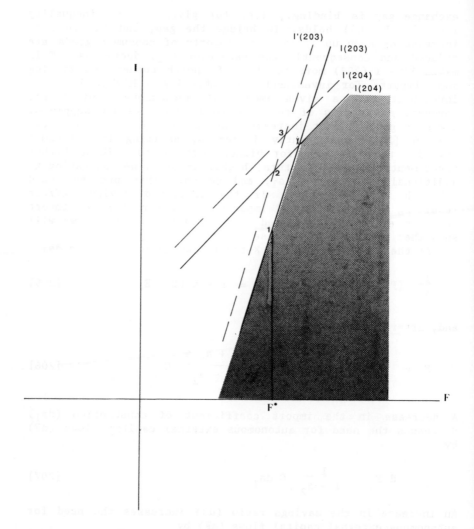

Figure 9.2. **The relation between the savings and the foreign exchange gap**

Consequently the savings rate increases by

$$d\ s\ =\ \frac{C}{C\ +\ E}\ d\ a_1 \qquad\qquad [209]$$

Substituting [209] in equation [208] we obtain the increased savings effect on autonomous capital inflows caused by a reduction in imports of consumer goods (da_1) as

$$d\ F\ =\ \frac{a_2}{1\ -\ a_2}\ C\ d\ a_1 \qquad\qquad [210]$$

Since a_2 is smaller than 1 the increased savings effect [210] is smaller than the decreased imports effect [207]. Hence the mechanism by which consumer imports are decreased in order to satisfy the foreign exchange constraint converges towards an equilibrium value.

Notes

[1]   But see Rodgers (1981), where an attempt is made to endogenise the supply constraint by introducing an economy-wide production function in order to simulate experiments with human capital. Also Anker and Knowles (1983) allow for an endogenous supply constraint based upon the level of agricultural exports, as discussed in Chapter 2.

[2]   As indicated in Chapter 2, we reserve the term "adjustment" to indicate the ways in which the economic system absorbs shocks, caused either by domestic policy intervention or by exogenous external events, as simulated in the scenario analysis.

[3]   In an earlier version of the model the rate of 100 per cent was applied; however, experiments showed that in certain sectors such a degree of over-investment took place that the excess capacity created was not removed even by the various convergency mechanisms and adjustment processes over the years.

[4]   It could be objected that the rationing mechanisms have left out all aspects of profit expectation. But as initial ex ante investment in each sector is determined both by the accelerator principle and by the possible excess demand, the initial amounts of ex ante investment already reflect the prospects for profits, and the assumption that investors in these sectors are willing to

pay higher costs for their investment. Thus rationing according to initial _ex_ _ante_ investment share reflects (through the magnitude of the shares) expected profits.

10 Behaviour on the foreign exchange market

Some aspects of the foreign exchange market have been covered earlier. Here we bring together all aspects in order to see what role foreign exchange (or shortage of foreign exchange) plays in the model. Major linkages within the foreign exchange subsystem as well as with other subsystems are indicated in figure 10.1.

Right at the beginning of each time period exports and additional available foreign exchange determine whether all demand for imports can be met. The maximum available amount of additional foreign exchange in the model is expressed as a percentage of total export proceeds (b) but whether this is fully used depends on import behaviour as indicated in section 8.4. Under the assumption that foreign investors and lenders follow a prudent policy in contributing foreign resources this percentage can be varied as part of a policy scenario reflecting changed international conditions. For the base run the percentage is set at 15 per cent, resulting in a fairly realistic balance of payments deficit during the first years of the operation of the model.

$$FE = EXP(t) + b \, EXP(t) \qquad \text{with } b = 0.15 \qquad [211]$$

In Chapter 8 we described how the total amount of foreign exchange influenced imports. If the total amount of foreign exchange is larger than warranted by import demand, all import demand is met and some of the available foreign capital is not used. However, if the demand for imports is higher than the

151

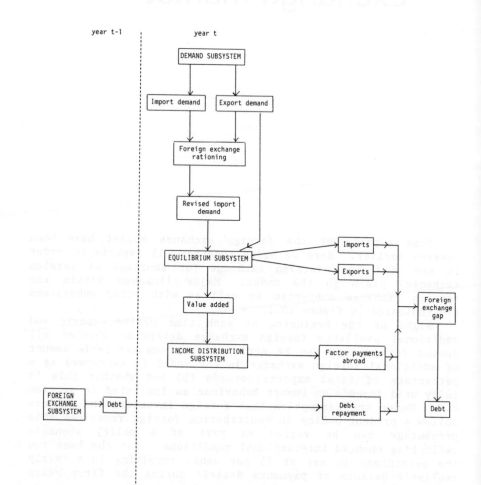

Figure 10.1. **Major linkages within the foreign exchange sub-system and between the subsystem and the rest of the model**

available foreign exchange, as is the case in the base run, the total amount of foreign exchange is rationed to the extent that imports of consumer goods are reduced to satisfy the foreign exchange constraint, as described in formula [118].

With the (eventually reduced) size of ex ante imports known, the model determines, through the convergency mechanism on the product market, the ex post values of imports, exports (Chapter 9) and factor payments abroad (Chapter 11). This allows the foreign exchange gap and the debt situation to be calculated:

$$\text{GAP} = \text{MPTA} - \text{TIMP} - \text{EXP} + \text{FACABR} + \text{REP} \qquad [212]$$

$$\text{MPTA} = (M^{1*} + M^2)^1 + (M^3)^1 \qquad [213]$$

$$\text{FACABR} = a \ \text{FORCAP} \qquad [214]$$

$$\text{FORCAP} = b \ \Sigma_i \ K_i \qquad [215]$$

$$\text{REP} = c \ \text{DEBT} \qquad [216]$$

$$\text{DEBT} = \text{GAP} + \text{DEBT} (t-1) - \text{REP} \qquad [217]$$

where

GAP	=	foreign exchange gap
EXP	=	total exports
MPTA	=	total imports adjusted
TIMP	=	import taxes
FACABR	=	factor income payment abroad
FORCAP	=	foreign capital
$(M^{1*})^1$	=	adjusted import of final consumer goods
$(M^2)^1$	=	adjusted import of capital goods
$(M^3)^1$	=	adjusted import of intermediate goods
REP	=	debt repayment
DEBT	=	total debt

For the flow of funds by sector (Chapter 11), we need to know the amount of factor income abroad by sector, which is calculated as follows:

$$\text{FACABR}_i = \frac{\text{VA}_i}{\Sigma_i \ \text{VA}_i} \ \text{FACABR} \qquad [218]$$

PLANNING FOR BASIC NEEDS

The Kenya basic needs model further allows for increased aid. Aid is provided as balance of payments support to the extent that a certain percentage of the foreign exchange gap does not need to be covered by external borrowing but is covered by additional balance of payments support.

If additional balance of payments support takes place formula [217] is replaced by the following formula:

$$DEBT = [1-d] \ GAP + DEBT(t-1) - REP \qquad [219]$$

in which d is the fraction of the foreign exchange gap for which balance of payments support is received.

11 Income distribution, the social accounting matrix and poverty determination

This subsystem determines the size, in terms of people and workers, of the various socio-economic groups and calculates the various value added components and the flow of funds for each sector, as well as for the economy as a whole. Various value added components are then mapped on to the socio-economic groups, for which incomes, transfer payments, taxes, savings and expenditure are determined. A condensed social accounting matrix is also calculated. The subsystem provides furthermore an indication of the amount of poverty in the various socio-economic groups. The major linkages within the subsystem as well as the linkages between the subsystem and the rest of the model over time are indicated in figure 11.1.

11.1 Determination of the different employment categories and socio-economic groups

The convergency mechanism in the labour market (Chapter 9, formulae [179]-[180]) determines the number of skilled and unskilled labour in each sector (LS_i and LU_i). Within the group of unskilled labour a further distinction is made between those working in the formal and informal sectors of the economy. The group of skilled labour is further divided into skilled workers and employers/professionals in the formal sector. Table 11.1 gives an overview of the various categories of labour in each sector.

A formal representation is as follows.

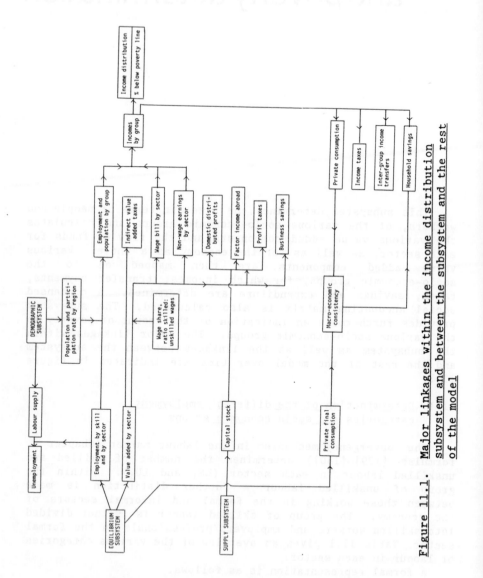

Figure 11.1. Major linkages within the income distribution subsystem and between the subsystem and the rest of the model

Table 11.1. **Overview of the various socio-economic groups in the Kenya basic needs model**

	Informal sector worker or peasant farmer	Unskilled worker	Skilled worker	Employer/ professional
1. Small-scale agriculture	x	x		
2. Large-scale agriculture		x	x	x
3. Mining		x	x	x
4. Food manufacturing	x	x	x	x
5. Non-food manufacturing	x	x	x	x
6. Modern building and construction		x	x	x
7. Traditional building and construction	x			
8. Transport and communications		x	x	x
9. Modern trade		x	x	x
10. Traditional trade and services	x			
11. Modern services		x	x	x
12. Government services (excluding 13)		x	x	x
13. Government services relating to education and health		x	x	x
14. Ownership of dwellings		x	x	x

157

$$WORKU_i \quad = \quad a_i \; LU_i \qquad\qquad [220]$$

$$WORKUIN_i \quad = \quad (1-a_i) \; LU_i \qquad\qquad [221]$$

$$WORKS_i \quad = \quad LS_i - EMP_i \qquad\qquad [222]$$

$$EMP_i \quad = \quad b_i \; (LS_i + LU_i) \qquad\qquad [223]$$

where

$WORKU_i$ = number of unskilled workers in sector i
$WORKUIN_i$ = number of informal sector workers in sector i
$WORKS_i$ = number of skilled workers in sector i
EMP_i = number of employers/professionals in sector i
LU_i = total unskilled labour in sector i
LS_i = total skilled labour in sector i

The division between employers/professionals and workers (b_i) is based upon a fixed percentage of the total labour force determined by the base year value (see table 11.2, column 1). Informal sector workers are found in five of the 14 economic sectors, as table 11.1 shows. For three sectors, the number of informal sector workers depends mainly or totally on the size of the workforce in the sector, viz. traditional agriculture (sector 1), traditional building and construction (sector 7) and traditional trade and services (sector 10). In the case of two manufacturing sectors, however, informal sector activities take place alongside formal sector activities, and the amount of economic activity in the sector as a whole determines the number of informal sector workers (see table 11.2, column 4).

The different categories of labour in the various sectors then form the basis for determining the socio-economic groups. It is assumed that the head of the household determines which socio-economic group the household belongs to,[1] and with the help of the different dependency ratios and household size figures from the demographic subsystem, the population is divided into the eight different socio-economic groups.

$$EAP_1 \quad = \quad \sum_{i=1}^{2} WORKUIN_i \qquad\qquad [224]$$

$$EAP_2 \quad = \quad \sum_{i=1}^{2} WORKS_i \qquad\qquad [225]$$

$$EAP_3 = \sum_{i=1}^{2} WORKU_i \qquad\qquad [226]$$

$$EAP_4 = \sum_{i=1}^{2} EMP_i \qquad\qquad [227]$$

$$EAP_5 = \sum_{i=3}^{14} WORKUIN_i \qquad\qquad [228]$$

$$EAP_6 = \sum_{i=3}^{14} WORKS_i \qquad\qquad [229]$$

$$EAP_7 = \sum_{i=3}^{14} WORKU_i \qquad\qquad [230]$$

$$EAP_8 = \sum_{i=3}^{14} EMP_i \qquad\qquad [231]$$

where

EAP_g = economically active population in socio-economic group g

and

$$POPGR_g = EAP_g * RDPR \qquad\qquad g = 1,\ldots,4 \qquad [232]$$

$$POPGR_g = EAP_g * UDPR \qquad\qquad g = 5,\ldots,8 \qquad [233]$$

where

$POPGR_g$ = population belonging to socio-economic group g
RDPR = rural dependency ratio (derived from the demographic subsystem)
UDPR = urban dependency ratio (derived from the demographic subsystem)

159

Table 11.2. Base year parameters of employment and income by sector

Sector	Employees as percentage of total employed	Per cent skilled (as % of employees)	Per cent unskilled (as % of employees)	Per cent informal sector	Per cent of wage bill in value added	Unskilled wage as per cent of skilled wage	Informal sector income as per cent of unskilled wage
1. AGTRAD	100.00	-	4.1	95.9	79.2	-	108.0
2. AGRMOD	86.41	3.7	96.3	-	22.2	7.8	-
3. MINING	100.00	26.4	73.6	-	52.2	13.2	-
4. MANFOOD	98.50	39.7	47.1	13.2	20.6	24.9	90.0
5. MANNONF	98.30	40.1	50.3	9.6	35.3	24.6	90.0
6. BUCOMOD	97.72	43.1	56.9	-	81.4	14.2	-
7. BUCOTRAD	100.00	-	-	100.0	100.0	-	-
8. TRANSP	95.55	57.8	42.2	-	63.4	33.5	-
9. TRAMOD	87.35	47.7	52.3	-	50.5	10.6	-
10. TRASETRA	100.00	-	-	100.0	100.0	-	-
11. SERMOD	90.95	44.0	56.0	-	52.6	22.5	-
12. GOVPUADM	100.00	21.1	78.9	-	98.3	12.2	-
13. GOVEDHE	100.00	80.0	20.0	-	100.0	39.6	-
14. OWNSDWELL	-	-	-	-	-	-	-

160

One problem which is frequently met in modelling socio-economic groups is the mobility of households between the socio-economic groups over time. Although the model does not track the movements of households separately, the changes in size of the different socio-economic groups reflect such mobility. During the simulation years the groups in the model change in size for various reasons: first, both migration and different growth rates for urban and rural population influence labour force growth and hence the size of urban and rural socio-economic groups. Second, the education system affects the supply of different skill levels and hence the size of the socio-economic groups. Third, changes in the sectoral composition of GDP alter the skill composition of the labour force.

The size of the various groups and the way they are determined in the base year is further explained in Appendix 1.

11.2 Value added components

Having determined the size of the various socio-economic groups, the subsystem divides value added for each sector into the following categories (leaving out the subscript i):

$$VA = W + COMP + TIND + FACABR + PRODIS + TDI + PROFSAV \qquad [234]$$

where

VA	=	value added
W	=	wage bill for unskilled, skilled and informal sector workers
COMP	=	compensation for employers
TIND	=	indirect taxes
FACABR	=	factor income sent abroad
PRODIS	=	distributed profits
TDI	=	profit tax
PROFSAV	=	retained profits

The wage share in each sector (LIC_i) is determined by institutional factors and can either be kept constant at 1976 values (see table 11.2, column 5) or determined behaviourally. In the latter case, which is applied in the model, we assume that with the evolution of society over time and increases in GDP the wage share in the economy increases. This assumption is confirmed by empirical research reported in Lecaillon et al. (1975), where a strong positive relation was found.

The determination of the wage share in the model is based upon a cross-country estimation by Moreland (1984, p. 98) involving 34 developed and developing countries. He found the

161

following relation:

$$\ln (LIC) = 2.63 + 0.1819 \ln \frac{VA}{POP} \atop (0.064)$$ [235]

$R^2 = 0.20$, $n = 34$ (standard error between brackets)

where

LIC = wage share in total value added in percentages

$\frac{VA}{POP}$ = per capita value added

This relation is used in the model. The constant term is adjusted in such a way that equation [235], expressed for per capita value added in the base year, generates the base year value of LIC which amounts to 37 per cent (excluding farm earnings in the small scale sector).

The wage share for each sector over time depends on the variation of the average wage share over time.

$$LIC_i(t) = LIC_i(0) \left(\frac{LIC(t)}{LIC(0)}\right)$$ [236]

where

$LIC_i(t)$ = wage share in sector i at time t

$LIC(t)$ = total wage share at time t

and we have

$$W_i = (LIC_i/100)VA_i$$ [237]

where

W_i = wage bill in sector i

The wage bill (W_i) is split up between the wage bill for skilled and for unskilled workers:

$$W_i = ws_i \, LS_i + wu_i \, LU_i$$ [238]

where

ws_i = wages for skilled labour in sector i
wu_i = wages for unskilled labour in sector i

LS_i and LU_i are already determined (see formulae

162

[179]-[180]), and it is further assumed that the ratio between skilled and unskilled wages (b_i) in each sector is a policy variable which in the base run is equal to the value in the base year (see table 11.2, column 6):

$$ws_i = b_i \ wu_i \qquad [239]$$

$$wu_i = \frac{W_i}{b_i \ LS_i + LU_i} \qquad [240]$$

For these sectors where workers belong entirely to the informal sector, we have

$$wuin_i = wu_i \qquad [241]$$

while for sectors with both formal and informal workers, informal earnings are a fraction a_i of formal earnings, based upon base year values.

$$wuin_i = a_i \ wu_i \qquad [242]$$

The compensation for employers in the value added (COMP) is calculated as the product of the number of employers times their average earnings, which are a fixed multiple of the skilled wage rate based upon base year rates, as can be deducted from table A1.1 in Appendix 1.

$$COMP_i = (c_i \ ws_i) \ EMP_i \qquad [243]$$

The non-wage payments of each sector, as indicated in formula [234] consist of indirect taxes, factor income paid abroad, distributed profits, profit taxes and profit savings.

Indirect taxes in each sector (TIND), as indicated in formula [140] of the public expenditure system, are determined as a percentage of value added.

Profits in each sector can thus be calculated (leaving out the subscripts) as follows:

$$PROFIT = VA - W - COMP - TIND \qquad [244]$$

Profits are then split up into factor income paid abroad (FACABR), domestically distributed profits (PRODIS), profit tax (TDI) and retained business savings (PROFSAV) calculated as a residual.

Thus we have (again leaving out the subscript i):

$$FACABR = f(FORCAP, \ VA), \ see \ formula \ [218]$$

PROFDIS   = c PROFIT   [245]

TDI   = b PROFIT, see formula [139]

PROFSAV   = PROFIT - FACABR - PRODIS - TDI   [246]

Factor income abroad (FACABR) for each sector depends on the amount of foreign capital and value added for each sector (as indicated in formula [218] in Chapter 10).

Domestically distributed profits (PRODIS) are determined as a fraction of total profits. The fraction in the base run is determined from values in the base year (see table 11.3).

Profit taxes (TDI), as indicated in formula [139] in Chapter 8, are also determined as a fraction of total profits (base run values are given in table 8.5).

Business savings (PROFSAV) are then calculated as a residual.

With this the flow of funds in the various sectors of the economy and the determination of the national account system is completed. The flow of funds for the base year is given in table 11.3.

11.3 Distribution of primary and secondary income among socio-economic groups

As indicated earlier, socio-economic groups are distinguished by employment characteristics (informal or subsistence, skilled, unskilled, employers/professionals) as well as sectoral criteria (agriculture versus non-agriculture). Their total income consists of labour income plus distributed "profits".

Since socio-economic groups are determined by skill and employment status, the mapping of labour income directly follows the composition of the socio-economic groups, as indicated in table 11.1. This gives the following relations.

$$WAGEGR_1 = \sum_{i=2}^{2} wuin_i \ WORKUIN_i \qquad [247]$$

$$WAGEGR_2 = \sum_{i=1}^{2} ws_i \ WORKS_i \qquad [248]$$

$$WAGEGR_3 = \sum_{i=1}^{2} wu_i \ WORKU_i \qquad [249]$$

164

$$WAGEGR_4 = \sum_{i=1}^{2} COMP_i \qquad [250]$$

$$WAGEGR_5 = \sum_{i=3}^{14} wuin_i\ WORKUIN_i \qquad [251]$$

$$WAGEGR_6 = \sum_{i=3}^{14} ws_i\ WORKS_i \qquad [252]$$

$$WAGEGR_7 = \sum_{i=3}^{14} wu_i\ WORKU_i \qquad [253]$$

$$WAGEGR_8 = \sum_{i=3}^{14} COMP_i \qquad [254]$$

where

$WAGEGR_g$ = labour income received by socio-economic group g

Other variables have been defined in sections 11.1 and 11.2.

The amount of distributed profits each group receives is determined as a fraction of total distributed profits. Most of the distributed profits are received by the employers/ professionals group in both urban and rural areas. Direct taxes are subtracted from total income, and transfers received or sent taken into account, in order to arrive at disposable income. Private consumption by sector is already determined by the convergency mechanism, as described in Chapter 9, which also determines, through the consumption matrix (table 8.2), the consumption of the different socio-economic groups. Savings of the socio-economic groups are then obtained as a residual.

This gives for each socio-economic group the following balance equation:

$$Y_g = WAGEGR_g + DIPR_g \qquad [255]$$

$$DIPR_g = a_g \sum_i PROFDIS_i \qquad [256]$$

165

Table 11.3. Flow of funds in the base year (1976) (K.£ million)

	1	2	3	4	5	6	7	8	9
	Value added	Wages	Indirect taxes	Profits (1-2-3)	Net factor payment abroad	National profits (4-5)	Distributed profits	Taxes	Business savings (6-7-8)
1. AGTRAD	370.04	293.18	0.00	76.86	0.00	76.86	39.21	14.03	23.62
2. AGRMOD	134.61	53.11	2.80	78.71	27.15	51.56	26.30	17.09	8.16
3. MINING	3.25	1.70	0.13	1.43	0.26	1.17	0.59	0.29	0.29
4. MANFOOD	94.57	20.89	42.54	31.14	5.40	25.74	12.73	6.24	6.77
5. MANNONF	167.71	63.92	48.79	55.00	9.58	45.42	22.48	11.01	11.92
6. BUCOMOD	46.52	40.92	0.43	5.17	0.80	4.37	2.11	1.04	1.21
7. BUCOTRAD	19.45	12.37	0.00	7.08	0.00	7.08	7.08	0.00	0.00
8. TRANSP	65.11	47.39	0.88	16.84	2.85	13.99	6.88	3.37	3.74
9. TRAMOD	109.07	79.06	2.50	27.51	4.85	22.66	11.24	5.50	5.91
10. TRASETRA	49.83	49.83	0.00	0.00	0.00	0.00	0.00	0.00	0.00
11. SERMOD	89.61	62.52	4.70	22.40	4.02	18.38	9.14	4.47	4.76
12. GOVPUADM	82.47	81.07	0.00	1.40	0.24	1.16	0.56	0.28	0.33
13. GOVEDHE	98.56	98.56	0.00	0.00	0.00	0.00	0.00	0.00	0.00
14. OWNSDWEL	75.12	0.00	6.62	68.50	11.09	57.41	27.98	13.15	15.47
TOTAL	1 405.92	904.5	109.38	392.03	67.05	324.98	166.33	76.47	82.19

$$DISP_g = Y_g - TRANF_g - TD_g \qquad [257]$$

$$TRANF_g = b_g\, Y_g \qquad g \geqslant 5 \qquad [258]$$

$$TRANF_g = c_g \sum_5^8 TRANF_g \qquad g \leqslant 4 \qquad [259]$$

$$TD_g = d_g\, Y_g \quad \text{see formula } [138]$$

$$SAGR_g = DISPg - PCGg \qquad [260]$$

$$PCG = [C]\; PC^1 \qquad [261]$$

where

Y_g	=	total income group g
$WAGEGR_g$	=	labour income received by socio-economic group g
$DIPR_g$	=	distributed profits received by socio-economic group g
$PROFDIS_i$	=	distributed profits of sector i (see formula [188])
$DISP_g$	=	disposable income of group g
$TRANF$	=	transfers between households
TD	=	direct income taxes
$SAGR_g$	=	savings by socio-economic group g
$PCGg$	=	private consumption of group g (element of vector PCG)
PCG	=	vector of private consumption by group
$[C]$	=	consumption matrix (dimension 14 x 8), mapping consumption by group on to consumption by sector (see table 8.2)
PC^1	=	vector of private consumption by sector after convergency, see formulae [159], [162], [165] and [167] in Chapter 9

According to the Social Accounting Matrix, transfer payments (receipts) are relatively small, accounting for 1.7 per cent of urban income and 2.4 per cent of rural income.[2] The same values have been applied in the basic needs model. Direct taxes represent 8.4 per cent of total income, although the richer groups pay more than the poorer groups. Total disposable household income is K.£988 million. Private savings represent 7.8 per cent of disposable income. Savings patterns differ between socio-economic groups, but the figures show clearly that the richer groups do not necessarily have a higher savings ratio than the poorer groups, especially if one takes the distinction between agriculture and non-agriculture into account. The various income components of the socio-economic groups are given in table 11.4.

The Gini ratios of inter-group inequality confirm a highly unequal distribution of income – although the distribution of disposable income is less unequal than that of wages and entrepreneurial income and of total income (a Gini ratio of 0.520 as compared to 0.531 and 0.555, respectively). That the latter figure is high is partly a result of the fact that distributed profits and incomes from capital are fully attributed to the various socio-economic groups, which is often not the case with income distribution figures, as Jamal (1982) has observed.

Having determined the income position of each socio-economic group and the relative size of each socio-economic group we can then calculate various average values needed in other parts of the model.

$$ERGR_g = \frac{WAGEGR_g}{EAP_g} \qquad\qquad [262]$$

$$YAPAE = \frac{\sum_{g=1}^{4} Y_g}{\sum_{g=1}^{4} POPAE_g} \qquad\qquad [263]$$

$$YNAPAE = \frac{\sum_{g=5}^{8} Y_g}{\sum_{g=5}^{8} POPAE_g} \qquad\qquad [264]$$

$$POPAE_g = POPGR_g \frac{RPOP - 0.5\ CHILDR}{RPOP} \qquad g = 1,\ldots,4 \qquad [265]$$

$$POPAE_g = POPGR_g \frac{UPOP - 0.5\ CHILDU}{UPOP} \qquad g = 5,\ldots,8 \qquad [266]$$

where

$WAGEGR_g$ labour income received by socio-economic group g
$ERGR_g$ =   average wage economically active person in socio-economic group g
$YAPAE$ =   income per adult equivalent in rural areas

168

Table 11.4. Primary and secondary income distribution by socio-economic group, 1976 (K.£ million)

	Wages and entrepreneurial compensation	Distributed operating surplus	Total income	Transfers	Taxes	Disposable income	Savings	Expenditure
1. Peasant farmers	294.49	39.47	333.96	+6.21	5.51	334.67	40.53	294.14
2. Agricultural workers, skilled	9.75	0.0	9.75	-	0.52	9.23	1.25	7.98
3. Agricultural workers, unskilled	31.20	0.0	31.20	+4.71	2.31	33.60	2.82	30.78
4. Agricultural employers/ professionals	23.21	38.15	61.36	-	14.48	46.89	4.15	42.74
5. Non-agricultural informal sector workers	52.81	5.59	58.40	-1.80	2.51	54.09	2.98	51.11
6. Non-agricultural workers, skilled	355.12	15.41	370.53	-5.00	21.16	344.37	11.19	333.18
7. Non-agricultural workers, unskilled	82.55	0.0	82.55	-2.10	3.29	77.16	4.65	72.51
8. Non-agricultural employers/ professionals	54.64	67.69	122.33	-2.02	32.81	87.51	9.05	78.46
TOTAL	903.76	166.33	1 070.09	0	82.58	987.51	76.61	910.89
Gini ratio	0.531	-	0.555	-	-	0.520	-	-

Source. Data base of Kenya basic needs model and Republic of Kenya, Central Bureau of Statistics (1981).

YNAPAE = income per adult equivalent in urban areas
$POPAE_g$ = adult equivalent population in socio-economic group g
CHILDR = number of children in rural areas
CHILDU = number of children in urban areas

11.4 Distributional effects of changes in rural-urban terms of trade

The level of income inequality between agricultural and non-agricultural sectors is partly determined by the terms of trade between agriculture and non-agriculture (henceforth called internal terms of trade). Since the model does not contain a full price system, although some "price effects", as discussed in Chapter 9, are included, we cannot explicitly introduce consequences of changes of internal terms of trade in the model. However, since internal terms of trade play an important role in the determination of living standards of the rural population, some aspects of changes in urban-rural terms of trade are introduced in the model.

Changing internal terms of trade in favour of agriculture has two effects for agricultural producers: a supply effect, to the extent that a higher price for agricultural products will increase supply, and an income effect to the extent that a higher price for a product means higher income for the agricultural producer. The supply effect is, however, difficult to determine. In the literature it is still debated whether an increase of the internal terms of trade will indeed have a substantial supply effect. One group argues that the supply effect is only noticeable in partial analysis, namely when prices of some crops change at the cost of prices of other crops. However, it is argued that when all agricultural prices change at the same time and with the same magnitude, the combined output effect is limited or non-existent. Others argue, however, that this reasoning may perhaps be valid in the short term, but not in the long term when as a consequence of higher agricultural prices investment may step up in agricultural sectors (Ghose, 1987).

In the preparation for the model various time series of changes in agricultural production and changes in urban-rural terms of trade were analysed, but a relation which was both satisfactory from a theoretical and from a statistical point of view could not be found. In consequence, the supply effect of a change in terms of trade was not modelled, but only the income effect whose effect is acknowledged by all authors. The following algorithm has been developed.

Before a change in the internal terms of trade takes place, the following relation exists.

$$Pa \ INCAG + Pb \ INCNAG = INCTOT \qquad [266]$$

with

$$\frac{Pa}{Pb} = 1 \qquad [267]$$

since we have no prices in the model.

where

Pa	=	price of agricultural product
Pb	=	price of non-agricultural product
INCAG	=	income in agriculture
INCNAG	=	income in non-agriculture
INCTOT	=	total income

Changing internal terms of trade implies changes in agricultural and non-agricultural prices.

$$\frac{P'a}{P'b} = C \neq 1 \qquad [268]$$

where

Pa = price of agricultural product after a change in internal terms of trade

Pb = price of non-agricultural product after a change in internal terms of trade

Under the restriction that overall income remains the same, the following equation needs to be satisfied:

$$P'a \ INCAG + P'b \ INCNAG = INCTOT \qquad [269]$$

By inserting [269], [268] and [267] in [266] we can develop the new price in terms of the old price and determine the new distributive income shares of agricultural and non-agricultural incomes.

$$\frac{P'a}{Pa} = \frac{INCAG + INCNAG}{INCAG + C(INCNAG)} \qquad [270]$$

$$\frac{P'b}{Pb} = C \ \frac{INCAG + INCNAG}{INCAG + C(INCNAG)} \qquad [271]$$

Based upon base year distributive shares and a value of 1.1 for C (as is used in various scenario experiments) we have the following values:

$$\frac{P'a}{Pa} = 1.063$$

$$\frac{P'b}{Pb} = 0.957$$

indicating that agricultural incomes would increase on average by 6.3 per cent and urban incomes would decrease on average by 4.3 per cent.

11.5 The social accounting matrix

After the convergency mechanism and the income distribution subsystem have determined the national accounts balances and the distribution of primary and secondary income between the various socio-economic groups, all relevant information is brought together by the model in the form of a social accounting matrix, which distinguishes between the various number of sectors (14), factors (4), socio-economic groups (8) and other actors (government and enterprises) as required.

In figure 11.2 we show only the presentation of the national accounts in a social accounting matrix framework. Each element of this matrix is further disaggregated as regards sector and socio-economic group. In the discussion on the base run results (Chapter 12) we will report the base year and the terminal year values for the elements of the social accounting matrix, as indicated in figure 11.2.

11.6 Determination of poverty

The extent of poverty is calculated for each socio-economic group. First the income per adult equivalent (AQERGR) is calculated:

$$AQERGR_g = DISP_g/POPAE_g \qquad for\ g = 1,...,8 \qquad [272]$$

where

$DISP_g$ = disposable income for socio-economic group g
$POPAE_g$ = population in terms of adult equivalents of socio-economic group g

The minimum basic needs income (POVLINE) is exogenous and differs for rural and urban areas. The values are discussed below.

The following algorithm is used to calculated the percentage of the population below the poverty line in each socio-economic group:

	Factors	Household and enterprises	Government	Production	Rest of the world	Capital — domestic	Capital — rest of the world	Totals
Factors				GDP at factor cost				
Household and enterprises	GNP at factor cost							
Government		Income and profit taxes		Indirect taxes	Import taxes			
Production		Domestic consumption	Public current expenditure	Intermediate production	Exports	Domestic investment goods		
Rest of the world	Factor income abroad	Imported consumer goods		Import of intermediate products		Imported investment goods		
Capital — domestic		Private and business savings	Public savings				Net capital inflow	
Capital — rest of the world					Balance of payments deficit			

Figure 11.2. **The national accounts of the Kenya basic needs model presented in a social accounting matrix framework**

$$f = \text{POVLINE/AQERGR} \qquad [273]$$

f is the ratio of the poverty line to the average income in each socio-economic group. We also need a measure of intra-group inequality for each group. At present this is exogenous in the model, and can be used as a policy parameter. It is assumed that average group income is log-normally distributed.

The fraction of the population below the poverty line is then calculated as follows:

$$P \ (X \leqslant \frac{1}{\sigma} \log f \ + \frac{1}{2} \sigma \ ) \qquad [274]$$

This is the probability of a normally distributed variate (X), while σ is the variance of the log-normal distribution.

The proof of this is as follows. Income is assumed to show a log-normal distribution within each socio-economic group:

$$y = \ \Lambda(y; \ \mu, \ \sigma^2) \qquad [275]$$

Hence, relative income (expressed as fraction or multiple of, the average income $\bar{y}$) is also log-normally distributed with the following parameters (Aitchison and Brown, 1957):

$$y/\bar{y} \ = \ \Lambda \ (y/\bar{y}; \ \mu - \log \bar{y}, \ \sigma^2) \qquad [276]$$

As y is log-normally distributed we have the following relation

$$\overline{\log y} \ = \ \log \bar{y} - \frac{1}{2} \ \sigma^2 \qquad [277]$$

and [276] can thus be written as

$$(y/\bar{y} \ ; \ \mu - \overline{\log y} - \frac{1}{2} \ \sigma^2 \ , \ \sigma^2) \qquad [278]$$

Further, $\overline{\log y}$ is a maximum likelihood estimator for μ , and we may therefore approach the log-normal distribution of $y/\bar{y}$ in [278] by

$$(y/\bar{y}; \ -\frac{1}{2} \ \sigma^2, \ \sigma^2) \qquad [279]$$

Transforming this to a standard normal distribution gives

$$N \ (\frac{\log y/\bar{y} + \frac{1}{2} \ \sigma^2}{\sigma} \ ; \ 0,1) \qquad [280]$$

$$N \ (\frac{1}{\sigma} \log \ ^y/\bar{y} + \frac{1}{2} \ \sigma \ ; \ 0,1) \hspace{3cm} [281]$$

Thus, if f is the poverty line expressed as a fraction of the average income then the fraction of the population below the poverty line is given by

$$P \ (X < \frac{1}{\sigma} \log f + \frac{1}{2} \ \sigma) \hspace{0.5cm} \text{where X is N (0,1)} \hspace{1cm} [282]$$

In some cases we do not know the variance σ of the log-normal distribution, but we know the value of the Gini ratio.

The variance σ can be calculated from the following relation:

$$G \ = \ 2 \ P \ (X \leqslant \ \sigma \ \sqrt{2}) \hspace{3cm} [283]$$

As formula [282] indicates, we need to introduce two parameters for each socio-economic group in order to calculate the percentage below the poverty line, namely the average income as a fraction of the poverty level and the inequality within the group, either expressed as the variance of a log-normal distribution or as the Gini ratio (assuming that the intra-group inequality is log-normally distributed).

Inequality figures for distribution within the eight socio-economic groups are not readily available, as most published income distribution data comprise a combination of various socio-economic groups.

For rural areas, however, we do have information based upon the Integrated Rural Survey for 1974-75 (IRSI) (see also Appendix 5 for a full description of the data base of the survey). Based upon this survey, Vandemoortele and van der Hoeven (1982) found a Gini ratio for household income of 0.382 for small-scale farmers. Information on inequality for the other three agricultural groups (skilled workers, unskilled workers and employers/professionals) is more difficult to come by. For the first two groups we have also assumed a moderate inequality with a Gini ratio of 0.38 as the groups are rather homogeneous. For the employers we have taken a greater inequality, with a Gini ratio of 0.45.

For the non-agricultural sector, assessment of inequality within groups is based upon that in urban areas. Vandemoortele and van der Hoeven (1982) found a Gini ratio of 0.52 for household incomes in urban areas, based upon an unpublished Nairobi household budget survey carried out in 1974. A considerable amount of this inequality, however, is the result of inter-group inequality between the four socio-economic groups (informal sector workers, skilled workers, unskilled workers and employers/professionals). For skilled and unskilled workers we have assumed an intra-group inequality with a Gini ratio of 0.45 and 0.38, respectively. For the informal sector workers we have assumed a greater degree of inequality, since activities and earnings vary a great deal in this sector (see, for example, House, 1978); we have therefore assumed a Gini ratio of 0.62. For non-agricultural employers, we have also assumed a higher level of inequality, with a Gini ratio of 0.47 (see table 11.5).

Table 11.5. Intra-group inequality

Group	Variance of log-normal distribution	Gini ratio
1. Peasant farmers	0.70	0.38
2. Agricultural workers, skilled	0.70	0.38
3. Agricultural workers, unskilled	0.70	0.38
4. Agricltural employers/professionals	0.85	0.45
5. Non-agricultural informal sector workers	1.25	0.62
6. Non-agricultural workers, skilled	0.85	0.45
7. Non-agricultural workers, unskilled	0.70	0.38
8. Non-agricultural employers/ professionals	0.90	0.47

The second input needed to calculate percentage below the poverty line, as indicated in formula [282], is average income expressed as a fraction of the basic needs income.

In earlier paragraphs we have described how average income has been calculated. Below we describe how the poverty line has been determined.

As discussed elsewhere (van der Hoeven, 1977), construction of a poverty line is fraught with conceptual difficulties, which stem partly from the interpretation of poverty (see, for example, Sen, 1983; for a useful overview of definitions of poverty lines see Hagenaars and van Praag, 1985). In the Kenya model we have, therefore, chosen a simple method of determining the poverty line, based upon nutritional standards.

Crawford and Thorbecke (1978) have calculated the cost of a simple diet in which 70 per cent of required calories is provided by maize and 30 per cent by beans, the required calorie intake per adult equivalent being set at 2,250 kilo-calories per day. Based on prices in urban and rural areas such a diet costs, in 1976 prices, K.£16.60 per adult equivalent in rural areas and K.£25.55 per adult equivalent in urban areas (Crawford and Thorbecke, 1978, pp. 11-13).

Having established the cost of a minimum diet, a usual practice is to calculate the poverty line by multiplying the diet with the inverse of the average share of food consumption in total income, or to impose normatively a food expenditure share, on the argument that the diet has also been determined normatively.[3] However, as indicated in van der Hoeven (1977), neither procedure would give a proper estimate of food poverty, since the relation between food consumption and total income is non-linear, following Engel's law. Rather than take an average food budget share, one should take the budget share as implied by the Engel curve at the level of required food intake.

Vandemoortele and van der Hoeven (1982) therefore established Engel curves for rural and urban areas. Data for rural and urban household consumption were derived from the IRS survey and the Nairobi household budget survey respectively (both took place in 1974). The following results were obtained:

Rural areas:

$$\ln(f) = -0.193 + 0.996 \ \ln(c) \qquad R^2 = 0.998 \qquad [284]$$
$$(66.42) \qquad\qquad N = 1533$$

Urban areas:

$$\ln(f) = 1.863 + 0.643 \ \ln(c) \qquad R^2 = 0.963 \qquad [285]$$
$$(12.40) \qquad\qquad N = 463$$

where

f = food consumption per adult equivalent (in K.sh.)
c = household income per adult equivalent (in K.sh.)

Introducing the above cost estimates of the "minimum diet" in the above equations gives us the estimates of the rural and the urban poverty line: K.£20.63 and K.£49.66 respectively. This implies a budget share for food of 80.5 per cent in rural areas and 51.5 per cent in urban areas: the average budget shares used by Crawford and Thorbecke (1978) were 78 per cent in rural areas and 41 per cent in urban areas.

Results are indicated in table 11.6.

Table 11.6. Calculation of poverty line: Kenya, 1976

	Annual cost of a diet providing 2,250 kcal per day per adult equivalent (K.£)	% food expenditure in low income budget	Minimum required income per adult equivalent per annum (K.£)
Urban	25.55	51.5	49.7
Rural	16.60	80.5	20.6

The poverty line calculated above for rural and for urban areas has been applied in the model.[4]

Notes

[1] In reality one can observe households in which one member is part of a particular employment category and another member part of another. Although it is possible to develop a system for categorising households according to multiple criteria, we thought this, for the purpose of the Kenya basic needs model, not worth the additional complexity as the eight different groups already provide a fair amount of stratification.

[2] Since more detailed information has become available it is generally acknowledged that this figure is an underestimation of the actual remittances between urban and rural areas. However, it remains difficult to estimate flows, as a large part of the flows represent intra-family remittances. Furthermore, this figure represents net remittances, while often only urban-rural remittances are reported.

[3] Crawford and Thorbecke (1978) have adopted the first method, while Collier and Lal (1980) and Jamal (1982) have opted for the second method by imposing a much higher food expenditure ratio resulting in a lower basic needs income for urban dwellers. Collier and Lal (1980), by positing an even more simple diet than Crawford and Thorbecke (1978) and Jamal (1982), arrive at the conclusion that urban poverty hardly exists.

[4] Although the calculation of the poverty line is a serious
     matter, for the purpose of the model its exact level is
     of limited relevance. We are interested firstly in the
     development over time, and want to know how much poverty
     increases or decreases over time. Secondly, we are
     interested in deviations from the time pattern in the
     base run as a consequence of policy changes or external
     shocks. In the case of both the time series analysis and
     the deviations caused by scenario changes, the change in
     poverty and the relative positions of the various
     socio-economic groups is of more interest than the
     absolute level.

PART III
RESULTS OF THE
ANALYSIS

12 Experimenting with the model: Scenario design and the base run

12.1 Introduction

As indicated in the previous chapters, the Kenya basic needs model is a simulation model. Taylor (1975) notices that in modelling the term "simulation" is used in different ways. Sometimes it is used to describe the process of making a number of solutions of a model in order to find out how the model responds to variations in parameters and other changes in specification. But, since one has to do this to make sense of any model, we agree with Taylor (1975) that it is better to use the term "exploration" or "numerical experimentation" for this process. This "exploration" phase takes place in the final phase of construction of the model; it is an iterative process which the modeller goes through in order to construct a meaningful model.[1]

The term "simulation" will thus be used in a more restrictive sense, namely to describe the numerical solution of a dynamic model made up of different equations which are too complex for analytical solutions or simple qualitative analysis – this is the case with the Kenya basic needs model.

The reasons for choosing to use a simulation model (touched upon in Chapter 2) are mainly based upon the fact that equations reflecting the consequences of basic needs policies cut across various parts of the model. They affect micro-economic behaviour, and result in non-linearities in the model. These cannot be approached by linearisation since the model has a long time frame. Such a long time frame is necessary, as we argued earlier, in order to calculate properly the consequences of basic needs policies.

The nature of the model implies the identification and use of a large number of variables. Following Tinbergen (1952) we can make for analytical models a distinction between endogenous variables, of which the value is determined by the relations in the model and which can be subdivided into target and irrelevant variables, and exogenous variables for which values have to be provided from outside the model, and which are split by Tinbergen into instruments and data. Cramer (1969) provides a somewhat more elaborate classification of the non-endogenous variables, called predetermined variables, which he splits up into non-economic variables, exogenous variables, lagged endogenous variables and instruments. Such a classification of the predetermined variables is useful in that it shows that for only one group of variables, the non-economic variables (i.e. rainfall), is the model builder truly barred from endogenising these within the model. All the others can be incorporated as endogenous variables by expanding the model and by assuming, in the case of instruments for policy-makers, behavioural relations (Cramer, 1969, p. 114).

Since we have included demographic (e.g. population growth) and basic needs (e.g. schooling) variables as endogenous variables in the model, the basic needs model does not contain non-economic variables as compared to most economic models. Regarding the other groups of variables, the model contains few exogenous variables. The exogenous variables it does contain are the rate of growth of export demand in the various economic sectors, disembodied technical progress in the various sectors, and age-specific male labour force participation rates in urban and rural areas. Expected government deficit as a percentage of gross domestic product is also predetermined, while the deficit in the foreign trade and services account is given an upper limit.

However, many of the predetermined variables in various equations are lagged endogenous variables (for example, all economic and basic needs access variables in the demographic subsystem). This, together with the fact that some of the subsystems can be solved recursively (for example, the income distribution subsystem and the basic needs subsystem), reduces the problems of the solution of the model. (It should be remembered, however, that other parts of the model cannot be solved recursively and that convergency mechanisms have been developed in order to deal with overdetermination in product, capital, labour and foreign exchange markets (see Chapter 9).)

Ideally, one might have liked to construct an optimisation model in which the satisfaction of basic needs - represented

either by a single item such as, for example, life expectancy
at birth or infant mortality, or by a composite index of
various items including literacy and calorie intake – is
maximised under various institutional, economic and exogenous
constraints. A normative interpretation of basic needs would
lend itself especially well to such an approach. But, as
indicated above, the many relations and the non-linear
character make a maximisation approach difficult to apply.
Nevertheless, by designing the experiments properly we can try
to get some answers to the question of optimisation, and the
results may perhaps be richer than can be achieved with an
optimisation model.

A temptation which is offered by the very nature of
simulation models is to keep changing the parameters of the
model and letting the model run under different circumstances.
As often noted, outcomes are unpredictable and the model
becomes a kind of "black box". If the model could truly
represent reality this would be acceptable. This is doubtful,
however, not only because one can never represent a living
economic system but also because changes in parameters affect
the system itself and it is difficult to judge what are
completely exogenous parameter values and which parameters can
be changed exogenously without affecting other parameters.

On the other hand, small changes in one exogenous variable
or one parameter often result in an outcome which is entirely
predictable, which often leads to the remark: "Does one need
such a large model in order to answer such a question? Could
this not be done without a model?" The controversy over
simulation models is still a subject of debate. Rodgers et
al. (1978) argue for large-scale modelling because of the
unexpected outcomes of the black box. Dervis et al. (1982)
also support large sectoral models. Taylor (1979), however,
argues that major behavioural patterns of large-scale models
can often be captured by smaller models.

The formulation of scenarios thus becomes a matter of
careful manoeuvring between the Scylla of the black box and
the Charybdis of oversimplicity. This is what has been
attempted in the following sections.

The purpose of the scenario analysis is to consider some
of the questions which were raised in the introductory
Chapters 1 and 2. The major questions here were whether basic
needs policies will be effective, both in the short run and in
the long run, and how the outcome of basic needs policies
relates over the long run to other policies such as a
continuation of present policies or policies with an increased
emphasis on growth.

The effects of different policies on satisfaction of basic
needs, poverty, income inequality, gross national product per

capita and external dependence interest us in particular, since looking at these elements allows us to interpret the success or failure of various policies in a broader (multi-dimensional) sense than is usually applied. The difficulty with such a multi-dimensional approach is that we cannot deduce whether one policy alternative is better than another (or generally more effective) unless results in all dimensions are worse for one given policy compared to another policy.

In order to answer the question of effectiveness, we need to formulate a social welfare function which gives different weights to various policy outcomes. This would solve dilemmas such as whether a one-year increase in average life expectancy is to be preferred to a 5 per cent higher GDP per capita. With this model, by introducing the effects on various socio-economic groups, we can investigate more complicated dilemmas such as whether a one-year increase in life expectancy in rural areas is to be preferred to a 5 per cent increase in GDP per capita in urban areas. Although various attempts have been made to introduce complicated sets of welfare functions (an overview is, for example, given in Fox et al., 1966), we would like to refrain from doing so. The advantage of a complicated welfare function is that one can rank the outcomes of various experiments in a unidimensional way. The disadvantage is that one has to rely on a process of determination of weights which is often very arbitrary. A more careful consideration of each scenario outcome and the reasons why one arrives at certain scenario outcomes is, in our view, more fruitful.

Another disadvantage of using a social welfare function is that its components are usually fixed targets. However, as Tinbergen (1952) has indicated, a distinction should be made between fixed and flexible targets. From the discussion it is clear that with a normative concept of basic needs, policy goals can best be expressed as flexible targets – bringing the percentage of the population whose income is inadequate to satisfy their basic needs at least below a level of X per cent over a certain period, increasing primary school enrolment at least up to B per cent, increasing life expectancy at least up to Q years, etc. Formulation of such goals almost excludes the application of an exclusive and unique social welfare criterion.

It is the function of simulation modelling, through various scenario experiments, to indicate the consequences of those scenarios on important target variables. Comparing the policy scenarios and their outcome provides an indication of the relative importance of the various policy scenarios. We will come back to this question in the concluding chapter (Chapter 15) when we discuss the scenario outcomes.

Before discussing the design of the scenarios we will briefly elaborate on the interpretation of the term "adjustment", which we first raised in Chapter 2. There we defined adjustment as the reaction of the economic system to exogenous shocks to the system, which can be either of an external (international) nature or of a domestic nature (changes in the structure or in the policy framework of the economy).

The questions related to adjustment are whether the economy will return to a stable growth pattern within a reasonable time, and whether this new growth pattern will be at a higher or lower level than the initial level. The situation becomes more complex, of course, if different shocks occur at the same time, either as a reaction to one another (an internal shock such as a reduction in government expenditure taking place as a reaction to an external shock causing decreased export proceeds) or taking place randomly. In this respect it is important to pose the question whether a less fluctuating growth pattern at a lower level of growth would be preferable to a more fluctuating growth pattern at a higher level.

Since the Kenya basic needs model is formulated in one-year time intervals, and since most shocks have effects lasting longer than one year, scenario analysis is, in principle, capable of showing adjustment patterns by looking at changes in variables in successive years, as we will show in the discussion on scenarios.

12.2 Scenario design in the model

Since the major emphasis of this study is on the effects of basic needs policies we have built up the various scenarios relating to basic needs in such a way that different aspects of basic needs policies are introduced separately in order to evaluate their consequences more precisely. Other scenarios also introduce changes in external circumstances and are more complex. These scenarios have been designed for the specific purpose of this analysis. Alternative sets of policy scenarios, however, can be equally dealt with in the model.

The base run describes the expected growth pattern of the Kenyan economy up to the year 2000, assuming the continuation of present policies and trends. Its assumptions and the actual outcome of the base run scenario are described in detail in section 12.3 and the following sections.

The first scenario deals with a policy experiment involving increased taxation in order to finance expanded public sector spending. The second scenario involves changes in the pattern of government expenditure in favour of basic needs services, as well as increased taxation. The third scenario, in addition to the policies of the second scenario, includes land redistribution as a means of improving the agricultural incomes of small-scale farmers, while the fourth scenario adds to the third scenario changes in the rural-urban terms of trade and increased productivity in small-scale agriculture. (A detailed description of these four scenarios is given in the next chapter.) In effect, the fourth scenario represents what we would like to call a broad-based basic needs policy approach. Policies are aimed at increasing the availability of and access to essential services, at redistributing assets (land) in order to promote equity and possibly growth, and at redistributing incomes (indirectly through price policies) in favour of the poorest socio-economic groups.

The fifth scenario represents policies to promote growth through decreases in income and profit taxes, through export subsidies, and through decreases in wages.

The sixth scenario reflects changes in international conditions. The concept of a viable deficit on the external goods and services account is broadened, resulting in larger capital inflows, while aid is also stepped up.

The basic needs policy approach scenario (scenario 4) and the growth policy scenario (scenario 5) reflect policies which are not necessarily mutually exclusive, but which can still be regarded as opposite to each other. The sixth scenario, however, reflects a change in international conditions. This could, like all scenarios, be extended by a whole range of domestic policy changes. However, we have refrained from doing so in order to present clearly the impact of the external changes on the behaviour of the economy as represented in the model.

Scenarios 7 and 8 deal with external and internal rigidities that prevent the economy from moving towards the production of more tradeables. In these scenarios the economy is externally constrained by inflexible demand for its export goods and internally by a standstill in import substitution of consumer imports (for a more detailed discussion of this see Chapter 14). Scenario 7 describes the effects of such rigidities in a situation of unchanged domestic policies (as reflected in the base run), while scenario 8 describes the effects of such rigidities in a situation where basic needs policies are applied (as reflected in scenario 4).

Figure 12.1 gives an overview of the various scenario experiments, while table 12.4 at the end of this chapter gives the exact parameter values of each policy scenario. The scenarios are described in more detail in Chapters 13 and 14, where we report on results. All scenario experiments start in

1984. Variables in all scenarios therefore have the same values between 1976 and 1984, the effects of scenario changes only being noticeable as from 1984 onwards.
The results of the various policy scenarios are discussed by comparing the major trends displayed by the scenarios. Given the sometimes weak data base on which this model had to be constructed, we felt it more important to proceed in this manner than to discuss the effects of each policy instrument separately as this might give a false impression of precision.

12.3 Base run: Introduction

As explained, the base run of the model tries to give a fairly realistic picture of Kenya's likely development over the last quarter of this century. It is not, however, intended as a fully-fledged projection of the Kenyan economy over this time period. As the words "base run" indicate, it gives an "expected" pattern of development which is used as a basis for comparison with different scenario experiments. As argued, the purpose of simulation models like this basic needs model is more to compare the outcome of the various scenario experiments with the base run and with each other than to provide through the base run, a detailed picture of future development.
It is nevertheless important to start with a description of the base run, not only because it gives a reference point when interpreting the results of the various scenarios, but also because it gives a good idea of how the model behaves.
The outcome of the base run and of the eight scenarios for some important variables is given in the annex to Chapter 15.
As explained in the description of the model in Part II, the model is mainly recursive and in consequence only a few exogenous trends need to be provided in order for the model to "run".
On the final demand side, the only exogenous variable is the growth rate of the demand for exports in those sectors which produce (or can produce) exportables. As explained in Chapters 8 and 9, supply bottlenecks may result in lower exports than demanded, although this does not take place in the base run, since the growth rates of demand for exports are not excessively high (see table 8.7, which gives the base run growth rates of export demand for five-year periods). The growth rates for the period 1976-80 are based on actual figures reported by the World Bank (1983), and these reports also provide the basis for the estimated growth rates for the period 1981-85. For the remaining five-year periods, growth rates are based on World Bank projections (World Bank, 1986). As can be seen in table 8.7, projected growth rates of export

189

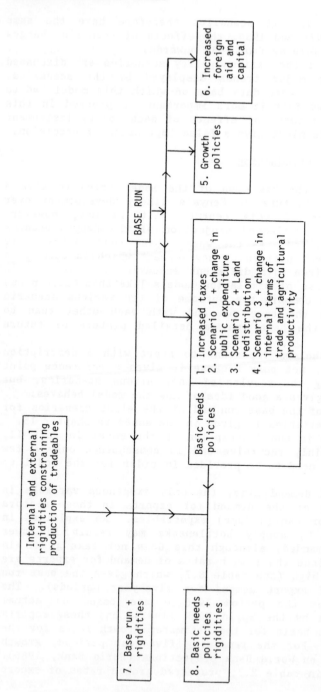

Figure 12.1. An overview of the various scenarios applied

Table 12.1. Shortfall in various basic needs categories at the beginning and end of the reference period (percentages)

	Basic needs income		Primary education		Secondary education		Health		Other basic needs	
	1976	2000	1976	2000	1976	2000	1976	2000	1976	2000
1. Peasant farmers	35	28	18	12	76	74	89	87	88	80
2. Agricultural workers, skilled	0	0	0	0	57	2	43	27	56	23
3. Agricultural workers, unskilled	24	9	14	0	68	60	57	44	73	46
4. Agricultural employers/ professionals	0	0	0	0	41	0	28	0	45	3
5. Non-agricultural informal sector workers	34	44	8	1	70	65	53	54	40	43
6. Non-agricultural workers, skilled	0	0	0	0	21	0	0	0	0	0
7. Non-agricultural workers, unskilled	10	22	5	0	64	39	26	19	17	11
8. Non-agricultural employers/professionals	0	0	0	0	5	0	0	0	0	0
All groups	31	25	15	9	73	64	78	72	78	65

agricultural sector.

The changes in relative income position result in an increase in the Gini ratio of disposable income from 0.520 to 0.542.

Within the group of small farmers the relative position of the three farm size groups also changes. Per capita value added of the peasant group with the smallest plots increases from K.£30.7 to K.£34.0, while that of the second and third groups remains stagnant.

Unemployment, which is residually determined in the model, is mainly an urban phenomenon. In rural areas unemployment is much less prevalent, but under-utilisation of the production factor labour (underemployment) results in continuing lower per capita output figures.

The unemployment rate in urban areas in the base year is around 9 per cent, for both skilled and unskilled workers. The unskilled unemployment rate goes up from 9 to 14 per cent over the reference run period and that of skilled unemployment from 9 to 21 per cent. The difference in these rates is mainly the consequence of increased supply of skilled workers in relation to unskilled workers, and the assumption of a fixed wage differential between skilled and unskilled workers (as was discussed in section 9.4). A 10 per cent reduction in the wage differential would result in an unemployment rate of 18 per cent for unskilled workers and 17 per cent for skilled workers in the year 2000 (unreported experiment).

12.7 Base run: Convergency mechanisms and social accounting matrix

As indicated in Chapter 9, the model deals with several aspects of disequilibrium and forces convergency on product, labour, capital and foreign exchange markets.

Imbalances in the labour market are reflected in unemployment figures and ratios, which were reported earlier.

The internal resource gap in 1976 reflects the disequilibrium on the capital market. Total savings, which are the sum of household savings (K.£76.6 million), business savings (K.£82.2 million) and government savings (K.£81.7 million), are equal to 17.1 per cent of total GDP. The share of public and private investments is 3.8 percentage points higher, which indicates the magnitude of the savings gap.

The external resource gap gives the disquilibrium on the foreign exchange market. Imports (minus import taxes) equal K.£436.9 million; together with factor payments abroad (K.£67 million) they equal K.£503.9 million. This is K.£52.4 million higher than the figure for export receipts, resulting in a balance of payments disequilibrium which is equal to the savings gap.

In the base run, the savings gap (and consequently the balance of payments gap) fluctuates slightly, but the trend is basically upward-moving, from 3.8 to 6.0 per cent of GDP.

The outcomes of the various equilibrating mechanisms are presented in a simple social accounting matrix (SAM).[2] Each element of the simplified SAM represents a condensed matrix of transactions. This simplified SAM has seven sectors: five sectors representing recurrent transitions; factors of production; households and enterprises; government; production; rest of the world. The latter two sectors represent the domestic capital account and the capital account of the rest of the world.

The SAM for the base year is presented in table 12.2. In line 1 we see that producers pay value added (which equals GDP minus indirect taxes) to factors. The value added received by the factors (K.£1,296.5 million) goes to households and enterprises (K.£1,229.5 million) and to the rest of the world (factor payments abroad, K.£67.0 million). This they "spend" on income taxes and profit taxes (K.£159.0 million), on domestic consumer goods (K.£819.1 million), on imported consumer goods (K.£91.8 million) and on savings (K.£159.5 million), which goes to the capital account. The government receives taxes from households and enterprises (K.£159.1 million), receives indirect taxes from production (K.£109.3 million), receives import taxes (K.£66.7 million) from the rest of the world and "spends" this amount on production (K.£253.4 million) and on savings (K.£81.7 million). Production receives K.£819.1 from consumers and investors, K.£253.4 million from the government, K.£1,291.8 from intermediate products, K.£451.6 million from exports and K.£202.5 million from capital formation. It spends its total receipts (K.£3,018.4 million) on payment of value added (K.£1,296.5 million), on indirect taxes (K.£109.3 million), on intermediate products (K.£1,291.8 million) and on imports of intermediate products (K.£320.8 million). The "rest of the world" receives K.£67.0 million as factor payments abroad, K.£91.8 million from imports of consumer goods, K.£320.8 million as imports of intermediate products and K.£91.0 million as imports of capital goods. The "rest of the world" spends this on import taxes, exports and on the balance of payments deficit of K.£52.3 million which is added to domestic savings.

Rather than presenting the same table for the year 2000, which would give a set of values for transactions which is difficult to interpret on its own, we provide a table (12.3) comparing the relative magnitudes of the cells of the social accounting matrix. All cells are expressed as percentages of their total row values both for 1976 and for the year 2000.

197

Table 12.2. Simplified social accounting matrix, 1976 (K.£ million)

	Factors	Households and enterprises	Government	Production	Rest of the world	Capital account	Capital account of the rest the world	Total
Factors				1 296.5				1 296.5
Households and enterprises	1 229.5							1 229.5
Government		159.1		109.3	66.7			335.1
Production		819.1	253.4	1 291.8	451.6	202.5		3 018.4
Rest of the world	67.0	91.8		320.8		91.0		570.6
Capital account		159.5	81.7				52.3	293.5
Capital account of rest of the world					52.3			52.3
Total	1 296.5	1 229.5	335.1	3 018.4	570.6	293.5	52.3	

Table 12.3. Comparison of SAM in 1976 and in the year 2000

	Factor 1976	Factor 2000	Households and enterprises 1976	Households and enterprises 2000	Government 1976	Government 2000	Production 1976	Production 2000	Rest of the world 1976	Rest of the world 2000	Capital account 1976	Capital account 2000	Capital account of rest of the world 1976	Capital account of rest of the world 2000	Total 1976	Total 2000
Factors							100.0	100.0							100.0	100.0
Household and enterprises	100.0	100.0													100.0	100.0
Government			47.5	47.6			32.6	33.0	19.9	19.4					100.0	100.0
Production			27.2	28.7	8.4	8.2	42.8	43.1	15.0	13.3	6.7	6.7			100.0	100.0
Rest of the world	11.7	14.9	16.1	8.0			56.2	60.6			15.9	16.5			100.0	100.0
Capital account			54.3	44.5	27.8	26.8							17.8	28.7	100.0	100.0
Capital account of rest of the world									100.0	100.0					100.0	100.0

1 All cells expressed as percentage of total row value.

199

The entries in table 12.3 for the years 1976 and 2000 differ substantially in some cases, slightly in others. Factor payments abroad increase from 11.7 to 14.9 per cent of total rest of the world receipts, which is a relative increase of 26 per cent, while imports of consumer goods drop from 16.1 per cent to 8.0 per cent of the rest of the world transaction, due to import restrictions prevailing in the base run. Receipts from exports drop by 1.7 percentage points, while capital inflow is 10.0 percentage points higher.

This shows that external influences affect the broad macro structure in the base run, but other structures remain fairly stable. The variation in incomes and basic needs satisfaction, as discussed earlier, comes rather from changes in the composition within each cell. As we explained, each cell is in effect a condensation of transaction matrices between sectors and/or between sectors and socio-economic groups.

12.8 Validation

A serious question that arises with this type of simulation model is that of validation of the model. Klein (1979) mentions five key ratios which are supposed to be constant over the longer time period, viz.:

> savings ratio,
> wage share,
> participation rate,
> capital output ratio,
> velocity of money.

However, in a process of structural change some of these ratios may well change over time.

In the base run of the model, the savings ratio, which is internally determined, oscillates slightly between 20.8 and 22 per cent (although the foreign and domestic components show more variation), and the wage share (behaviourally determined) increases by 1 percentage point to 59 per cent. The participation rate depends on various factors and varies over time. Male labour force participation rates are constant, but different for different cohorts so that the average value is not fixed. Female labour force participation rates are, however, behaviourally determined, going down from 55 to 53 per cent in rural areas, while increasing from 18 to 19 per cent in the urban areas. The capital-output ratio is also an outcome of the model rather than a constant, and increases from 2.3 to 2.9 in the year 2000. As the model does not contain monetary variables, the constancy of the velocity of money is not relevant.

The changes over time in some of these ratios show that the model is capable of capturing structural changes in the economy.

Another way of ascertaining the validity of the model is to look at how the model behaves over the time period already covered.

Figures 12.2 to 12.5 provide a comparison between the actual value and the base run result of some GDP components for the years 1976-84.

Total GDP compares rather well with the actual values. In the years 1977 and 1978 a steeper increase in actual values is noticeable, being the effect of the so-called coffee boom. The effect of the coffee boom is also noticeable in agricultural GDP.

Actual private consumption, after some sharp increases in 1978-79, is in 1981 almost back in line with the base run value, after which it increases slightly more than in the base run values. Actual public consumption shows a less erratic pattern. For a number of years it is higher than the base run results; however, the consequences of credit restraint bring public consumption back more or less to its base run values in 1982.

Gross capital formation (figure 12.4) in particular is smoother in the model than in reality. The actual values for 1976-84 oscillate around the base run trend. As discussed in the description of the model, investment is an adjustment mechanism and behaves quite smoothly in the model because of the imposed savings equals investment condition.

A first thing to notice when looking at the figures for exports and imports is that the model results and the actual values for 1976 differ slightly. This is the consequence of a recent revision of the import and export figures in the national accounts which was not included in the input-output tables for 1976, from which the data base of the Kenya model is derived. Actual export figures up to 1980 compare rather well with the model results, which is not surprising since the growth rate of export demand, being an exogenous value, has been calibrated upon actual figures. After 1980 the model results for exports are somewhat higher than actual values. Actual import figures after 1980 are considerably lower than the model results, reflecting the serious attempts to adjust the economy by import reduction.

It is, of course, difficult to draw firm conclusions from a comparison between the results of a long-term model and the actual values for some initial years, which may not be representative of long-term trends. The graphs in figures 12.2 to 12.5 show, however, that on the whole model results compare well with actual values.

Notes

[1] Examples of this type of activity can be found amongst
     others in Chapter 6 where we describe how definitions of
     skilled and unskilled workers have to be interpreted
     differently over time in order to avoid non-meaningful
     solutions.

[2] Chapter 11 discusses the way a social accounting matrix
     is generated within the framework of the model. Bigsten
     (1981b)   and   Vandemoortele   (1987)   provide   further
     discussion   on   the   Social   Accounting   Matrix   (SAM)
     constructed by the Central Bureau of Statistics and some
     attempts to improve that Social Accounting Matrix.

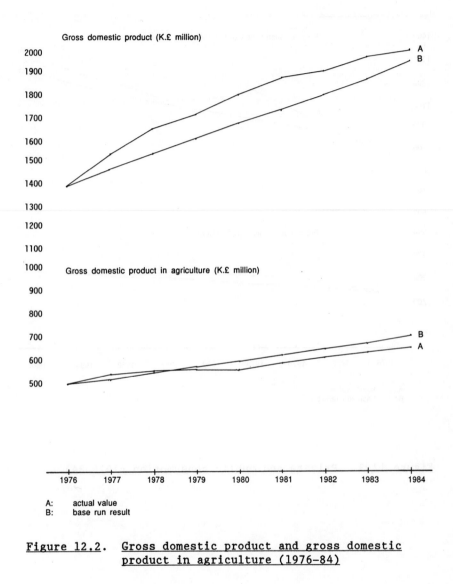

Figure 12.2. <u>**Gross domestic product and gross domestic product in agriculture (1976-84)**</u>

203

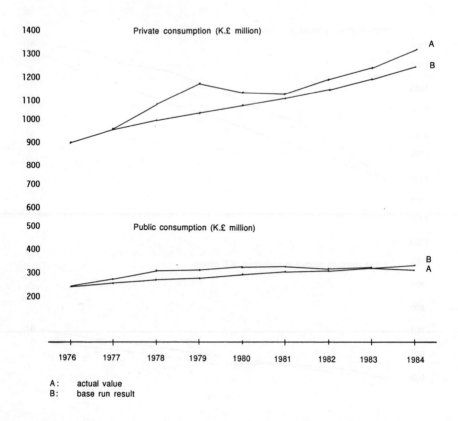

A: actual value
B: base run result

Figure 12.3. Private and public consumption (1976–84)

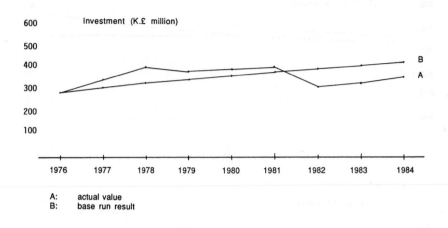

A: actual value
B: base run result

Figure 12.4. Investment (1976-84)

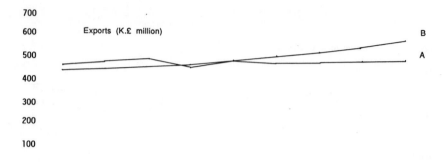

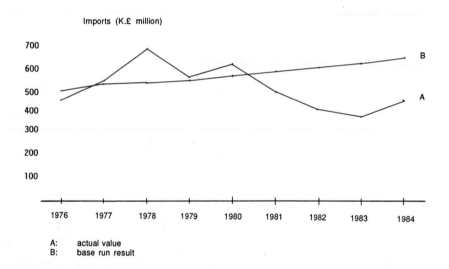

A: actual value
B: base run result

Figure 12.5.   Exports and imports (1976-84)

Table 12.4. **An overview of parameter changes in the eight scenarios**

Scenario	Scenario value	Base run value	Formula
1. Increased taxes and government expenditure	$a_4 = 0.30$ $a_8 = 0.30$ $b_i = 0.25$ $e_i = 0.05$	$a_4 = 0.24$ $a_8 = 0.27$ $b_i = 0.20$ for i=1,...,14 $e_i = 0.00$ for i=1,...,14	[138] [138] [139] [142]
2. Increased attention to basic needs	All changes in scenario 1 + $c_{12} = 0.50$ $c_{13} = 0.50$	 $c_{12} = 0.55$ $c_{13} = 0.45$	 [135]
3. Land redistribution	All changes in scenario 2 + $a = 0.60$	 $a = 0.56$	 [116]
4. Agricultural urban-rural terms of trade Increased rural productivity (Basic needs policies)	All changes in scenario 3 + $c = 1.1$ $t_{1,j} = 0.01$	 $c = 1.0$ $t_{1,j} = 0.005$ for j=1,...,3	 [268] [119]
5. Growth policies	$a_4 = 0.20$ $a_8 = 0.20$ $b_i = 0.15$ $e_i = -0.05$ LIC = 0.9 LIC	$a_4 = 0.24$ $a_8 = 0.27$ $b_i = 0.20$ for i=1,...,14 $e_i = 0.00$ for i=1,...,14	[138] [138] [139] [142] [236]
6. Increased aid and foreign capital	$d = 0.20$ $b = 0.25$	$d = 0.00$ $b = 0.15$	[219] [211]
7. Internal and external rigidities constraining production of tradeables under base run policies	$a = 0.00$ formula [151] instead of formula [152]	$a = 0.10$	[150]
8. Internal and external rigidities constraining production of tradeables under basic needs policies	All changes in scenario 4 + $a = 0.00$ formula [151] instead of formula [152]	 $a = 0.10$	 [150]

13 Experimenting with the model: Domestic scenarios

13.1 Introduction

In the domestic scenarios we want to contrast policies aiming at increasing satisfaction of basic needs with other policies, loosely labelled growth policies. We have included several sets of government policies in the scenario analysis.

First we have <u>fiscal policies and government expenditure policies</u>. These can include various forms of tax increases or decreases, and allocation of more or less funds to those public sector categories which provide basic needs services.

A second set of policies deals more directly with the poorer groups, the majority of whom are still to be found in the rural areas. These policies deal both with the access of the poorer groups to production factors (<u>land redistribution policies</u>) and with the prices farmers get for their products (<u>agricultural pricing policies</u>).

A final set of policies deals mainly with remuneration of the urban sector and relates to <u>wage and labour market policies</u> (which in our model can also be regarded, when combined with policies for import and export taxes, as proxies for adjustment and stabilisation policies since we do not explicitly have the price of foreign exchange in the model) (Branson, 1983).

Through the scenario experiments, we will look at four sets of policies relating to basic needs provision (scenarios 1 to 4) and one related to growth (scenario 5). The basic needs policies are introduced cumulatively in the scenarios.

The first scenario experiment reflects fiscal policy. Government revenue is augmented through the introduction of a 5 per cent export tax, a 25 per cent increase in corporate tax and an increase in personal taxation of 12.5 per cent for the richest rural group and 36 per cent for the richest urban group. Government expenditure increases by the same amount while keeping the percentage-wise allocation of it unchanged.

The second scenario experiment additionally reflects changes in government expenditure. Non-basic needs expenditure is decreased by 9 per cent and basic needs expenditure is increased by 10 per cent, leaving the total amount of government expenditure at the level of the first scenario.

The third and fourth scenario experiments reflect agricultural policies as well. In the third policy experiment the government also distributes land from large-scale farmers to small-scale farmers. The percentage of land owned by large-scale farmers decreases from 44 to 40 per cent.

In the fourth policy experiment the government intervenes further in agricultural policies by changing agricultural and non-agricultural prices. The urban-rural terms of trade decrease by 10 per cent from their base run value, while the government manages, through its more effective expenditure pattern, to augment the productivity of land of small-scale farmers by 0.5 per cent per annum.

The fifth policy experiment reflects the traditional growth scenario. It mainly comprises policies to stimulate private production by providing export subsidies of 5 per cent and by reducing corporate taxes by 25 per cent. In order to increase investible surpluses, the government also intervenes in the wage labour market to reduce wage costs by 10 per cent from the base run value.

As indicated, the relevant changes in the model parameters are given in table 12.4, while detailed outcomes of the base run and all scenarios are reported in the tables in the annex to Chapter 15.

13.2 Increase in government expenditure (scenario 1)

In the first scenario, reflecting an increase in taxes and consequent increases in public expenditure, we notice slight macro-economic changes. GDP in the year 2000 is 0.5 per cent lower than in the base run with primary sector GDP 1.3 per cent lower, secondary sector GDP 2.2 per cent lower and tertiary sector GDP 1.4 per cent higher. Changes in final demand categories in the year 2000 are somewhat larger. Private consumption is 1.3 per cent lower, investment demand 7.6 per cent lower, and public consumption 6.5 per cent higher, exports are 3 per cent and imports 2.7 per cent lower. All three import categories are more or less equally affected. Imports of consumer goods are 3.3 per cent lower, imports of intermediate products 2.3 per cent lower and imports of capital goods 3.9 per cent lower in the year 2000 than in the base run.

Increased taxation also results in a drop in the total savings rate in the year 2000 from 21.1 per cent in the base run to 20.4 per cent under this scenario. This is mainly caused by a drop in the domestic savings rate, since the foreign savings rate remains quite stable (it drops slightly from 6 per cent in the base run to 5.9 per cent under this scenario in the year 2000).

The increase in taxation causes an exogenous shock to the economy to which it has to adjust. Thus, after the change in the taxation parameters, which was introduced experimentally in 1984, government expenditure is higher in 1985 than in the base run. This causes an increase in the annual GDP growth rate from 4.5 to 5.2 per cent, since other final demand components remain at the same level in a situation of slight excess supply. As a consequence, the domestic savings rate drops from 16.6 to 14.9 per cent. In later years, however, the decrease in the savings ratio causes lower investment which in turn results in lower growth, to the extent that from 1987 to 1992 the GDP growth rate is lower than in the base run (base run GDP growth in 1990 is 4.4 per cent compared to 4.0 per cent under this scenario experiment). After 1992 the growth rate under the scenario is slightly higher (in 1995, for example, 4.5 per cent under the scenario, compared to 4.4 per cent in the base run), converging again at the end of the century to the base run growth pattern (figure 13.1). Broadly concluding, one can say that according to the model it takes seven years for the economy to adjust to a shock caused by increases in taxation.

Increased government expenditure also results in increased expenditure on basic needs categories. In consequence, the percentage of children attending primary school in the year 2000 increases to 95 per cent as compared to 91 per cent in the base run. The percentage of the total population without access to health facilities drops only slightly, however. Access does increase for groups other than peasant farmers (the percentage of urban skilled workers without access drops, for example, from 19.5 per cent in the base run to 18 per cent in this scenario experiment). However, since peasant farmers form the largest group their position very much influences the national average.

As a result the influence on the basic needs indicators is only limited. The percentage of the population with primary

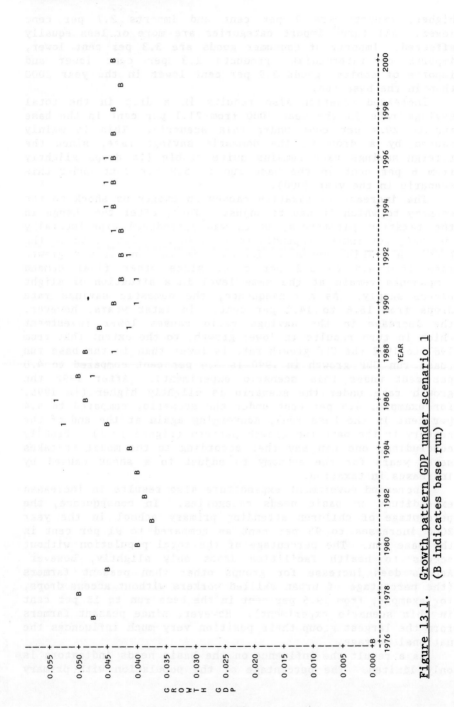

Figure 13.1. Growth pattern GDP under scenario 1
(B indicates base run)

schooling increases from 80 to 81 per cent, female life expectancy in the year 2000 remains constant in the rural areas, while in the urban areas it is 9.5 months higher than in the base run. Population growth is hardly affected in either urban or rural areas, nor are migration rates affected by this experiment.

Since both GDP and population in the year 2000 remain the same under this scenario, per capita GDP remains unchanged also. The somewhat larger drop in value added in the secondary sector referred to above causes a slight drop in non-agricultural GDP per capita, which is K.£346.4 as compared to K.£348.5 in the base run, but the changes are not large enough to influence the pattern of income distribution. The Gini ratio for total income remains at 0.575 but that for disposable income goes down from 0.542 to 0.538 (since tax increases are not proportionally applied). Since the economic structure remains the same, unemployment rates differ only slightly under this scenario experiment. In the year 2000 the unemployment rate of the urban unskilled is 13.9 per cent under this scenario as compared to 14.2 per cent in the base run, and that of urban skilled workers 20.7 per cent as compared to 21.4 per cent.

13.3 Changes in government expenditure (scenario 2)

The second scenario experiment builds upon the first scenario experiment by additionally changing the pattern of government expenditure and allocating more expenditure to basic needs. In the first scenario expenditure on basic needs items in the year 2000 is 6.5 per cent higher than in the base run because of the general increase in government expenditure. With the changes in the public expenditure pattern in this experiment, basic needs expenditure in the year 2000 is 17.6 per cent higher than in the base run.

The macro-economic effects are not much different from the first scenario. Total GDP and the composition of GDP are much the same as under scenario 1. The final demand components, however, differ slightly from scenario 1. Private consumption is 1.7 per cent lower in the year 2000 than in the base run compared to a decrease of 1.3 per cent under scenario 1. Investment demand is 5.9 per cent lower as compared to 7.6 per cent lower under scenario 1. There are also slight differences in import demand. Imports of consumer goods are 5.2 per cent lower compared to the base run in the year 2000, while under scenario 1 they were 3.2 per cent lower. Imports of intermediate goods are 2.4 per cent lower under both scenarios as compared to the base run, but imports of capital goods are 2.6 per cent lower under scenario 2, while they were 3.8 per

213

cent lower in scenario 1.

Since the economic structure and pattern of final demand change so little, the savings and investment picture is almost the same under this scenario as under the previous one. The domestic savings ratio is a fraction higher – 14.7 per cent under this scenario compared to 14.5 per cent under the first scenario, and 15 per cent in the base run.

The areas where we notice direct changes are, of course, those regarding the provision of basic needs. Primary school attendance becomes 100 per cent after 1990 and the percentage of population without medical facilities in the year 2000 goes down from 71.9 in the base run to 70.1 in the experiment. Both urban and rural areas are affected. Increases in basic needs expenditure categories also cause the output indicators to increase. The percentage of adult population with completed primary education goes up from 80 per cent in the base run to 85 per cent in this experiment, mainly due to improvements in educational achievement in the rural areas. Rural female life expectancy in the year 2000 becomes 57.6 years compared to the base run value of 57 years, and urban female life expectancy becomes 64.6 years instead of 63.7 in the base run.

The increased satisfaction of basic needs does not, however, have much effect on population growth. We notice a slight increase in the rural–urban migration rate to 5.0 per thousand of rural population in the year 2000 as compared to 4.7 per thousand in the base run, which results in a total rural population of 27 million in the year 2000 as compared to 27.2 million in the base run. The urban population amounts to 6.4 million compared to 6.3 million. Because of the increased urban population and increases in government activities which demand more skilled persons, the unemployment rate of the unskilled is somewhat higher – 15.8 per cent in the year 2000 compared to 14.2 per cent in the base run – and that of skilled workers somewhat lower – 19.4 per cent as compared to 21.4 per cent. The effects are, however, too small to cause a change in the Gini ratio.

As economic structure and population have not changed, compared to scenario 1, the incomes and the income shares of the various socio–economic groups remain unaltered compared to scenario 1 and the base run. Consequently, the percentage of population below the poverty line remains at 25 per cent.

13.4 Land redistribution (scenario 3)

The third scenario adds institutional agricultural changes to the two previous scenarios of fiscal policy and government expenditure. This takes the form of land redistribution, in

which the amount of land belonging to the large-scale farmers
is reduced by 7 per cent of its original value and added to
the land stock of the small-scale farmers, among whom it is
distributed according to existing patterns of land distribution.[1] The primary aim of land redistribution is to
improve the standard of living of the small-scale farming
class.

As a consequence of the land redistribution, GDP in the
year 2000 is 1.9 per cent higher under this scenario than in
the base run. However, compared to previous policy experiments
with increased taxes and increased expenditure on basic needs,
and thus reflecting the consequences of land redistribution
rather than the combined package, GDP is 2.4 per cent higher
in the year 2000. Higher GDP under this scenario is mainly
caused by a higher GDP in the primary sector; this is 2.2 per
cent higher than in the base run and 3.5 per cent higher than
in the previous policy experiment. Value added in the
secondary sector in the year 2000 is 0.2 per cent lower than
in the base run and 2.0 per cent lower compared to the
previous scenario experiment. GDP in the tertiary sector is
3.1 per cent higher than in the base run, but only 1.5 per
cent higher compared to the previous scenario. Since we have
not applied any policies affecting the secondary and tertiary
sectors in this scenario, all the changes in these sectors are
due to linkages through changes in level and composition of
consumption, investment and savings among the various
socio-economic groups in the model.

Private consumption in the year 2000 is 1 per cent higher
than in the base run and 2.6 per cent higher than under the
previous scenario. Investment demand is 1.3 per cent lower
than in the base run, but 4.5 per cent higher than in the
previous scenario. Public consumption is 7.8 per cent higher
than in the base run, but only 1.2 per cent higher compared to
the previous scenario. Despite higher private consumption,
total imports of consumer goods are 6.5 per cent lower than in
the base run and 1.3 per cent lower compared to the previous
scenario since import coefficients of consumption by the
various socio-economic groups are different. Imports of
intermediate products are also lower than in the base run (0.7
per cent) but 1.6 per cent higher compared to the previous
scenario. Imports of capital goods are 1 per cent higher than
in the base run but 3.6 per cent higher compared to the
previous scenario.

Land redistribution does not result in a substantial drop
in exports. On the contrary, exports in the year 2000 are 0.9
per cent higher than in the previous scenario.

The total savings rate in the year 2000 under this
scenario is almost identical to that in the base run (20.9 per

cent compared to 21.1 per cent), but it is higher than in the previous scenario (20.9 per cent compared to 20.6 per cent). The "good" performance is almost entirely due to a better performance of the domestic savings rate, which in itself is mainly the consequence of increased household savings.

Regarding access to basic needs facilities, this scenario reflects very much the same pattern as the previous one, and the basic needs outcomes are consequently the same. The percentage of adult population with completed primary education in the year 2000 is 85 per cent, the same as in the previous scenario, while rural female life expectancy is 57.8 years compared to 57.6 years in the previous scenario and 57 years in the base run. Urban female life expectancy is the same as under the previous scenario - 64.6 years. The area where this scenario does differ appreciably from the previous scenario is that of poverty incidence and income inequality. The percentage of the total population below the poverty line in the year 2000 is 22.4 per cent compared to 25.2 per cent in the base run. This is to a large extent due to a fall in poverty incidence among small-scale farmers. The decrease in poverty among small-scale farmers also results in a drop in the Gini ratio for total income, which in the year 2000 is 0.560 under this experiment as compared to 0.575 in the base run. The drop in the Gini ratio for disposable income is slightly more pronounced (the ratio being 0.524 under this experiment as compared to 0.542 in the base run).

The changes in final demand and in sectoral output also result in changes in the unemployment pattern in urban areas. The unemployment rate for unskilled workers in the year 2000 is 14.4 per cent as compared to 15.8 per cent in the previous experiment and 14.2 per cent in the base run. The unemployment rate for skilled workers is 18.1 per cent as compared to 19.4 per cent in the previous experiment and 21.5 per cent in the base run. The decrease in the unemployment rate for both urban and rural workers compared to the previous scenario is mainly the consequence of increased activities in the non-agricultural sector and of an increase in demand for more labour-intensive products.

13.5 Other agricultural policies (scenario 4)

In the fourth scenario we add to the previous scenarios of fiscal policies, changes in government expenditure patterns and land distribution a more active agricultural policy in the form of a 10 per cent improvement in the rural-urban terms of trade. We further assume that government expenditure is targeted more to agriculture, leading to an improvement in land productivity of small-scale farmers of 0.5 per cent per year. These policy changes are carried out over and above those in the previous policy experiment. This policy experiment can, therefore, be regarded as reflecting a broad basic needs strategy in that it involves increased access to basic needs services, asset redistribution in the form of land distribution, and income redistribution through changing the rural-urban terms of trade.

Under this scenario GDP in the year 2000 is 2.3 per cent higher than in the base run. But the structure of GDP has changed more. Value added in the primary sector in the year 2000 is 5.5 per cent higher as compared to the base run and 3.2 per cent as compared to the previous scenario. Value added in the secondary sector is virtually the same as in the base run (an increase of 0.1 per cent), while value added in the tertiary sector is 1.2 per cent higher than in the base run, but 1.9 per cent lower compared to the previous experiment; the latter drop is mainly a consequence of lower tax receipts. Private consumption in the year 2000 is 3.0 per cent higher than in the base run and 2 per cent higher compared to the previous scenario. Investment demand is 1.7 per cent higher than in the base run and 3.0 per cent higher compared to the previous scenario, while public consumption is 6.7 per cent higher than in the base run but 1 per cent lower compared to the previous scenario.

Income redistribution appears to have a negative effect on exports, which are 2.1 per cent lower as compared to the previous scenario and 4.2 per cent lower compared to the base run. A change in consumption patterns and a decrease in exports also result in changes in imports. Imports of intermediate goods are 1.2 per cent lower than in the base run, but imports of capital goods are 3.0 per cent and imports of consumer goods are 3.6 per cent higher. Since the drop in imports of intermediate products cannot compensate for the increase in the two other categories the foreign savings rate increases; under this experiment it is 0.4 percentage points higher than in the base run. Consequently, the total foreign debt increases, and is 7.3 per cent higher in the year 2000 under this scenario than in the base run. But since GDP under this scenario is also higher, the debt/GDP ratio in the year 2000 is only 4.9 per cent higher than in the base run.

The domestic savings rate in the year 2000 is only 0.2 percentage point lower, and in consequence the total savings rate under this experiment is slightly higher than in the base run.

The introduction of land redistribution (performed under the previous scenario experiment), and of other agricultural policies in addition to land redistribution in this scenario, cause an exogenous shock to the system. As with the exogenous shock caused by changes in fiscal policy in the first scenario, we look at how long it takes the model to adjust to this shock. The introduction of increased taxation and government expenditure, initially not compensated for by lower domestic savings, caused economic growth to increase in 1985 from 4.5 to 5.2 per cent, as we saw in figure 13.1. The effects of land redistribution and changes in the terms of trade, added to this, cause growth to increase further to 5.6 per cent (figure 13.2). The higher growth rate resulting from the latter experiment is quickly lowered again, however, and remains below the base run level of growth until 1990, from which time on it remains at a level somewhat higher than in the base run. Adjustment under this experiment thus occurs more quickly than with the experiment involving increased government expenditure alone.

Provision of basic needs services remains virtually the same under this experiment as in the previous one; it includes a 100 per cent primary school attendance rate before 1990, and a 30 per cent coverage rate of population with respect to health facilities. However, since for some socio-economic groups access to basic needs services also depends on their own expenditure (notably on health and secondary education) and since the distribution of income has favoured the agricultural sector more under this experiment, shortfall rates are, in the case of health and education, lower for agricultural skilled and unskilled workers, as well as for agricultural employers/professionals. Shortfall rates are higher, however, for urban socio-economic groups. (Shortfall in access to health facilities in the year 2000, for example, for agricultural unskilled workers is 28.3 per cent under this experiment, and 37.8 per cent under the previous experiment, while shortfall in access for urban unskilled workers is 10.2 per cent under this experiment as compared to 9.4 per cent under the previous experiment.)

Average levels of basic needs satisfaction in the year 2000 are, however, at the same level as under the previous experiment. Again, we notice hardly any change in population growth under this experiment.

Policies to stimulate agriculture have, however, had a positive impact on poverty and income distribution (and thus indirectly on consumption and savings patterns, as we indicated above). The percentage population below the poverty line in the year 2000 reaches a level of 17.6 per cent in this experiment as compared to a value of 22.4 per cent under the previous experiment, and a value of 25.2 per cent under the base run experiment. The higher level of rural per capita income (K.£52.4 in the year 2000 compared to K.£49.6 under the base run) also results in reduced income inequality. The Gini

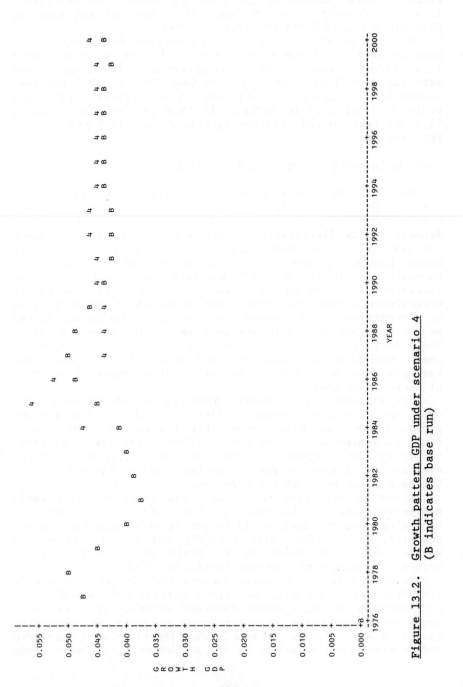

Figure 13.2. Growth pattern GDP under scenario 4
(B indicates base run)

ratio of total income in the year 2000 under this experiment is 0.521 compared to 0.575 under the base run and that of disposable income 0.484 compared to 0.542.

Changes in final demand and production patterns, rather than changes in labour force participation rates, also result in a different composition of unemployment. The unemployment rate for unskilled workers in the year 2000 is 15.1 per cent as compared to 14.4 per cent under the previous experiment, while that of skilled workers is 18.0 per cent compared to 18.1 per cent in the previous experiment and 21.5 per cent in the base run.

13.6 Efficiency in basic needs delivery

One of the outcomes of the broad-based basic needs scenario (scenario 4) is a rapid increase in access to basic needs services. Access to basic needs goods and services depends on the distribution of the use of the services among the various socio-economic groups, on the unit cost of basic needs provision, and on the level of total basic needs expenditure. In the scenario analysis the latter amount was increased, both through increased allocation within the public expenditure budget and through increased public expenditure as a consequence of increased tax receipts following faster economic growth or deliberate policies to increase tax rates. These factors, as indicated, cause a rapid increase in basic needs satisfaction. But, as indicated, this is under the assumption of constant recurrent and capital costs of delivery of basic needs goods.

For at least two reasons, however, it is unlikely that costs will remain constant. First of all, as the economy grows, tastes and preferences will change and people will often no longer accept the same quality of services. Pressure is put on the government to increase the quality of services, even before it has achieved a coverage rate of 100 per cent at the more basic level of the services.

A second important reason why unit costs of basic needs provision tend to increase is that when a programme is expanding rapidly, such as is happening under the basic needs scenario, inefficiency will increase and the recurrent and capital costs of provision of basic needs will increase because of management problems (Arellano, 1985).

We simulated an increase in quality (or an increase in inefficiency) by assuming that the recurrent and capital costs of provision of basic needs increase annually by 1 per cent when the complete set of basic needs policies is introduced (scenario 4). Figures 13.3-13.5 show the effects of increased unit costs on the behaviour of the demographic and basic needs

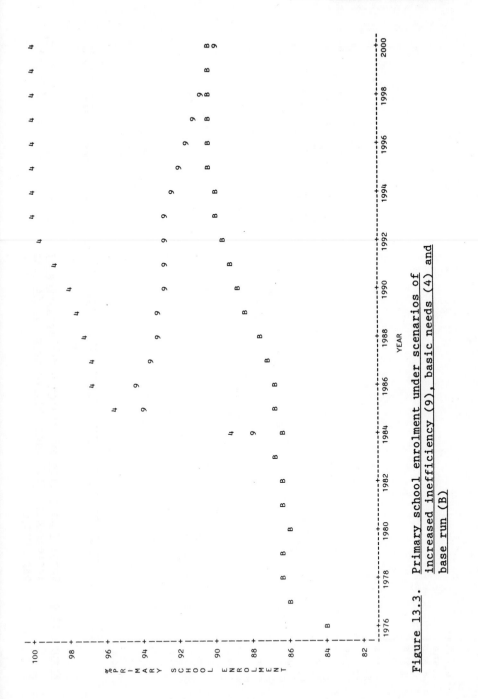

Figure 13.3. Primary school enrolment under scenarios of increased inefficiency (9), basic needs (4) and base run (B)

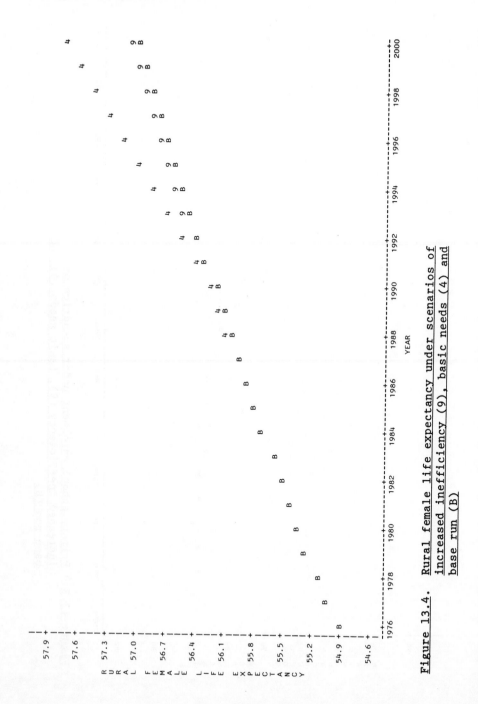

Figure 13.4. Rural female life expectancy under scenarios of increased inefficiency (9), basic needs (4) and base run (B)

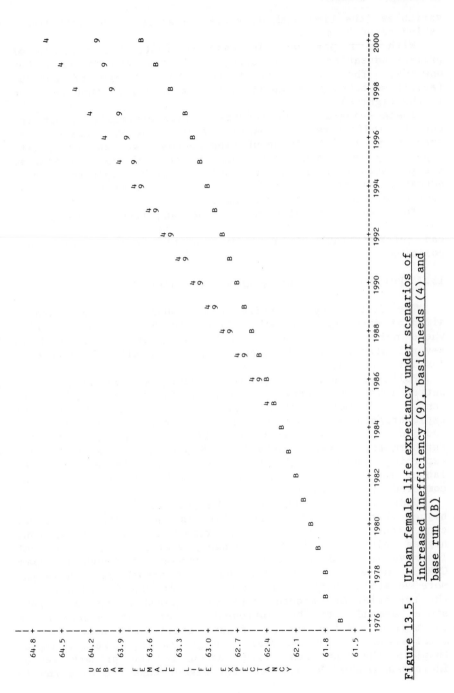

<u>Figure 13.5.</u> <u>Urban female life expectancy under scenarios of</u>
<u>increased inefficiency (9), basic needs (4) and</u>
<u>base run (B)</u>

223

variables (the time path of variables affected by inefficiency is indicated by a 9).

With a 1 per cent increase in costs the coverage of primary education becomes worse than in the base run from 1999 onwards. The turning point for the coverage of medical facilities takes place earlier, viz. around 1989 (not reported in the figures).

These changes in the coverage ratios naturally affect the output indicators of basic needs. Urban female life expectancy at birth is about nine months lower and rural life expectancy ten months lower than in the basic needs scenario. The percentage of the adult population with completed primary education in the year 2000 is 80 per cent compared to 85 per cent under the basic needs scenario.

These outcomes point to an important result, namely that insufficient care in the management of basic needs programmes can quickly result in unwinding positive results from other policies.

13.7 Policies to stimulate growth (scenario 5)

The fifth scenario reflects a number of policy changes aimed at encouraging growth. Unlike in the previous scenarios where policies relating to basic needs were introduced in several stages, in this scenario we apply all policy changes deviating from the base run at once.

Policies under the growth scenario aim at providing a better investment climate by reducing profit taxes by 25 per cent. Income taxes paid by the group of employers/professionals in urban and rural areas are also reduced by 34 per cent and 18 per cent respectively. Furthermore, an export subsidy of 5 per cent is given to all exporting sectors. The government also intervenes in the labour market and reduces the wage bill by 10 per cent as compared to the base run value.

Under this scenario GDP in the year 2000 is 4.1 per cent higher than in the base run. This is the result of 10.5 per cent higher value added in the primary sector, 5.9 per cent higher value added in the secondary sector and 2.6 per cent lower value added in the tertiary sector. Although a higher GDP is achieved in the year 2000, the growth pattern is far more volatile than in the base run. At the introduction of the scenario, GDP growth drops as compared to the base run, since demand at the introduction of the scenario is constrained, while supply effects still need some time to materialise. After two years GDP growth is, however, higher than in the base run, value added in the primary sector increases gradually (4.5 per cent higher than the base run in

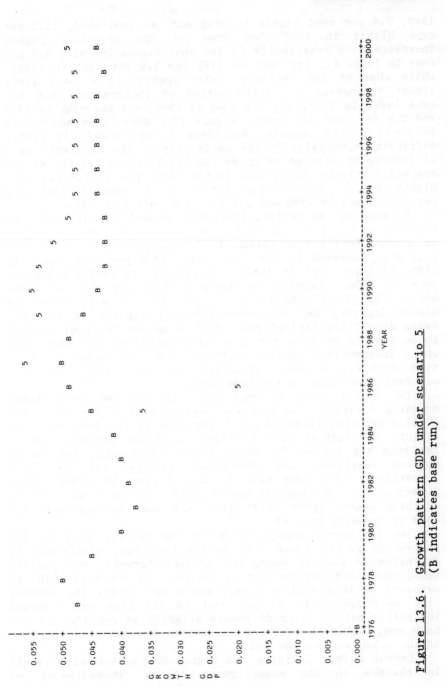

Figure 13.6. Growth pattern GDP under scenario 5
(B indicates base run)

225

1990, 7.4 per cent higher in 1995 and, as indicated, 10.5 per cent higher in 2000) but that of the secondary sector increases more erratically (2 per cent higher in 1985, 0.7 per cent in 1990, 4.1 per cent in 1995 and 5.9 per cent in 2000), while that of the tertiary sector remains at a lower level almost throughout the whole period of observation (4.6 per cent lower in 1985, 8.1 per cent in 1990, 4.4 per cent in 1995 and 2.6 per cent in 2000). Figure 13.6 shows that adjustment to these policy changes, according to the model, is rather difficult, especially in the early years. The difficult path of adjustment also shows up in the final demand sectors of the economy. Private consumption in the year 2000 is 2.8 per cent higher than in the base run, but 2 per cent lower in 1985, 2.2 per cent lower in 1990 and 0.8 per cent higher in 1995.

Because of tax relief, investment demand also increases as compared to the base run and its value is 27.1 per cent higher in 2000. Public consumption is lower, because of lower tax receipts, compared to the base run: 13.9 per cent lower in 1985, 14.2 per cent in 1990, 10.6 per cent in 1995 and 8.6 per cent in 2000. Exports in the year 2000 are 8.7 per cent higher than in the base run. Higher exports also allow for higher imports, but the composition of imports is changed. Heavy demand for capital goods pushes up the level of capital goods imports by 17.6 per cent as compared to the base run, while intermediate imports increase by 6.1 per cent. This in turn results in a lower level of imports of consumer goods (1 per cent lower than in the base run).

The higher level of investment is financed from higher domestic savings. The domestic savings rate in the year 2000 is 17.3 per cent compared to 15 per cent in the base run. In effect, the savings rate is higher than the savings rate in the base run during the whole policy experiment, but as we noticed earlier, the increased savings and increased investments took some time to materialise in higher GDP. Consequently, the capital-output ratio in the year 2000 is slightly higher under this experiment than in the base run (3.1 as compared to 2.9).

The percentage population below the poverty line is 3.6 percentage points lower than in the base run, mainly due to decreases in poverty among the peasant farmers, but poverty among unskilled workers has increased; in the year 2000, 24 per cent of this socio-economic group fall below the poverty line as compared to 22 per cent in the base run. Income inequality before taxes decreases slightly as compared to the base run, since the farmers' situation has improved but that of the urban workers has not.

Labour market policies and higher GDP growth also result in changes in the unemployment rates. Unemployment of unskilled workers in the year 2000 is 13.5 per cent as compared to 14.9 per cent in the base run, while unemployment of skilled workers is 21.7 per cent as compared to 21.5 per cent in the base run.

Regarding access to basic needs services, this scenario shows more or less the same results as the base run scenario; the percentage of the adult population with completed primary education and the number of years of female life expectancy therefore do not improve over the base run values.

Note

[1] The model also allows for a change in land distribution within the small-scale farming class, but such experiments are not performed here.

14 Experimenting with the model: Scenarios reflecting external influences and domestic rigidities

14.1 External aid and capital inflow (scenario 6)

The sixth scenario reflects changes in external conditions affecting the foreign exchange situation.

First, an additional inflow of balance of payments support equal to financing 20 per cent of the current account deficit is made available. Furthermore, the margin of imports over exports, which is financed by foreign borrowing, is increased from 15 per cent in the base run to 25 per cent. All other policy parameters and trends are the same as in the base run.

The inflow of additional foreign resources from 1984 onwards allows the economy to grow without a foreign exchange constraint until 1992, which results in 4.8 per cent higher GDP than in the base run in 1995. After this period, growth does not accelerate any more but stays at the same level as under the base run (figure 14.1). The higher GDP is entirely due to higher GDP in the secondary and tertiary sectors (up by 4.2 and 9.1 per cent respectively in the year 2000 as compared to the base run). The lifting of the foreign exchange constraint benefits consumers more than producers. Private consumption under this scenario is 12 per cent higher in the year 2000 than in the base run, while investment demand is only 1.8 per cent higher. Public consumption is 6.5 per cent higher, while exports are 1.3 per cent lower. The relatively large increase in private consumption (in relation to the increase in GDP) results in a lower domestic savings rate which in the year 2000 is 10.9 per cent as compared to 15 per

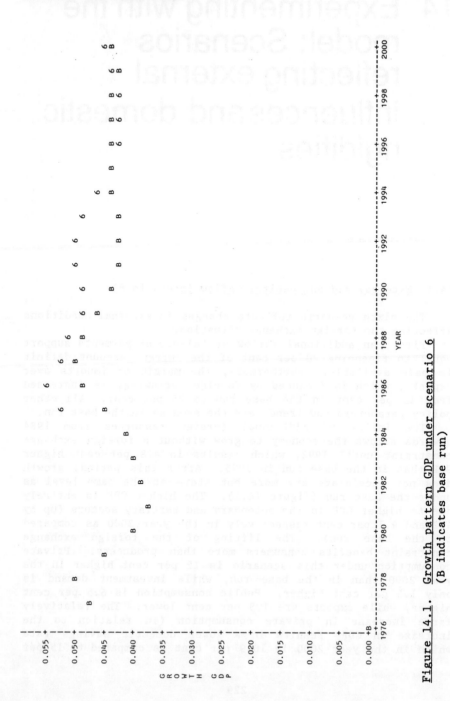

Figure 14.1. Growth pattern GDP under scenario 6
(B indicates base run)

230

cent in the base run. The fall in domestic savings is partly compensated for by a higher foreign savings rate (which, under this experiment, is 7.9 per cent as compared to 6 per cent in the base run) and by additional aid (which amounts to 2 per cent of GDP as compared to zero per cent in the base run). Because of the higher foreign savings rate the total foreign debt in the year 2000 is 32 per cent higher under this scenario than in the base run and consequently debt repayments are higher too.

More foreign resources result in increased imports which under this scenario are 12.8 per cent higher in the year 2000 than in the base run. The increase in the level of imports over the base run level mainly takes place from the introduction of the policies in 1984 until 1990, when the increase becomes much smaller. This increase in imports is mainly due to an increase in imports of consumer goods which, in the absence of the foreign exchange constraint, are 98.5 per cent higher than in the base run in the year 2000, while imports of intermediate products and capital goods are 4.3 per cent and 3.1 per cent higher as compared to the base run.

Since government expenditure under this scenario is higher than in the base run because of a higher tax base, access to some basic needs facilities is improved. The percentage of children attending primary school in the year 2000 is 95 per cent compared to 90 per cent in the base run. The improvement in enrolment rates is, however, too low to have an appreciable effect on the percentage of the adult population with completed primary education in the year 2000, which in this experiment only goes up from 80 to 81 per cent. Female life expectancy at birth in the year 2000 is also much the same under this scenario as in the base run, for both rural and urban areas. For urban areas it is nine months higher, mainly due to higher urban incomes.

As we noticed above, the higher GDP under this scenario is mainly the result of increases in GDP in the secondary and tertiary sectors. In consequence, per capita incomes in the non-agricultural sector are higher in this experiment than in the base run (K.£369.8 in the year 2000 as compared to K.£348.5), but agricultural incomes remain at the same levels as in the base run. Although migration increases somewhat, this hardly affects the per capita agricultural/non-agricultural differences. The urban population in the year 2000 is only 1 per cent higher in this experiment than in the base run.

Regarding poverty levels, we notice in this experiment a somewhat higher percentage of the population below the poverty line in the year 2000 than in the base run (26.1 per cent compared to 25.1 per cent). This is entirely due to a worsening of the income position of small-scale farmers compared to other agricultural and non-agricultural groups. In effect, the Gini ratio for total income is, in the year 2000, 0.586 under this experiment as compared to 0.575 in the base run. The increased activities in the secondary and tertiary sectors result, however, in a lower urban unemployment rate. In the year 2000 the unemployment rate of skilled workers is 18.1 per cent as compared to 21.5 per cent in the base run and that of unskilled workers 8 per cent as compared to 14.2 per cent in the base run.

14.2 Policy experiments under rigid internal and external circumstances (scenarios 7 and 8)

In the last two experiments we investigate what happens when the economy cannot switch into production of more tradeables both because of domestic institutional problems and because of non-accommodating foreign demand. The effects of these rigidities are modelled as follows. First, we have assumed a fixed trend in export demand each year rather than applying a growth factor to realised exports, which might be higher than initial export demand for a given year because of favourable supply conditions (see the discussion around formulae [151] and [152] in Chapter 8). Second, we have set the parameter for import substitution at zero as an indication that increased production of tradeables has been made difficult (see formula [150] in Chapter 8 for more details).

The effects of these rigidities where base run standard policies are being applied are reported in scenario 7, while the effects of the rigidities alongside basic needs policies (as in scenario 4) are reported in scenario 8.

The rigidities have a negative effect on the national income. Applied to base run policies the rigidities result in a 7.2 per cent lower GDP in the year 2000 (scenario 7). However, when rigidities are applied to basic needs policies GDP in the year 2000 is only 3.8 per cent lower as compared to the base run. The constraints are noticeable in the secondary sector (9.5 per cent lower for the year 2000 under scenario 7 and 7.2 per cent lower under scenario 8) and in the tertiary sector (11.1 per cent lower for the year 2000 under scenario 7 and 7.9 per cent lower under scenario 8) rather than in the primary sector where effects are negligible or positive (only 0.5 per cent lower in the year 2000 under scenario 7, and 4.1 per cent higher under scenario 8). The relative strength of the agricultural sector, and especially the support provided to it under the basic needs policy package scenario provide a stable basis for the growth of the economy under conditions of rigidities.

The final demand picture when rigidities are applied to base run policies (scenario 7) is not much different from the base run, with two exceptions. First, the decrease in investment demand is lower than the decrease in private and public consumption (4.6 per cent lower in the year 2000 compared to 9.4 per cent and 7.8 per cent lower). Second, imports of consumer goods are higher at the expense of imports of intermediate goods and investment goods, indicating a lower level of domestic production, as has already been noticed above. However, the different consumption patterns when basic needs policies are applied mitigate the effect of increased imports of consumer goods considerably (in the year 2000 imports of consumer goods are 35.6 per cent higher under scenario 7, but only 10.6 per cent higher under scenario 8), which shows the strong effect of basic needs policies on import levels and import patterns.

Savings rates in the case of rigidities are slightly higher than in the base run. In the year 2000 the domestic savings rate is 15.9 per cent under scenario 7 and 15.5 per cent under scenario 8 compared to 15.0 per cent in the base run.

Under scenario 7, access to basic needs services remains the same as in the base run with a similar percentage of children in primary school and a similar proportion of the population having access to health facilities. Access is higher under scenario 8, reaching almost the same level as in the "normal" basic needs scenario (scenario 4). Patterns of life expectancy and percentage of adult population with primary school education also correspond to the above picture.

Poverty levels are slightly higher under rigidities with base run policies (scenario 7) than in the base run proper (26.9 per cent compared to 25.2 per cent in the year 2000) but much lower under rigidities with basic needs policies (19.4 per cent compared to 17.6 per cent under the basic needs scenario proper). However, because non-agricultural activity levels are lower, incomes and employment levels are lower. The unemployment rate for urban unskilled workers in the year 2000 is 22.5 per cent under scenario 7 compared to 14.2 per cent in the base run, and that of skilled workers 28.5 per cent compared to 21.5 per cent in the base run. Under scenario 8 the figures for skilled workers approach the base run level, but this is not the case for unskilled workers.

Income inequality is only slightly lower under scenario 7 than in the base run, but much lower under scenario 8.

15 Conclusions

In this last chapter we first draw some general
conclusions from the outcomes of the various policy scenarios
described in the previous chapters. Then we discuss more
generally the outcome of this modelling exercise and see
whether we have been able to reply satisfactorily to the
questions raised in Chapters 1 and 2. Finally we look at the
implications of this work for future research activities.

15.1 Interpretation of the results
of the various policy scenarios

Increased allocation to basic needs activities of
government expenditure financed through increased taxes does
result in better performance not only for the input but also
for the output indicators of basic needs satisfaction. The
composition of GDP changes somewhat, since tax increases are
mainly financed out of profit income and by higher income
groups. Total private consumption decreases less than
investment, for example, since consumption patterns change.
Imported consumer goods decrease more than other imports as
compared to the base run values. Despite the change in
composition of GDP, however, total GDP is hardly affected.
But when such changes in public expenditure are supported
by policies to increase the production possibilities and
income position of small-scale peasant farmers, through land
redistribution and changes in the terms of trade, the effects
of such combined policies on macro-economic variables are

strongly positive.

The effects of increased government expenditure and improved agricultural policies on the macro-economic variables work through several mechanisms. First, the increased taxes, both profit taxes and direct taxes in the higher income brackets, manage to redistribute part of the investible surplus to public sector final demand. Second, as public sector demand is less import-intensive than private investment demand, the pressure on foreign exchange is less in the basic needs scenarios. The import reducing effect is supported by changes in private consumption caused by the decrease in disposable incomes of the two richest socio-economic groups which have the highest import coefficients.

The consequences of the policies concerning the peasant farmers work more through the supply side. Production as well as incomes increase through a productivity increase and through favourable changes in the rural-urban terms of trade. The supply effects are fully utilised as no excess capacity exists in the peasant agricultural sector, where a large part of what is produced is still consumed by the household itself and where possibilities for increasing exports exist. The increased incomes of the rural peasant farming sector also lessen income inequality and contribute to the earlier described changes in consumption patterns.

The traditional growth scenario - the opposite policy response to basic needs policies - which aims for increased production mainly in the secondary sector, through export incentives and reduced taxation, results in a higher GDP than in the base run or in the basic needs scenario, but does not result in a noticeable increase in basic needs satisfaction.

The scenarios also show that the economy, as reflected in the basic needs model, is able to "adjust" to the "shocks" caused by policy changes and by changes in external events. After a period of five to seven years, depending on the shocks, many economic variables return to a regular trajectory, similar or parallel to that of the base run. The shocks caused by the introduction of basic needs policies are less volatile than the shocks caused by the introduction of growth policies and the economy returns more quickly to a stable growth path.

Another important and somewhat disturbing conclusion is that inefficiency (or increases in unit costs) in basic needs delivery has a significant influence on the level of basic needs satisfaction. A cumulative efficiency loss of 1 per cent per year could wipe out much of the positive results in increasing access to basic needs. This indicates that besides allocating more funds to basic needs expenditure items, equally or even more important is the design and control of the programme. Too rapid increases in public expenditure may well jeopardise this.

The results of the aid-cum-capital inflow scenario show us that an increase in international involvement can have a stimulating effect on the economy in the form of higher GDP, but that basic needs levels are not automatically affected; the percentage of the population below the poverty line, despite the higher GDP, is higher than under either the basic needs or the growth scenario. The question is, of course, whether the aid-cum-capital inflow scenario could be combined with a basic needs scenario. An argument against this is that increased profits in certain sectors may reinforce "traditional" political interests, which make it more difficult to propose and carry through desirable changes in policies to stimulate access to and increased satisfaction of basic needs. However, this model, as any model, is unable to handle the question as to whether such a combination of scenarios is feasible. This depends very much on the political economy of the country, as will be discussed later.

Comparing the results of the basic needs, the growth and the aid-cum-capital scenarios, it becomes clear that the relevant variables do not show a uniform pattern of change. In consequence, it is not possible to argue that one scenario performs uniformly better than another. We concentrate the discussion, therefore, on a few areas and make a more formal comparison of the outcome of the three scenarios. The following areas have been chosen for comparison:

(a) economic development, represented by the level of GDP;
(b) education, represented by the primary school enrolment rate;
(c) health, represented by rural female life expectancy;
(d) poverty, represented by the percentage of population not meeting their basic needs income.

In figure 15.1 we have depicted these four areas on the four axes, where the scale of the axis is determined by the highest and lowest score in each of the four variables (the absolute values are given in table 15.1). By combining the different scenario results on the four axes through straight lines we get three "diamonds" of unequal size. The shape of these gives us a good picture of the relationship between the four areas.

An objection could be that we actually try to construct here a social welfare function. Indeed, if the distances on the axes could represent societal preferences in relation to the four items (e.g. 1 percentage point in the drop of poverty equals K.£1 million in GDP, etc.), then the surface of the

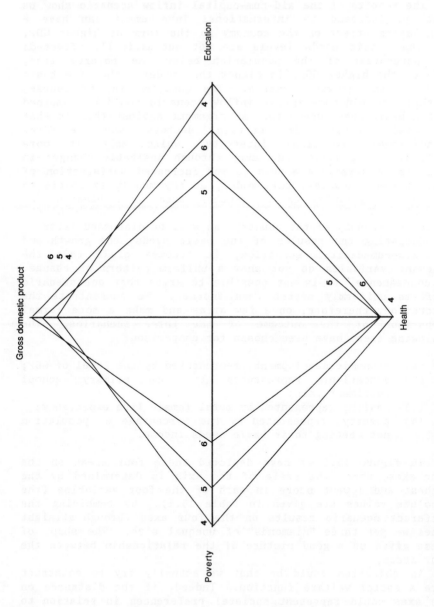

Figure 15.1. A comparison of three scenarios

diamonds would indicate an ordering of social welfare and the diamond with the largest surface would represent the optimal situation.

Table 15.1. A comparison of three scenarios

	Base run scenario	Scenario		
		4 Basic needs strategy	5 Growth strategy	6 Aid-cum- capital inflow
Gross domestic product (K.£ millions)	3 956	4 046	4 118	4 140
Primary school enrolment rate (%)	90	100	90	95
Rural female life expectancy (years)	57.0	57.8	57.0	57.0
Population not meeting basic needs income (%)	25.1	17.5	21.6	26.1
Urban skilled unemployment rate (%)	22	18	22	19
Urban unskilled unemployment rate (%)	14	15	14	8
Some important ratios				
Debt/GDP ratio	0.47	0.49	0.49	0.59
Domestic savings ratio	0.15	0.15	0.17	0.11
Gini ratio	0.54	0.48	0.54	0.55

However, as we discussed earlier, we do not intend to propose any such trade-off between the four items. We have therefore put the same distance between the highest and the lowest score in percentage terms for each item on each of the four axes. As we do not put any "weights" on the four items, the discussion is restricted to considering whether the boundaries of the four diamonds intersect or not. The crossing of sides of diamonds indicates that we are able to order on an ordinal scale but not on a cardinal scale.

As can be seen from the figure, no scenario scores on all four areas optimally. The basic needs scenario (scenario 4) scores best on education, health and poverty, but not on GDP, which is 2.3 per cent lower than the "best" score on GDP, that of scenario 6, and 1.7 per cent lower than that of scenario 5. The growth scenario (scenario 5) scores the least on education, with scenario 6 in an intermediate position. Poverty is highest, however, under the aid-cum-capital inflow scenario (scenario 6) (8.5 percentage points more than under scenario 4 despite a 2.3 per cent higher GDP). Scenarios 5 and 6 score equally badly on health (a 10-month lower rural female life expectancy at birth than under scenario 4).

Thus, taking all four criteria into account we cannot say that any of the scenarios is absolutely better. If a decrease in poverty, and improvements in education and health, are taken to be the most significant variables, then the basic needs scenario must be seen as optimal. And the question then, as discussed earlier, is how much of a drop in GDP growth one is willing to accept and still regard the situation as better. If, for example, one were to include a boundary condition that GDP may not be lower than the trend value (as expressed in the base run), then the outcome of the basic needs scenario could still be regarded as optimal since GDP under the basic needs scenario is still 2.3 per cent higher than in the base run.

A final conclusion is therefore that basic needs policies can have a positive effect both on growth and on basic needs satisfaction, but that they will not necessarily lead to maximum feasible growth since other policies could be superior on this criterion.

Another point which arises from comparing the different scenarios is that urban unemployment rates remain fairly high (see table 15.1). Under the basic needs scenario and the aid-cum-capital inflow scenario the skilled unemployment rate is somewhat lower. This is the result of increased demand for government services in the first case and of increased demand for general government and private services in the second case. In that case we also notice a decrease in unskilled unemployment. However, since the urban population forms only a small part of the total population these (limited) changes in the unemployment rate do not affect poverty or inequality estimates.

As noted in the previous chapter, the effect on basic needs provision did not change very much when we looked at the outcomes of scenario experiments 7 and 8, which represent in effect the base run scenario and the basic needs scenario (4) under conditions of increased external and internal rigidities in the production of tradeables. We also saw that both these scenarios performed worse than the same scenarios with less rigidities. It is interesting, however, that with increased rigidities the basic needs scenario (scenario 8) performed relatively better compared with the base run scenario (scenario 7) than in a situation with less rigidities (scenario 4 compared to the base run). GDP in the year 2000 is 3.6 per cent higher in scenario 8 as compared to scenario 7, while in scenario 4 it is only 2.3 per cent higher as compared to the base run. The unemployment rate for unskilled urban workers in the year 2000 is 0.8 percentage points lower under scenario 8 as compared to scenario 7, while in scenario 4 it is 1 percentage point higher than in the base run. The unemployment rate of unskilled workers in the situation of increased rigidities is 4.5 percentage points lower when basic needs policies are applied, while in the situation of less rigidities it is only 3.4 percentage points lower. The relatively better performance of basic needs policies in a situation of increased rigidities is explained by the stimulus of stronger final demand on the economy, which reduces the effect of disquilibrium (excess supply in the year 2000 is 3.5 per cent under scenario 7 and 2.4 per cent under scenario 8).

Treatment of disequilibrium in economies ("the absence of the Walrasian auctioneer") is still in its infancy, however. Although in our opinion the situation in developing countries calls for more disequilibrium analysis than the situation in developed economies, it is mainly for developed economies that new theories are being developed. These new developments, often an extension of Keynesian analysis, attempt to explain rigidities in the labour market. Cuddington (1984) provides a useful overview of the development of disequilibrium economics advancing the discussion of Barro and Grossmann (1976) and Benassy (1982) while Balassa (1982) and Krueger (1982) discuss some aspects in relation to developing countries. It is interesting to note the different approaches of Balassa and Krueger. While Balassa discusses "distortions" on product, factor and foreign exchange markets and argues that removal of distortions would always be optimal, Krueger, through a review of the literature, deals with the more relevant questions concerning the consequences of removing distortions in a disequilibrium situation. She argues that results may be quite different from those that are obtained when distortions are removed in an equilibrium situation.

Focusing on the labour and commodity market one can distinguish between:

- classical unemployment, with an excess supply of labour and an excess demand for commodities;

- Keynesian unemployment, with an excess supply of labour and an excess supply of commodities (Cuddington, 1984, p. 24).

Two other possible situations are an excess demand for labour and an excess demand for goods (repressed inflation) and an excess demand for labour with an excess supply of goods (underconsumption). In the case of a basic needs model for developing countries, clearly the first two situations are more relevant.

What happens in scenario 7 of the model is that (through the rationing of imports) an initial decrease in actual private consumption aspirations, coupled with unemployment, gives the impression of a situation of classical unemployment. However, the rationing on the foreign exchange market is only part of the convergency mechanism. In another convergency mechanism the excess of savings, assuming a neo-classical investment function, leads to higher investment and finally to excess supply on the domestic product market. As we assume that only some imports are competitive some upward movement in consumption expenditure takes place, but we may still end up with a situation of excess supply of domestic goods. Thus what initially, because of foreign exchange shortage and consequent forced saving, looked like a situation of classical unemployment actually turns out to be a situation of Keynesian unemployment. Experiments with increased basic needs financing through increased taxes (which reduces savings), as carried out under scenario 8, increase economic output through the Keynesian mechanisms.

This illustrates that the outcomes of various macro-economic policies cannot be predicted beforehand but depend to a large extent on the kind of disequilibrium situation which exists at the time the policies are introduced.

15.2 Lessons drawn: Reflections on results

What do the outcomes of the various policy scenarios teach us in the light of the questions we posed in the first chapters of this book? The major questions here were whether basic needs policies will be effective both in the short run and in the long run and how the outcomes of basic needs policies relate over the long run to other policies such as a continuation of present policies or policies with an increased emphasis on growth.

We noticed from the experiments with the sce
application of a broad-based package of basic ne
increases not only basic needs satisfaction but a:
GDP. The increase in GDP is, however, mainly th
the application of basic needs-oriented supply side policies
in the agricultural sector based upon land redistribution, an
improvement in the rural-urban terms of trade and an increase
in agricultural productivity. The increase in basic needs
satisfaction, apart from increases in household income, is
mainly the consequence of increased government expenditure on
the various basic needs expenditure items. Since increases in
government expenditure are financed by targeted tax increases,
the direct effect on macro-economic behaviour is, as we
noticed, rather limited. The greatest changes are in effect
the result of changes in the composition of domestic final
demand.

We are therefore able to state that increases in government
expenditure on basic needs do not hamper economic growth. Nor
do they appear to have a very significant positive impact on
growth. The main reason for this is that increased
satisfaction of basic needs does not have a positive influence
on productivity in most parts of the model. As discussed in
Chapter 6, although such an influence has been noted in
various micro-economic relationships, we were unable to
develop such links for most sectors of the model because of
the lack of an adequate data base. In effect, as indicated in
Chapter 7, we were only able to introduce such a relationship
into the production functions for small-scale agriculture, but
not into the production functions for other sectors. What the
model presents is thus an underestimation rather than an
overestimation of the macro-economic consequences of increased
government basic needs expenditure.

What the policy experiments also teach us is that income
and asset redistribution in favour of agriculture greatly
reduces absolute poverty levels without jeopardising GDP
growth; a structural approach to solving poverty problems
thus appears to be feasible. However, although basic needs
policies can increase both basic needs satisfaction and
absolute levels of GDP, such policies will not maximise
growth. Explicit growth policies, according to the model, can
push up GDP higher than other scenarios. Increased foreign
resources (aid and capital) can also push up GDP without
automatically increasing basic needs satisfaction.

These outcomes lead, of course, to the question as to what
extent these exercises with the model can help us in
understanding the real world "problematique".

A first reflection is that of modesty. What we have tried

to show with the model analysis is an interaction between certain policy measures and the socio-economic situation. The functioning of the economic framework depends to a large extent on the behaviour of economic actors. It is difficult, however, to model the behaviour of economic actors in reaction to various policy measures. Little is known about how especially deprived groups react towards changes in their situation. Will they react more or less the same at different levels of basic needs satisfaction? Will they accommodate easily to lower levels? What will their reaction be to increased levels of basic needs satisfaction? Will they resist these levels being lowered again in the wake of austerity programmes, as many examples of recent riots have suggested? Such experiences would indicate that vigorous pursuit of a growth scenario may not in fact be feasible because of the strong influence the outcome of the scenario may have on the behaviour of economic actors – in particular on those aspects that are not built into the model.

Fox et al. (1966), for example, describe an agrarian reform policy model for Peru, where political stability is included in a composite welfare function. Since political stability is difficult to measure Fox et al. suggest using the Gini ratio of income inequality as a proxy for political stability or, if such a ratio is lacking, a ratio of regional income differences (as was done for Peru) and include it in the welfare function as an independent variable, which, as we argue above, it is not. Rather we need to explain the behaviour of economic actors as a consequence of political stability. Hopkins and van der Hoeven (1984) have, in this vein, proposed including a variable representing the bargaining power of socio-economic groups. An increase in bargaining power would depend, according to a first hypothesis, on absolute income and on levels of basic needs satisfaction. Increases in bargaining power would then affect income formation within various sectors and the allocation of investment to different sectors. This mechanism would in effect proxy the aspect of participation of socio-economic groups in the process of national decision-making. Quantification of such a process, however, proved to be too difficult for meaningful inclusion in a socio-economic model as yet.

It is not only the behaviour of economic actors that might be affected by the different scenarios. More technical relationships may also change considerably. In Chapter 13 we referred to the problem of efficiency in basic needs delivery. A mere increase in allocation of government expenditure to a certain project is often a necessary, but not always a sufficient condition to improve the population's access to basic needs services. Social commitment of those involved is as important as financial transfers. Furthermore, the relation between increased funds and delivery of services might very well not be linear. Sudden increases in funds might lead to less efficient behaviour and force civil servants to be occupied with administration rather than delivery of services. Our experiment in Chapter 13 showed how sensitive delivery of services is to decreases in efficiency and how crucial the assumption of constant unit costs in basic needs delivery is.

15.3 Lessons drawn: Future research activities

The discussion of the results of the model and the reflections above lead as a matter of course to a discussion of future research on the conditions for and consequences of basic needs policies. We would suggest four major themes which can themselves be subdivided into more detailed themes.

The first theme is essential to any quantitative exercise and relates to the macro-economic functioning of a developing country's economy. It is often argued that national accounts statistics do not adequately reflect production and consumption of many goods and services. The introduction of the concept of the informal sector in the early 1970s, and the research that has been done on subsistence economies, clearly bear this out. Yet production and consumption in these under-reported sectors might, and can, greatly enhance basic needs satisfaction. More research is needed to estimate the size and structure of these sectors in order to complement GDP statistics.

However, it is not only the measurement of these sectors that is important but also their relationship with other sectors in the economy. Is their development complementary to that of other sectors or not? That is to say, when activities in other sectors shrink, such as at times of austerity programmes, will informal and subsistence activities expand, or conversely, when other sectors expand will they do so at the cost of these unrecorded activities? In such a situation of complementarity, the actual consequences of basic needs policies on production and consumption in these sectors might in fact be less than recorded by GDP statistics.

A second theme is that of international influences. We noticed that prima facie increased aid and capital inflows do not automatically contribute to increased basic needs satisfaction. An important question is whether increased external support could be accompanied by increased attention to basic needs satisfaction, and also whether the national authorities, accepting this increased reliance on international influences, would nevertheless be free to pursue at the same time policies aimed at increasing basic needs satisfaction. Looked at purely as a matter of shifting resources in a national accounting framework, nothing would preclude a shifting of the additional resources earned from favourable external influences to expenditure on basic needs services. However, political reality is often different and, as indicated above, the behaviour of many economic (and political) actors may mean that such a policy option is not feasible. More needs to be said about the conditions under which such a process would be feasible.

A third theme for research is the influence of basic needs satisfaction on productivity. Generally, it has been shown that a higher level of basic needs satisfaction enhances growth, but the targeting of basic needs expenditure is also important. Will increased basic needs satisfaction in a certain socio-economic group enhance their productivity directly or indirectly? As will be discussed in Appendix 5, some authors argue that an increase in the education levels of the farming population does not increase their agricultural productivity, but rather increases their access to urban labour markets and enhances their integration in the formal economy, which allows for receiving increased credit and funds to be put into more innovative and risky farming activities yielding higher returns.

This example demonstrates clearly that the lines of causality are not always straightforward, and that cross-country comparisons may reflect for certain countries complex relations between various sectors and actors. Yet such inter-related processes are important, as they determine the absolute and relative position of the various socio-economic groups. Country-specific or perhaps even area-specific research would be warranted.

A fourth theme for further research is the question of the behaviour of the various socio-economic groups, and especially the deprived groups, as a consequence of economic development and economic policies. What makes worker groups more vocal in demanding a larger share of the national income and increased access to basic needs services? Do these groups need to possess production factors or skills which have become scarce in the development process, as Adelman (1978) suggests? In effect this theme cuts across the other themes discussed above. In the discussion of the consequences of external influences we looked at the role of economic and political actors reacting to increased revenues from outward-looking activities. Are the socio-economic conditions prevalent which would result in political behaviour favouring increased expenditure on basic needs and programmes to decrease poverty? Would such behaviour be fully dependent on a redistribution of assets and skills, as Adelman suggested, or

are societal structures much more important?   These and other
questions still need resolving.

* * *

What we have tried to do in this analysis is to unveil
certain aspects of the relationship between basic needs
satisfaction and the working of a macro-economic system, for
which we took Kenya as an example.   We realise that we have
only been able to add a (perhaps infinitesimally) small part
to the discussion but we hope this may contribute to a change
in policy thinking and a change of direction in the research
geared towards the needs of those many millions in the world
for whom the word "development" is still a big unknown.

Annex to Chapter 15

Results of the various scenarios and the base run
for some important social and economic variables

CONCLUSIONS

Scenarios

B = base run
1 = increased taxation
2 = 1 + increased expenditure on basic needs
3 = 2 + land reform
4 = 3 + improvement in rural-urban terms of trade and agricultural productivity
5 = growth policies
6 = increased aid and capital
7 = base run under internal and external rigidities
8 = scenario 4 under internal and external rigidities

abs = absolute value of variable
rel = percentage deviation from base run value

KENYA MODEL SCENARIO COMPARISON

TYPE	YEAR	B GROWTH GDP	1 GROWTH GDP	2 GROWTH GDP	3 GROWTH GDP	4 GROWTH GDP	5 GROWTH GDP	6 GROWTH GDP	7 GROWTH GDP	8 GROWTH GDP
ABS.	1976	0.0000	0.0000	0.0000	0.0000	0.0000	0.0000	0.0000	0.0000	0.0000
	1980	3.9548	3.9548	3.9548	3.9548	3.9548	3.9548	3.9548	3.9548	3.9548
	1985	4.5435	5.1949	5.3330	5.7114	5.5665	3.5661	5.2908	4.2679	5.3183
	1990	4.4335	3.9777	3.9642	3.7848	4.4732	5.5308	4.8911	3.8946	4.0621
	1995	4.3748	4.5148	4.5356	4.3997	4.5027	4.7052	4.4149	3.9528	4.0744
	2000	4.3832	4.4230	4.4321	4.4580	4.5778	4.8806	4.5451	4.0218	4.1560
REL.	1976	0.0000	0.0000	0.0000	0.0000	0.0000	0.0000	0.0000	0.0000	0.0000
	1980	0.0000	0.0000	0.0000	0.0000	0.0000	0.0000	0.0000	0.0000	0.0000
	1985	0.0000	14.3373	17.3768	25.7057	22.5165	-21.5121	16.4479	-6.0658	17.0541
	1990	0.0000	-10.2804	-10.5859	-12.2419	0.8957	24.7511	10.3217	-12.1546	-8.3702
	1995	0.0000	3.1988	3.6755	0.5696	2.9219	7.5525	0.9166	-9.6476	-6.8681
	2000	0.0000	0.9079	1.1164	1.7068	4.4408	11.3491	3.6951	-8.2445	-5.1835

KENYA MODEL SCENARIO COMPARISON

TYPE	YEAR	B GROSS DOMESTIC PRODUCT	1 GROSS DOMESTIC PRODUCT	2 GROSS DOMESTIC PRODUCT	3 GROSS DOMESTIC PRODUCT	4 GROSS DOMESTIC PRODUCT	5 GROSS DOMESTIC PRODUCT	6 GROSS DOMESTIC PRODUCT	7 GROSS DOMESTIC PRODUCT	8 GROSS DOMESTIC PRODUCT
ABS.	1976	1405.92	1405.92	1405.92	1405.92	1405.92	1405.92	1405.92	1405.92	1405.92
	1980	1681.73	1681.73	1681.73	1681.73	1681.73	1681.73	1681.73	1681.73	1681.73
	1985	2052.61	2065.40	2069.68	2085.95	2083.40	2033.42	2067.28	2047.20	2078.50
	1990	2587.94	2575.97	2571.02	2619.70	2602.20	2555.98	2653.57	2494.64	2554.03
	1995	3196.00	3177.38	3179.56	3253.41	3249.34	3259.43	3349.06	3025.85	3114.49
	2000	3956.18	3936.34	3937.46	4029.68	4046.27	4118.39	4140.83	3670.45	3804.26
REL.	1976	0.00	0.00	0.00	0.00	0.00	0.00	0.00	0.00	0.00
	1980	0.00	0.62	0.83	1.62	1.50	-0.93	0.71	-0.26	1.26
	1985	0.00	-0.46	-0.65	.23	.55	-1.24	2.54	-3.61	-1.31
	1990	0.00	-0.58	-0.51	1.80	1.67	1.98	4.79	-5.32	-2.55
	2000	0.00	-0.50	-0.47	1.86	2.28	4.10	4.67	-7.22	-3.84

Scenarios

B = base run
1 = increased taxation
2 = 1 + increased expenditure on basic needs
3 = 2 + land reform
4 = 3 + improvement in rural-urban terms of trade and agricultural productivity
5 = growth policies
6 = increased aid and capital
7 = base run under internal and external rigidities
8 = scenario 4 under internal and external rigidities

abs = absolute value of variable
rel = percentage deviation from base run value

KENYA MODEL SCENARIO COMPARISON

TYPE	YEAR	B VALUE ADDED PRIM.SECTOR	1 VALUE ADDED PRIM.SECTOR	2 VALUE ADDED PRIM.SECTOR	3 VALUE ADDED PRIM.SECTOR	4 VALUE ADDED PRIM.SECTOR	5 VALUE ADDED PRIM.SECTOR	6 VALUE ADDED PRIM.SECTOR	7 VALUE ADDED PRIM.SECTOR	8 VALUE ADDED PRIM.SECTOR
ABS.	1976	504.6445	504.6445	504.6445	504.6445	504.6445	504.6445	504.6445	504.6445	504.6445
	1980	607.4753	607.4753	607.4753	607.4753	607.4753	607.4753	607.4753	607.4753	607.4753
	1985	747.9434	748.1118	748.5571	760.5393	766.2644	750.8086	751.5007	745.7754	763.6338
	1990	904.2869	891.1384	888.4624	916.0571	924.5488	944.7761	893.3689	895.5703	917.9019
	1995	1082.1216	1064.0525	1062.8926	1098.3787	1119.9631	1161.8123	1077.0640	1070.3821	1107.6707
	2000	1280.5388	1263.9543	1263.1948	1308.5400	1350.3970	1415.3359	1277.8745	1274.0417	1333.1748
REL.	1976	0.0000	0.0000	0.0000	0.0000	0.0000	0.0000	0.0000	0.0000	0.0000
	1980	0.0000	0.0000	0.0000	0.0000	0.0000	0.0000	0.0000	0.0000	0.0000
	1985	0.0000	0.0225	0.0821	1.6841	2.4495	0.3831	0.4756	-0.2899	2.0978
	1990	0.0000	-1.4540	-1.7499	1.1016	2.2407	4.4775	-1.2074	-0.9639	1.5056
	1995	0.0000	-1.6698	-1.7770	1.5023	3.4970	7.3643	-0.4674	-1.0849	2.3610
	2000	0.0000	-1.2951	-1.3544	2.1867	5.4544	10.5266	-0.2081	-0.5074	4.1105

KENYA MODEL SCENARIO COMPARISON

TYPE	YEAR	B VALUE ADDED SEC.SECTOR	1 VALUE ADDED SEC.SECTOR	2 VALUE ADDED SEC.SECTOR	3 VALUE ADDED SEC.SECTOR	4 VALUE ADDED SEC.SECTOR	5 VALUE ADDED SEC.SECTOR	6 VALUE ADDED SEC.SECTOR	7 VALUE ADDED SEC.SECTOR	8 VALUE ADDED SEC.SECTOR
ABS.	1976	396.6064	396.6064	396.6064	396.6064	396.6064	396.6064	396.6064	396.6064	396.6064
	1980	471.9597	471.9597	471.9597	471.9597	471.9597	471.9597	471.9597	471.9597	471.9597
	1985	572.5046	564.4543	564.1016	566.4246	566.0205	584.3809	575.4141	570.7063	564.9705
	1990	728.3860	714.9163	713.1958	725.0503	721.9326	733.4526	749.0747	696.5696	706.4963
	1995	907.2695	887.4988	887.4131	906.7615	906.7468	944.5920	949.9319	845.1772	861.0327
	2000	1135.3843	1110.3123	1110.0039	1132.6689	1136.4368	1202.8379	1182.5017	1027.0962	1052.5806
REL.	1976	0.0000	0.0000	0.0000	0.0000	0.0000	0.0000	0.0000	0.0000	0.0000
	1980	0.0000	-1.4062	-1.4678	-1.0620	-1.1326	2.0744	0.5082	-0.3141	-1.3160
	1985	0.0000	-1.8493	-2.0855	-0.4580	-0.8860	0.6956	2.8404	-4.3681	-3.0052
	1990	0.0000	-2.1791	-2.1886	-0.0560	-0.0576	-1.137	-0.7023	-6.8439	-5.0963
	2000	0.0000	-2.2082	-2.2354	-0.2392	0.0927	5.9410	4.1499	-9.5376	-7.2930

251

PLANNING FOR BASIC NEEDS

Scenarios

B = base run
1 = increased taxation
2 = 1 + increased expenditure on basic needs
3 = 2 + land reform
4 = 3 + improvement in rural-urban terms of trade and agricultural productivity
5 = growth policies
6 = increased aid and capital
7 = base run under internal and external rigidities
8 = scenario 4 under internal and external rigidities

abs = absolute value of variable
rel = percentage deviation from base run value

KENYA MODEL SCENARIO COMPARISON

VALUE ADDED TERT. SECTOR

TYPE	YEAR	B	1	2	3	4	5	6	7	8
ABS.	1976	504.6689	504.6689	504.6689	504.6689	504.6689	504.6689	504.6689	504.6689	504.6689
	1980	602.2966	602.2966	602.2966	602.2966	602.2966	602.2966	602.2966	602.2966	602.2966
	1985	732.1636	752.8350	757.0294	758.9863	751.1130	698.2322	740.3691	730.7188	749.8958
	1990	955.2659	969.9163	969.3579	978.5940	955.7224	877.7471	1011.1218	902.5029	929.6309
	1995	1206.6116	1225.8267	1229.2527	1248.2690	1222.6311	1153.0269	1322.0623	1110.2927	1145.7830
	2000	1540.2598	1562.0767	1564.2563	1588.4758	1559.4375	1500.2129	1680.4556	1369.3108	1418.5056
REL.	1976	0.0000	0.0000	0.0000	0.0000	0.0000	0.0000	0.0000	0.0000	0.0000
	1980	0.0000	0.0000	0.0000	0.0000	0.0000	0.0000	0.0000	0.0000	0.0000
	1985	0.0000	2.8233	3.3957	3.6635	2.5861	-4.6344	1.1207	-0.1973	2.4219
	1990	0.0000	1.5336	1.4752	2.4421	0.0478	-8.1149	5.8472	-5.5234	-2.6835
	1995	0.0000	1.5925	1.8764	3.4524	1.3276	-4.4409	9.5682	-7.9826	-5.0413
	2000	0.0000	1.4164	1.5581	3.1304	1.2451	-2.6000	9.1021	-11.0987	-7.9048

KENYA MODEL SCENARIO COMPARISON

PRIVATE CONSUMPTION

TYPE	YEAR	B	1	2	3	4	5	6	7	8
ABS.	1976	910.8918	910.8918	910.8918	910.8918	910.8918	910.8918	910.8918	910.8918	910.8918
	1980	1072.5359	1072.5359	1072.5359	1072.5359	1072.5359	1072.5359	1072.5359	1072.5359	1072.5359
	1985	1316.8267	1333.3735	1333.8081	1356.1699	1363.3059	1289.3191	1368.1821	1305.1003	1349.5515
	1990	1686.2815	1658.5581	1647.3542	1685.3906	1680.2703	1647.8386	1857.3643	1590.0530	1620.4438
	1995	2085.1260	2063.1450	2057.3154	2111.2930	2126.6636	2102.9072	2345.8118	1933.2942	1982.0647
	2000	2602.6223	2568.1282	2558.9666	2629.5464	2681.2346	2677.6499	2917.4519	2357.9719	2437.3545
REL.	1976	0.0000	0.0000	0.0000	0.0000	0.0000	0.0000	0.0000	0.0000	0.0000
	1980	0.0000	0.0000	0.0000	0.0000	0.0000	0.0000	0.0000	0.0000	0.0000
	1985	0.0000	1.2566	1.2896	2.9877	3.5296	-2.0889	3.8999	-0.8905	2.4851
	1990	0.0000	-1.6441	-2.3085	-0.0528	-0.3565	-2.2797	10.1456	-5.7066	-3.9043
	1995	0.0000	-1.0302	-1.3338	1.2549	1.9921	0.8528	12.5022	-7.2817	-4.9927
	2000	0.0000	-1.3254	-1.6774	1.0345	3.0205	2.8828	12.0966	-9.4001	-6.3501

Scenarios

B = base run
1 = increased taxation
2 = 1 + increased expenditure on basic needs
3 = 2 + land reform
4 = 3 + improvement in rural-urban terms of trade and agricultural productivity
5 = growth policies
6 = increased aid and capital
7 = base run under internal and external rigidities
8 = scenario 4 under internal and external rigidities

abs = absolute value of variable
rel = percentage deviation from base run value

KENYA MODEL SCENARIO COMPARISON

					SCENARIO				
	B	1	2	3	4	5	6	7	8
TYPE|YEAR	PUBLIC CONSUMPTION	PUBLIC CONSUMPTION	PUBLIC CONSUMPTION	PUBLIC CONSUMPTION	PUBLIC CONSUMPTION	PUBLIC CONSUMPTION	PUBLIC CONSUMPTION	PUBLIC CONSUMPTION	PUBLIC CONSUMPTION
ABS. 1976	253.4280	253.4280	253.4280	253.4280	253.4280	253.4280	253.4280	253.4280	253.4280
1980	302.7488	302.7488	302.7488	302.7488	302.7488	302.7488	302.7488	302.7488	302.7488
1985	363.8066	395.4473	395.8865	397.9290	396.8661	313.4976	366.2466	363.8066	396.8613
1990	463.5981	494.7373	493.1589	496.3525	489.4431	397.6150	481.3601	444.0313	480.5530
1995	572.1902	609.9453	610.1299	617.2886	610.5215	511.4001	609.5313	538.8320	583.5386
2000	708.4570	754.6541	754.2896	763.5537	756.0269	647.4722	755.0933	652.9766	708.3372
REL. 1976	0.0000	0.0000	0.0000	0.0000	0.0000	0.0000	0.0000	0.0000	0.0000
1980	0.0000	0.0000	0.0000	0.0000	0.0000	0.0000	0.0000	0.0000	0.0000
1985	0.0000	8.6971	8.8178	9.3792	9.0858	-13.8285	0.6707	0.0000	9.0858
1990	0.0000	6.7168	6.3764	7.0653	5.5749	-14.2328	0.6260	-4.2207	3.6572
1995	0.0000	6.5984	6.6306	7.8817	6.6990	-10.6241	6.5260	-5.6299	-.9831
2000	0.0000	6.5208	6.4693	7.7701	6.7146	-8.6081	6.5828	-7.8312	-0.0169

KENYA MODEL SCENARIO COMPARISON

					SCENARIO				
	B	1	2	3	4	5	6	7	8
TYPE|YEAR	INVESTMENT DEMAND	INVESTMENT DEMAND	INVESTMENT DEMAND	INVESTMENT DEMAND	INVESTMENT DEMAND	INVESTMENT DEMAND	INVESTMENT DEMAND	INVESTMENT DEMAND	INVESTMENT DEMAND
ABS. 1976	213.9000	213.9000	213.9000	213.9000	213.9000	213.9000	213.9000	213.9000	213.9000
1980	272.8994	272.8994	272.8994	272.8994	272.8994	272.8994	272.8994	272.8994	272.8994
1985	332.6738	291.1101	297.4136	302.1487	303.9480	398.8323	329.4829	332.6738	303.9480
1990	407.5454	380.2463	387.4548	403.5492	407.6482	496.3811	408.6252	403.0430	406.2207
1995	499.0496	459.0845	467.4565	493.2832	502.5325	628.8950	513.5913	484.5559	494.1523
2000	613.2927	566.5369	577.1052	605.0571	623.7073	779.7666	624.3564	584.9429	604.2458
REL. 1976	0.0000	0.0000	0.0000	0.0000	0.0000	0.0000	0.0000	0.0000	0.0000
1980	0.0000	0.0000	0.0000	0.0000	0.0000	0.0000	0.0000	0.0000	0.0000
1985	0.0000	-12.4938	-10.5990	-9.1757	-8.6348	19.8869	-0.9592	-0.0000	-8.6348
1990	0.0000	-6.6984	-4.9297	-0.9815	0.0252	21.7977	0.2650	-1.1048	-0.3250
1995	0.0000	-8.0082	-6.3306	-1.1555	0.6979	26.0185	2.9139	-2.9043	-0.9813
2000	0.0000	-7.6237	-5.9005	-1.3428	1.6981	27.1443	1.8040	-4.6226	-1.4751

Scenarios

B = base run
1 = increased taxation
2 = 1 + increased expenditure on basic needs
3 = 2 + land reform
4 = 3 + improvement in rural-urban terms of trade and agricultural productivity
5 = growth policies
6 = increased aid and capital
7 = base run under internal and external rigidities
8 = scenario 4 under internal and external rigidities

abs = absolute value of variable
rel = percentage deviation from base run value

KENYA MODEL SCENARIO COMPARISON

		SCENARIO								
TYPE	YEAR	B IMPORTS	1 IMPORTS	2 IMPORTS	3 IMPORTS	4 IMPORTS	5 IMPORTS	6 IMPORTS	7 IMPORTS	8 IMPORTS
ABS.	1976	503.5444	503.5444	503.5444	503.5444	503.5444	503.5444	503.5444	503.5444	503.5444
	1980	565.0183	565.0183	565.0183	565.0183	565.0183	565.0183	565.0183	565.0183	565.0183
	1985	689.3887	689.0642	688.4063	687.7141	687.5410	689.9658	718.9475	679.9541	675.9646
	1990	866.5222	841.7634	840.6711	852.0037	847.2888	891.8792	953.8401	834.0481	830.4817
	1995	1071.1692	1043.0759	1043.0410	1060.7122	1060.9602	1131.5137	1190.5547	1022.8899	1017.4568
	2000	1334.3298	1298.1707	1298.6504	1322.4216	1335.6726	2436.6194	1505.6152	1264.1680	1256.2002
REL.	1976	0.0000	0.0000	0.0000	0.0000	0.0000	0.0000	0.0000	0.0000	0.0000
	1980	0.0000	0.0000	0.0000	0.0000	0.0000	0.0000	0.0000	0.0000	0.0000
	1985	0.0000	-0.0471	-0.1425	-0.2429	-0.2680	0.0837	4.2877	-1.3685	-1.9472
	1990	0.0000	-2.8573	-2.9833	-1.6755	-2.1196	2.9263	10.0768	-3.7476	-4.1592
	1995	0.0000	-2.6227	-2.6259	-0.9762	-0.9531	5.6335	11.1453	-4.5072	-5.0184
	2000	0.0000	-2.7099	-2.6740	-0.8924	0.1006	7.6660	12.8368	-5.2582	-5.8553

KENYA MODEL SCENARIO COMPARISON

		SCENARIO								
TYPE	YEAR	B EXPORTS	1 EXPORTS	2 EXPORTS	3 EXPORTS	4 EXPORTS	5 EXPORTS	6 EXPORTS	7 EXPORTS	8 EXPORTS
ABS.	1976	451.5544	451.5544	451.5544	451.5544	451.5544	451.5544	451.5544	451.5544	451.5544
	1980	495.7324	495.7324	495.7324	495.7324	495.7324	495.7324	495.7324	495.7324	495.7324
	1985	604.9351	603.5513	601.9712	589.1938	586.7195	609.2471	603.1257	599.1987	578.0503
	1990	753.3013	728.3220	727.3000	729.5864	718.2854	780.3762	728.3560	737.0073	709.5876
	1995	930.3579	898.8123	898.6921	904.1514	886.9490	987.6858	894.0195	903.9961	862.4121
	2000	1147.2881	1112.6550	1113.1790	1123.2354	1099.4531	1249.0015	1132.1733	1113.4590	1051.7676
REL.	1976	0.0000	0.0000	0.0000	0.0000	0.0000	0.0000	0.0000	0.0000	0.0000
	1980	0.0000	0.0000	0.0000	0.0000	0.0000	0.0000	0.0000	0.0000	0.0000
	1985	0.0000	-0.2288	-0.4899	-2.6021	-3.0112	0.7128	-0.2991	-0.9483	-4.4442
	1990	0.0000	-3.3160	-3.4516	-3.1481	-4.6483	3.5942	-1.3115	-1.6304	-5.8029
	1995	0.0000	-3.3907	-3.4036	-2.8168	-4.6658	6.1619	-3.9058	-2.8335	-7.3032
	2000	0.0000	-3.0187	-2.9730	-2.0965	-1.1694	8.8655	-1.3174	-2.9486	-8.3258

Scenarios

B	=	base run
1	=	increased taxation
2	=	1 + increased expenditure on basic needs
3	=	2 + land reform
4	=	3 + improvement in rural–urban terms of trade and agricultural productivity
5	=	growth policies
6	=	increased aid and capital
7	=	base run under internal and external rigidities
8	=	scenario 4 under internal and external rigidities
abs	=	absolute value of variable
rel	=	percentage deviation from base run value

KENYA MODEL SCENARIO COMPARISON

Imports of Intermediate Products

TYPE	YEAR	B	1	2	3	4	5	6	7	8
ABS.	1976	320.8459	320.8459	320.8459	320.8459	320.8459	320.8459	320.8459	320.8459	320.8459
	1980	381.8516	381.8516	381.8516	381.8516	381.8516	381.8516	381.8516	381.8516	381.8516
	1985	467.0662	462.9392	462.3545	462.4658	461.8950	473.4329	469.5098	465.1489	460.5330
	1990	599.8840	587.9983	586.4192	594.0015	589.4675	601.8862	616.1721	570.8425	574.8411
	1995	753.7842	736.2363	736.0698	749.2156	744.9734	783.7478	788.1008	696.3630	702.7856
	2000	950.7024	928.5847	928.1902	943.8447	939.0200	1008.7070	991.4792	850.4875	861.6047
REL.	1976	0.0000	0.0000	0.0000	0.0000	0.0000	0.0000	0.0000	0.0000	0.0000
	1980	0.0000	0.0000	0.0000	0.0000	0.0000	0.0000	0.0000	0.0000	0.0000
	1985	0.0000	-0.8836	-1.0088	-0.9849	-1.1072	1.3631	0.5232	-0.4105	-1.3988
	1990	0.0000	-1.9813	-2.2446	-0.9806	-1.7364	0.3338	2.7152	-4.8412	-4.1746
	1995	0.0000	-2.3280	-2.3502	-0.6061	-1.1689	3.9751	4.5526	-7.6177	-6.7657
	2000	0.0000	-2.3265	-2.3680	-0.7213	-1.2288	6.1012	4.2891	-10.5411	-9.3718

KENYA MODEL SCENARIO COMPARISON

Imports of Consumer Goods

TYPE	YEAR	B	1	2	3	4	5	6	7	8
ABS.	1976	91.7584	91.7584	91.7584	91.7584	91.7584	91.7584	91.7584	91.7584	91.7584
	1980	69.4308	69.4308	69.4308	69.4308	69.4308	69.4308	69.4308	69.4308	69.4308
	1985	84.0475	97.6107	95.2443	92.3648	92.2000	62.6327	111.9019	76.5978	82.1640
	1990	95.5511	88.0807	86.4860	84.7894	83.8680	97.9610	164.7279	95.5529	83.0302
	1995	107.4467	105.4474	102.9773	98.7164	100.7615	103.6419	184.7711	124.5328	104.7267
	2000	125.0428	120.9216	118.5585	117.0205	129.6588	123.8139	248.2312	169.6473	138.3111
REL.	1976	0.0000	0.0000	0.0000	0.0000	0.0000	0.0000	0.0000	0.0000	0.0000
	1980	0.0000	0.0000	0.0000	0.0000	0.0000	0.0000	0.0000	0.0000	0.0000
	1985	0.0000	16.1375	13.3219	9.8959	9.6998	-25.4795	33.1412	-8.8638	-2.2410
	1990	0.0000	-7.8182	-9.4871	-11.2628	-12.2271	2.5222	72.3978	0.0019	-13.1038
	1995	0.0000	-1.8608	-4.1597	-8.1252	-6.2220	-3.5411	71.9653	15.9019	-2.5315
	2000	0.0000	-3.2958	-5.1857	-6.4156	3.6915	-0.9827	98.5170	35.6714	10.6110

Scenarios

B = base run
1 = increased taxation
2 = 1 + increased expenditure on basic needs
3 = 2 + land reform
4 = 3 + improvement in rural-urban terms of trade and agricultural productivity
5 = growth policies
6 = increased aid and capital
7 = base run under internal and external rigidities
8 = scenario 4 under internal and external rigidities

abs = absolute value of variable
rel = percentage deviation from base run value

KENYA MODEL SCENARIO COMPARISON

SCENARIO

TYPE|YEAR	B IMPORTS OF CAPITAL GOODS	1 IMPORTS OF CAPITAL GOODS	2 IMPORTS OF CAPITAL GOODS	3 IMPORTS OF CAPITAL GOODS	4 IMPORTS OF CAPITAL GOODS	5 IMPORTS OF CAPITAL GOODS	6 IMPORTS OF CAPITAL GOODS	7 IMPORTS OF CAPITAL GOODS	8 IMPORTS OF CAPITAL GOODS
ABS. 1976	90.9405	90.9405	90.9405	90.9405	90.9405	90.9405	90.9405	90.9405	90.9405
1980	114.0215	114.0215	114.0215	114.0215	114.0215	114.0215	114.0215	114.0215	114.0215
1985	138.4848	128.6850	130.6810	132.3469	132.8006	154.0880	137.7335	138.4848	132.8006
1990	171.3954	165.9669	168.0468	173.3433	173.9423	192.5006	173.4585	168.0962	172.6349
1995	210.3161	201.6067	204.2188	212.9180	215.1254	244.6337	218.4557	202.5789	209.9030
2000	258.9756	248.9836	252.2229	261.7852	266.8318	304.6240	266.9419	244.7922	256.1609
REL. 1976	0.0000	0.0000	0.0000	0.0000	0.0000	0.0000	0.0000	0.0000	0.0000
1980	0.0000	0.0000	0.0000	0.0000	0.0000	0.0000	0.0000	0.0000	0.0000
1985	0.0000	-7.0764	-5.6352	-4.4322	-4.1046	11.2676	-0.5425	0.0000	-4.1046
1990	0.0000	-3.1673	-1.9537	-1.1365	1.4860	12.3138	1.2037	-1.9249	0.7232
1995	0.0000	-4.1411	-2.8991	1.2372	2.2867	16.3172	3.8702	-3.6788	-0.1964
2000	0.0000	-3.8583	-2.6075	1.0849	3.0336	17.6265	3.0761	-5.4767	-1.0869

KENYA MODEL SCENARIO COMPARISON

SCENARIO

TYPE|YEAR	B DEBT/GDP RATIO	1 DEBT/GDP RATIO	2 DEBT/GDP RATIO	3 DEBT/GDP RATIO	4 DEBT/GDP RATIO	5 DEBT/GDP RATIO	6 DEBT/GDP RATIO	7 DEBT/GDP RATIO	8 DEBT/GDP RATIO
ABS. 1976	0.2185	0.2185	0.2185	0.2185	0.2185	0.2185	0.2185	0.2185	0.2185
1980	0.2937	0.2937	0.2937	0.2937	0.2937	0.2937	0.2937	0.2937	0.2937
1985	0.3540	0.3522	0.3516	0.3539	0.3554	0.3575	0.3524	0.3555	0.3555
1990	0.4006	0.4018	0.4019	0.4063	0.4151	0.4058	0.4390	0.3947	0.4148
1995	0.4382	0.4394	0.4381	0.4406	0.4547	0.4510	0.5320	0.4234	0.4524
2000	0.4674	0.4647	0.4639	0.4662	0.4902	0.4859	0.5911	0.4551	0.4830
REL. 1976	0.0000	0.0000	0.0000	0.0000	0.0000	0.0000	0.0000	0.0000	0.0000
1980	0.0000	0.0000	0.0000	0.0000	0.0000	0.0000	0.0000	0.0000	0.0000
1985	0.0000	-0.5087	-0.6772	-0.0222	0.3977	0.9815	-0.4481	-0.1367	-0.1097
1990	0.0000	0.3019	0.3329	1.4257	3.6171	1.3088	9.5929	-1.4722	3.5457
1995	0.0000	0.2770	-0.0285	0.5488	3.7551	2.9108	21.4024	-3.3955	3.2221
2000	0.0000	-0.5759	-0.7404	-0.2519	4.8873	3.9662	26.4772	-4.6693	3.3459

256

KENYA MODEL SCENARIO COMPARISON

| | | SCENARIO | | | | | | | | |
| | | B | 1 | 2 | 3 | 4 | 5 | 6 | 7 | 8 |
TYPE	YEAR	CAPITAL OUTPUT RATIO	CAPITAL OUTPUT RATIO	CAPITAL OUTPUT RATIO	CAPITAL OUTPUT RATIO	CAPITAL OUTPUT RATIO	CAPITAL OUTPUT RATIO	CAPITAL OUTPUT RATIO	CAPITAL OUTPUT RATIO	CAPITAL OUTPUT RATIO
ABS.	1976	2.2649	2.2649	2.2649	2.2649	2.2649	2.2649	2.2649	2.2649	2.2649
	1980	2.5576	2.5576	2.5576	2.5576	2.5576	2.5576	2.5576	2.5576	2.5576
	1985	2.7941	2.7534	2.7561	2.7472	2.7628	2.8579	2.7758	2.8010	2.7676
	1990	2.8560	2.8294	2.8485	2.8134	2.8327	3.0398	2.8060	2.9471	2.8806
	1995	2.9210	2.8606	2.8739	2.8415	2.8353	3.0965	2.8684	3.0341	2.9304
	2000	2.9302	2.8525	2.8699	2.8435	2.8199	3.1127	2.9459	3.0800	2.9365
REL.	1976	0.0000	0.0000	0.0000	0.0000	0.0000	0.0000	0.0000	0.0000	0.0000
	1980	0.0000	0.0000	0.0000	0.0000	0.0000	0.0000	0.0000	0.0000	0.0000
	1985	0.0000	-1.4562	-1.3570	-1.6756	-1.1191	2.2851	-0.6552	0.2492	-0.9486
	1990	0.0000	-0.9304	-0.2627	-1.4919	-0.8146	6.4361	-1.7494	3.1925	0.8614
	1995	0.0000	-2.0650	-1.6103	-2.7199	-2.9322	6.0102	-1.8007	3.8729	0.3234
	2000	0.0000	-2.6510	-2.0567	-2.9566	-4.0347	6.2286	0.5366	5.1149	0.2167

KENYA MODEL SCENARIO COMPARISON

| | | SCENARIO | | | | | | | | |
| | | B | 1 | 2 | 3 | 4 | 5 | 6 | 7 | 8 |
TYPE	YEAR	TOTAL SAVINGS RATE	TOTAL SAVINGS RATE	TOTAL SAVINGS RATE	TOTAL SAVINGS RATE	TOTAL SAVINGS RATE	TOTAL SAVINGS RATE	TOTAL SAVINGS RATE	TOTAL SAVINGS RATE	TOTAL SAVINGS RATE
ABS.	1976	20.8294	20.8294	20.8294	20.8294	20.8294	20.8294	20.8294	20.8294	20.8294
	1980	21.8282	21.8282	21.8282	21.8282	21.8282	21.8282	21.8282	21.8282	21.8282
	1985	21.7212	20.0559	20.3255	20.4246	20.5199	24.4076	20.1630	21.7790	20.5685
	1990	21.3204	20.7402	21.0414	21.3019	21.5198	24.2552	19.2070	21.6939	21.7621
	1995	21.1832	20.4239	20.6750	21.0674	21.3131	24.1702	19.0727	21.5540	21.6984
	2000	21.0710	20.3591	20.6187	20.9116	21.2283	23.8184	18.7754	21.4711	21.6788
REL.	1976	0.0000	0.0000	0.0000	0.0000	0.0000	0.0000	0.0000	0.0000	0.0000
	1980	0.0000	0.0000	0.0000	0.0000	0.0000	0.0000	0.0000	0.0000	0.0000
	1985	0.0000	-7.6670	-6.4256	-5.9693	-5.5306	12.3674	-7.1738	0.2657	-5.3072
	1990	0.0000	-2.7210	-1.3086	-0.0864	0.9355	13.7656	-9.9122	1.7522	2.0717
	1995	0.0000	-3.5843	-2.3990	-0.5467	0.6133	14.1009	-9.9630	1.7505	2.4322
	2000	0.0000	-3.3783	-2.1463	-0.7564	-0.7465	13.0390	-10.8946	1.8990	2.8849

Scenarios

B = base run
1 = increased taxation
2 = 1 + increased expenditure on basic needs
3 = 2 + land reform
4 = 3 + improvement in rural-urban terms of trade and agricultural productivity
5 = growth policies
6 = increased aid and capital
7 = base run under internal and external rigidities
8 = scenario 4 under internal and external rigidities

abs = absolute value of variable
rel = percentage deviation from base run value

Scenarios

B = base run
1 = increased taxation
2 = 1 + increased expenditure on basic needs
3 = 2 + land reform
4 = 3 + improvement in rural-urban terms of trade and agricultural productivity
5 = 4 + growth policies
6 = 5 + increased aid and capital
7 = base run under internal and external rigidities
8 = scenario 4 under internal and external rigidities

abs = absolute value of variable
rel = percentage deviation from base run value

KENYA MODEL SCENARIO COMPARISON

| | | | | | SCENARIO | | | | |
TYPE/YEAR	B DOMESTIC SAVINGS RATE	1 DOMESTIC SAVINGS RATE	2 DOMESTIC SAVINGS RATE	3 DOMESTIC SAVINGS RATE	4 DOMESTIC SAVINGS RATE	5 DOMESTIC SAVINGS RATE	6 DOMESTIC SAVINGS RATE	7 DOMESTIC SAVINGS RATE	8 DOMESTIC SAVINGS RATE
ABS: 1976	17.1053	17.1053	17.1053	17.1053	17.1053	17.1053	17.1053	17.1053	17.1053
1980	17.1083	17.1083	17.1083	17.1083	17.1083	17.1083	17.1083	17.1083	17.1083
1985	16.5789	14.8980	15.1627	14.9368	14.9300	19.2870	15.0170	16.7650	15.0448
1990	15.7352	15.1916	15.5096	15.7293	15.7589	18.3283	11.8660	16.5281	16.1606
1995	15.4389	14.6850	14.9478	15.2855	15.1985	17.9336	11.3769	16.2452	15.8561
2000	15.0106	14.4498	14.7144	14.9756	14.7515	17.3269	10.8776	15.9749	15.5332
REL: 1976	0.0000	0.0000	0.0000	0.0000	0.0000	0.0000	0.0000	0.0000	0.0000
1980	0.0000	0.0000	0.0000	0.0000	0.0000	0.0000	0.0000	0.0000	0.0000
1985	0.0000	-10.1387	-8.5425	-9.9047	-9.9459	16.3347	-9.4212	1.1223	-9.2533
1990	0.0000	-3.4552	-1.4339	-0.0375	0.1505	16.4790	-24.5894	5.0390	2.7030
1995	0.0000	-4.8835	-3.1813	-0.9938	-1.5577	16.1580	-26.3101	5.2220	2.7020
2000	0.0000	-3.7361	-1.9732	-0.2335	-1.7260	15.4309	-27.5339	6.4240	3.4810

KENYA MODEL SCENARIO COMPARISON

| | | | | | SCENARIO | | | | |
TYPE/YEAR	B FOREIGN SAVINGS RATE	1 FOREIGN SAVINGS RATE	2 FOREIGN SAVINGS RATE	3 FOREIGN SAVINGS RATE	4 FOREIGN SAVINGS RATE	5 FOREIGN SAVINGS RATE	6 FOREIGN SAVINGS RATE	7 FOREIGN SAVINGS RATE	8 FOREIGN SAVINGS RATE
ABS: 1976	3.7241	3.7241	3.7241	3.7241	3.7241	3.7241	3.7241	3.7241	3.7241
1980	4.7199	4.7199	4.7199	4.7199	4.7199	4.7199	4.7199	4.7199	4.7199
1985	5.1423	5.1578	5.1628	5.4878	5.5899	5.1205	5.1460	5.0140	5.5236
1990	5.5851	5.5487	5.5318	5.5726	5.7609	5.9270	7.3410	5.1658	5.6015
1995	5.7443	5.7390	5.7272	5.7819	6.1147	6.2367	7.6958	5.3089	5.8423
2000	6.0603	5.9093	5.9043	5.9360	6.4767	6.4915	7.8977	5.4962	6.1457
REL: 1976	0.0000	0.0000	0.0000	0.0000	0.0000	0.0000	0.0000	0.0000	0.0000
1980	0.0000	0.0000	0.0000	0.0000	0.0000	0.0000	0.0000	0.0000	0.0000
1985	0.0000	0.3020	0.3993	6.7185	8.7047	-0.4231	-1.0718	-2.4960	7.4153
1990	0.0000	-0.6525	-0.9554	-0.2243	3.1470	6.1205	31.4386	-7.5082	0.2930
1995	0.0000	-0.0926	-0.2964	0.6553	0.4482	8.5720	33.9732	-7.5799	1.7071
2000	0.0000	-2.4920	-2.5753	-2.0515	6.8704	7.1142	30.3184	-9.3068	1.4083

Scenarios

B	=	base run
1	=	increased taxation
2	=	1 + increased expenditure on basic needs
3	=	2 + land reform
4	=	3 + improvement in rural-urban terms of trade and agricultural productivity
5	=	growth policies
6	=	increased aid and capital
7	=	base run under internal and external rigidities
8	=	scenario 4 under internal and external rigidities
abs	=	absolute value of variable
rel	=	percentage deviation from base run value

KENYA MODEL SCENARIO COMPARISON

TYPE	YEAR	B TOTAL POPULATION	1 TOTAL POPULATION	2 TOTAL POPULATION	3 TOTAL POPULATION	4 TOTAL POPULATION	5 TOTAL POPULATION	6 TOTAL POPULATION	7 TOTAL POPULATION	8 TOTAL POPULATION
ABS.	1976	13.5279	13.5279	13.5279	13.5279	13.5279	13.5279	13.5279	13.5279	13.5279
	1980	15.7602	15.7602	15.7602	15.7602	15.7602	15.7602	15.7602	15.7602	15.7602
	1985	19.0094	19.0094	19.0094	19.0094	19.0094	19.0094	19.0094	19.0094	19.0094
	1990	22.9255	22.9257	22.9231	22.9231	22.9233	22.9258	22.9256	22.9254	22.9234
	1995	27.6995	27.7010	27.6876	27.6912	27.6924	27.7029	27.7014	27.6998	27.6915
	2000	33.4953	33.5000	33.4807	33.4918	33.4949	33.5048	33.4993	33.4965	33.4944
REL.	1976	0.0000	0.0000	0.0000	0.0000	0.0000	0.0000	0.0000	0.0000	0.0000
	1980	0.0000	0.0000	0.0000	0.0000	0.0000	0.0000	0.0000	0.0000	0.0000
	1985	0.0000	0.0000	0.0000	0.0000	0.0000	0.0000	0.0000	0.0000	0.0000
	1990	0.0000	0.0007	-0.0106	-0.0105	-0.0097	0.0010	0.0068	0.0005	-0.0095
	1995	0.0000	0.0055	-0.0429	-0.0301	-0.0256	0.0122	0.0118	0.0010	-0.0289
	2000	0.0000	0.0140	-0.0435	-0.0106	-0.0122	0.0283	0.0361	0.0036	-0.0027

KENYA MODEL SCENARIO COMPARISON

TYPE	YEAR	B POPULATION GROWTH	1 POPULATION GROWTH	2 POPULATION GROWTH	3 POPULATION GROWTH	4 POPULATION GROWTH	5 POPULATION GROWTH	6 POPULATION GROWTH	7 POPULATION GROWTH	8 POPULATION GROWTH
ABS.	1976	3.9279	3.9279	3.9279	3.9279	3.9279	3.9279	3.9279	3.9279	3.9279
	1980	3.8432	3.8432	3.8432	3.8432	3.8432	3.8432	3.8432	3.8432	3.8432
	1985	3.8096	3.8096	3.8099	3.8100	3.8099	3.8096	3.8096	3.8096	3.8099
	1990	3.8411	3.8417	3.8350	3.8352	3.8354	3.8422	3.8416	3.8408	3.8361
	1995	3.8702	3.8777	3.8666	3.8706	3.8721	3.8730	3.8713	3.8703	3.8711
	2000	3.8767	3.8801	3.8813	3.8852	3.8862	3.8805	3.8764	3.8768	3.8881
REL.	1976	0.0000	0.0000	0.0000	0.0000	0.0000	0.0000	0.0000	0.0000	0.0000
	1980	0.0000	0.0000	0.0000	0.0000	0.0000	0.0000	0.0000	0.0000	0.0000
	1985	0.0000	0.0000	0.0084	0.0105	0.0084	0.0000	0.0000	0.0000	0.0000
	1990	0.0000	0.0166	-0.1575	-0.1524	-0.1463	0.0302	0.0135	-0.0081	-0.1292
	1995	0.0000	0.0401	-0.0938	0.0116	0.0484	0.0717	0.0302	-0.0033	0.0232
	2000	0.0000	0.0342	0.1187	0.2198	0.2456	0.0985	-0.0711	0.0023	0.2941

Scenarios

B = base run
1 = increased taxation
2 = 1 + increased expenditure on basic needs
3 = 2 + land reform
4 = 3 + improvement in rural-urban terms of trade and agricultural productivity
5 = growth policies
6 = increased aid and capital
7 = base run under internal and external rigidities
8 = scenario 4 under internal and external rigidities

abs = absolute value of variable
rel = percentage deviation from base run value

KENYA MODEL SCENARIO COMPARISON

		B	1	2	3	4	5	6	7	8
TYPE	YEAR	URBAN POPULATION	URBAN POPULATION	URBAN POPULATION	URBAN POPULATION	URBAN POPULATION	URBAN POPULATION	URBAN POPULATION	URBAN POPULATION	URBAN POPULATION
ABS.	1976	1.6101	1.6101	1.6101	1.6101	1.6101	1.6101	1.6101	1.6101	1.6101
	1980	2.1253	2.1253	2.1253	2.1253	2.1253	2.1253	2.1253	2.1253	2.1253
	1985	2.8853	2.8853	2.8853	2.8853	2.8853	2.8853	2.8853	2.8853	2.8853
	1990	3.8038	3.8107	3.8107	3.8156	3.8121	3.7789	3.8096	3.8009	3.8108
	1995	4.9310	4.9501	4.9703	4.9709	4.9588	4.8662	4.9591	4.9109	4.9468
	2000	6.3186	6.3584	6.4123	6.4138	6.3908	6.2072	6.3867	6.2660	6.3505
REL.	1976	0.0000	0.0000	0.0000	0.0000	0.0000	0.0000	0.0000	0.0000	0.0000
	1980	0.0000	0.0000	0.0000	0.0000	0.0000	0.0000	0.0000	0.0000	0.0000
	1985	0.0000	0.0000	0.0000	0.0000	0.0000	0.0000	0.0000	0.0000	0.0000
	1990	0.0000	0.1818	0.1818	0.3116	0.2187	-0.6528	0.1518	-0.0767	0.1837
	1995	0.0000	0.3889	0.7985	0.8109	0.5651	-1.3132	0.5715	-0.4067	0.3208
	2000	0.0000	0.6312	1.4838	1.5074	1.1439	-1.7630	1.0792	-0.8319	0.5056

KENYA MODEL SCENARIO COMPARISON

		B	1	2	3	4	5	6	7	8
TYPE	YEAR	RURAL POPULATION	RURAL POPULATION	RURAL POPULATION	RURAL POPULATION	RURAL POPULATION	RURAL POPULATION	RURAL POPULATION	RURAL POPULATION	RURAL POPULATION
ABS.	1976	11.9178	11.9178	11.9178	11.9178	11.9178	11.9178	11.9178	11.9178	11.9178
	1980	13.6349	13.6349	13.6349	13.6349	13.6349	13.6349	13.6349	13.6349	13.6349
	1985	16.1241	16.1241	16.1241	16.1241	16.1241	16.1241	16.1241	16.1241	16.1241
	1990	19.1217	19.1150	19.1083	19.1075	19.1112	19.1468	19.1161	19.1245	19.1126
	1995	22.7686	22.7509	22.7173	22.7202	22.7336	22.8367	22.7423	22.7889	22.7447
	2000	27.1768	27.1416	27.0684	27.0780	27.1041	27.2977	27.1125	27.2305	27.1439
REL.	1976	0.0000	0.0000	0.0000	0.0000	0.0000	0.0000	0.0000	0.0000	0.0000
	1980	0.0000	0.0000	0.0000	0.0000	0.0000	0.0000	0.0000	0.0000	0.0000
	1985	0.0000	0.0000	0.0000	0.0000	0.0000	0.0000	0.0000	0.0000	0.0000
	1990	0.0000	-0.0353	-0.0705	-0.0746	-0.0551	0.1310	-0.0297	0.0146	-0.0479
	1995	0.0000	-0.0776	-0.2252	-0.2122	-0.1536	0.2992	-0.1155	0.0893	-0.1047
	2000	0.0000	-0.1295	-0.3986	-0.3635	-0.2674	0.4448	-0.2364	0.1979	-0.1209

Scenarios

B = base run
1 = increased taxation
2 = 1 + increased expenditure on basic needs
3 = 2 + land reform
4 = 3 + improvement in rural-urban terms of trade and agricultural productivity
5 = growth policies
6 = increased aid and capital
7 = base run under internal and external rigidities
8 = scenario 4 under internal and external rigidities

abs = absolute value of variable
rel = percentage deviation from base run value

KENYA MODEL SCENARIO COMPARISON

SCENARIO — FEMALE RURAL LIFE EXPECTANCY

TYPE	YEAR	B	1	2	3	4	5	6	7	8
ABS.	1976	54.8800	54.8800	54.8800	54.8800	54.8800	54.8800	54.8800	54.8800	54.8800
	1980	55.3352	55.3352	55.3352	55.3352	55.3352	55.3352	55.3352	55.3352	55.3352
	1985	55.7806	55.7806	55.7805	55.7819	55.7819	55.7806	55.7806	55.7806	55.7819
	1990	56.2066	56.2197	56.2197	56.2688	56.2664	56.2104	56.2052	56.2054	56.2634
	1995	56.6216	56.6529	56.6732	57.0067	57.0008	56.6285	56.6304	56.6180	56.9260
	2000	57.0243	57.0763	57.0498	57.8477	57.7815	57.0358	57.0570	57.0188	57.6990
REL.	1976	0.0000	0.0000	0.0000	0.0000	0.0000	0.0000	0.0000	0.0000	0.0000
	1980	0.0000	0.0000	0.0000	0.0000	0.0000	0.0000	0.0000	0.0000	0.0000
	1985	0.0000	0.0000	-0.0001	0.0023	0.0024	0.0000	0.0000	0.0000	0.0024
	1990	0.0000	0.0232	0.0232	0.1071	0.1064	0.0067	-0.0025	-0.0021	0.1010
	1995	0.0000	0.0552	0.4444	0.6801	0.6697	0.0121	0.0154	-0.0064	0.5376
	2000	0.0000	0.0912	1.0969	1.3336	1.3280	0.0202	0.0574	-0.0096	1.1832

KENYA MODEL SCENARIO COMPARISON

SCENARIO — FEMALE URBAN LIFE EXPECTANCY

TYPE	YEAR	B	1	2	3	4	5	6	7	8
ABS.	1976	61.6800	61.6800	61.6800	61.6800	61.6800	61.6800	61.6800	61.6800	61.6800
	1980	61.9715	61.9715	61.9715	61.9715	61.9715	61.9715	61.9715	61.9715	61.9715
	1985	62.2962	62.2962	62.3674	62.3667	62.3666	62.2962	62.2962	62.2962	62.3666
	1990	62.7113	62.7073	63.0074	63.1576	63.1432	62.6649	62.8915	62.6698	63.1245
	1995	63.0991	63.7508	63.8899	63.9086	63.8997	63.1031	63.6723	63.0352	63.8523
	2000	63.7044	64.5072	64.6400	64.6553	64.6503	63.7201	64.4176	63.3964	64.5827
REL.	1976	0.0000	0.0000	0.0000	0.0000	0.0000	0.0000	0.0000	0.0000	0.0000
	1980	0.0000	0.0000	0.0000	0.0000	0.0000	0.0000	0.0000	0.0000	0.0000
	1985	0.0000	0.0000	0.1142	0.1131	0.1130	0.0000	0.0000	0.0000	0.1130
	1990	0.0000	0.0000	0.4721	0.7118	0.6887	-0.0739	0.2874	-0.0661	0.6589
	1995	0.0000	1.0329	1.2533	1.2830	1.2689	0.0065	0.9085	-0.1012	1.1937
	2000	0.0000	1.2602	1.4686	1.4926	1.4847	0.0246	1.1194	-0.4835	1.3787

Scenarios

B = base run
1 = increased taxation
2 = 1 + increased expenditure on basic needs
3 = 2 + land reform
4 = 3 + improvement in rural-urban terms of trade and agricultural productivity
5 = growth policies
6 = increased aid and capital
7 = base run under internal and external rigidities
8 = scenario 4 under internal and external rigidities

abs = absolute value of variable
rel = percentage deviation from base run value

KENYA MODEL SCENARIO COMPARISON

					SCENARIO				
	B	1	2	3	4	5	6	7	8
TYPE/YEAR	RURAL-URBAN MIGRATION	RURAL-URBAN MIGRATION	RURAL-URBAN MIGRATION	RURAL-URBAN MIGRATION	RURAL-URBAN MIGRATION	RURAL-URBAN MIGRATION	RURAL-URBAN MIGRATION	RURAL-URBAN MIGRATION	RURAL-URBAN MIGRATION
ABS. 1976	5.4000	5.4000	5.4000	5.4000	5.4000	5.4000	5.4000	5.4000	5.4000
1980	5.2030	5.2030	5.2030	5.2030	5.2030	5.2030	5.2030	5.2030	5.2030
1985	4.8117	4.8117	4.8234	4.8252	4.8270	4.8117	4.8117	4.8117	4.8270
1990	4.7506	4.8541	4.9607	4.9446	4.8776	4.3742	4.9053	4.6314	4.8241
1995	4.6773	4.8024	4.9890	4.9930	4.9224	4.4129	4.9455	4.4917	4.7653
2000	4.6732	4.8276	5.0450	5.0376	4.9829	4.4105	4.9573	4.4010	4.7445
REL. 1976	0.0000	0.0000	0.0000	0.0000	0.0000	0.0000	0.0000	0.0000	0.0000
1980	0.0000	0.0000	0.0000	0.0000	0.0000	0.0000	0.0000	0.0000	0.0000
1985	0.0000	0.0000	0.2432	0.2819	0.3183	0.0000	0.0000	0.0000	0.3183
1990	0.0000	0.0000	2.1797	4.0839	2.6744	-7.9228	3.2560	-2.5081	1.5476
1995	0.0000	0.0000	2.6743	6.7484	5.2391	-5.6535	5.7339	-3.9677	1.8814
2000	0.0000	0.0000	3.3034	7.9574	6.6271	-5.6210	6.0807	-5.8249	1.5270

KENYA MODEL SCENARIO COMPARISON

					SCENARIO				
	B	1	2	3	4	5	6	7	8
TYPE/YEAR	%POP BELOW BASIC NEEDS INCOME	%POP BELOW BASIC NEEDS INCOME	%POP BELOW BASIC NEEDS INCOME	%POP BELOW BASIC NEEDS INCOME	%POP BELOW BASIC NEEDS INCOME	%POP BELOW BASIC NEEDS INCOME	%POP BELOW BASIC NEEDS INCOME	%POP BELOW BASIC NEEDS INCOME	%POP BELOW BASIC NEEDS INCOME
ABS. 1976	31.2212	31.2212	31.2212	31.2212	31.2212	31.2212	31.2212	31.2212	31.2212
1980	27.7720	27.7720	27.7720	27.7720	27.7720	27.7720	27.7720	27.7720	27.7720
1985	26.3729	26.3617	26.2388	23.9723	20.8966	26.6163	26.0921	26.4988	21.0841
1990	25.3452	25.6236	25.6703	22.9582	19.7325	23.2527	26.6880	26.2378	20.4175
1995	25.1846	25.4840	25.3655	22.5103	18.5689	22.2450	26.4955	26.4959	19.8879
2000	25.1849	25.4234	25.2553	22.3884	17.5807	21.6232	26.1255	26.8767	19.3680
REL. 1976	0.0000	0.0000	0.0000	0.0000	0.0000	0.0000	0.0000	0.0000	0.0000
1980	0.0000	0.0000	0.0000	0.0000	0.0000	0.0000	0.0000	0.0000	0.0000
1985	0.0000	-0.0425	-0.5086	-9.1026	-20.7649	0.9229	-1.0647	0.4773	-20.0540
1990	0.0000	1.0982	1.2825	-9.4179	-22.1449	-8.2562	1.3526	3.5216	-19.4425
1995	0.0000	1.1886	0.7180	-10.6190	-26.2691	-11.6723	-0.3148	5.2067	-21.0317
2000	0.0000	0.9471	0.2795	-11.1037	-30.1934	-14.1424	3.7348	6.7175	-23.0968

Scenarios

B = base run
1 = increased taxation
2 = 1 + increased expenditure on basic needs
3 = 2 + land reform
4 = 3 + improvement in rural-urban terms of trade and agricultural productivity
5 = growth policies
6 = increased aid and capital
7 = base run under internal and external rigidities
8 = scenario 4 under internal and external rigidities

abs = absolute value of variable
rel = percentage deviation from base run value

KENYA MODEL SCENARIO COMPARISON

		B	1	2	3	4	5	6	7	8
		%SCHOOL AGED IN PRIM.SCHOOL	%SCHOOL AGED IN PRIM.SCHOOL	%SCHOOL AGED IN PRIM.SCHOOL	%SCHOOL AGED IN PRIM.SCHOOL	%SCHOOL AGED IN PRIM.SCHOOL	%SCHOOL AGED IN PRIM.SCHOOL	%SCHOOL AGED IN PRIM.SCHOOL	%SCHOOL AGED IN PRIM.SCHOOL	%SCHOOL AGED IN PRIM.SCHOOL
TYPE	YEAR									
ABS.	1976	84.1711	84.1711	84.1711	84.1711	84.1711	84.1711	84.1711	84.1711	84.1711
	1980	86.1334	86.1334	86.1334	86.1334	86.1334	86.1334	86.1334	86.1334	86.1334
	1985	86.6242	87.8958	95.3527	95.7427	95.5333	86.5598	86.6092	86.6212	95.5339
	1990	88.8750	91.8068	99.0541	99.1737	98.1167	88.6921	89.3864	88.5754	97.5860
	1995	90.2707	93.5217	100.0000	100.0000	100.0000	90.1487	93.5339	89.8006	98.7186
	2000	90.5724	94.9025	100.0000	100.0000	100.0000	90.4952	94.9670	89.9707	98.9106
REL.	1976	0.0000	0.0000	0.0000	0.0000	0.0000	0.0000	0.0000	0.0000	0.0000
	1980	0.0000	0.0000	0.0000	0.0000	0.0000	0.0000	0.0000	0.0000	0.0000
	1985	0.0000	1.4679	10.7664	10.5265	10.2848	-0.0743	-0.0172	-0.0035	10.2855
	1990	0.0000	3.2987	11.4532	11.5878	10.3985	-0.2059	0.5754	-0.3372	9.8014
	1995	0.0000	3.6014	10.7779	10.7779	10.7779	-0.1352	3.6149	-0.5208	9.3584
	2000	0.0000	4.7807	10.4089	10.4089	10.4089	-0.0852	4.8520	-0.6643	9.2061

KENYA MODEL SCENARIO COMPARISON

		B	1	2	3	4	5	6	7	8
		%POP WITHOUT MED.FACILIT-IES	%POP WITHOUT MED.FACILIT-IES	%POP WITHOUT MED.FACILIT-IES	%POP WITHOUT MED.FACILIT-IES	%POP WITHOUT MED.FACILIT-IES	%POP WITHOUT MED.FACILIT-IES	%POP WITHOUT MED.FACILIT-IES	%POP WITHOUT MED.FACILIT-IES	%POP WITHOUT MED.FACILIT-IES
TYPE	YEAR									
ABS.	1976	78.2733	78.2733	78.2733	78.2733	78.2733	78.2733	78.2733	78.2733	78.2733
	1980	76.4266	76.4266	76.4266	76.4266	76.4266	76.4266	76.4266	76.4266	76.4266
	1985	74.6824	74.6123	73.7003	73.4756	73.5096	74.7707	74.6935	74.6855	73.5089
	1990	73.5815	73.4065	72.2409	72.0324	72.1207	73.7106	73.5766	73.5762	72.2488
	1995	72.6589	72.4215	71.1593	70.9105	71.0198	72.9063	72.5223	72.7028	71.2516
	2000	71.8605	71.5253	70.1466	69.8925	70.0150	72.2114	71.5912	71.9788	70.3854
REL.	1976	0.0000	0.0000	0.0000	0.0000	0.0000	0.0000	0.0000	0.0000	0.0000
	1980	0.0000	0.0000	0.0000	0.0000	0.0000	0.0000	0.0000	0.0000	0.0000
	1985	0.0000	-0.0938	-1.3150	-1.6159	-1.5703	0.1183	0.0149	0.0041	-1.5713
	1990	0.0000	-0.2379	-1.8220	-2.1054	-1.9853	0.1754	-0.0067	-0.0073	-1.8113
	1995	0.0000	-0.3267	-2.0638	-2.4062	-2.2559	0.3405	-0.1800	0.0604	-1.9368
	2000	0.0000	-0.4664	-2.3851	-2.7387	-2.5682	0.4883	-0.3748	0.1645	-2.0528

Scenarios

B = base run
1 = increased taxation
2 = 1 + increased expenditure on basic needs
3 = 2 + land reform
4 = 3 + improvement in rural-urban terms of trade and agricultural productivity
5 = growth policies
6 = increased aid and capital
7 = base run under internal and external rigidities
8 = scenario 4 under internal and external rigidities

abs = absolute value of variable
rel = percentage deviation from base run value

KENYA MODEL SCENARIO COMPARISON

UNEMPLOYMENT URBAN SKILLED

TYPE	YEAR	B	1	2	3	4	5	6	7	8
ABS.	1976	0.0875	0.0875	0.0875	0.0875	0.0875	0.0875	0.0875	0.0875	0.0875
	1980	0.1289	0.1289	0.1289	0.1289	0.1289	0.1289	0.1289	0.1289	0.1289
	1985	0.1799	0.1565	0.1306	0.1258	0.1290	0.2178	0.1732	0.1829	0.1311
	1990	0.1850	0.1738	0.1547	0.1434	0.1515	0.2276	0.1582	0.2244	0.1721
	1995	0.2073	0.1965	0.1785	0.1657	0.1686	0.2251	0.1708	0.2603	0.2126
	2000	0.2149	0.2070	0.1938	0.1812	0.1805	0.2169	0.1866	0.2853	0.2403
REL.	1976	0.0000	0.0000	0.0000	0.0000	0.0000	0.0000	0.0000	0.0000	0.0000
	1980	0.0000	0.0000	0.0000	0.0000	0.0000	0.0000	0.0000	0.0000	0.0000
	1985	0.0000	-13.0239	-27.4060	-30.0688	-28.2965	21.0679	-3.7399	1.6239	-27.1249
	1990	0.0000	-6.0740	-16.3678	-22.4842	-18.0916	23.0097	-14.4742	21.2954	-6.9665
	1995	0.0000	-5.1792	-13.8777	-20.0512	-18.6362	8.5798	-17.5771	25.6008	2.5655
	2000	0.0000	-3.6425	-9.8021	-15.6769	-15.9994	0.9332	-13.1379	32.7779	11.8363

KENYA MODEL SCENARIO COMPARISON

UNEMPLOYMENT URBAN UNSKILLED

TYPE	YEAR	B	1	2	3	4	5	6	7	8
ABS.	1976	0.0875	0.0875	0.0875	0.0875	0.0875	0.0875	0.0875	0.0875	0.0875
	1980	0.1177	0.1177	0.1177	0.1177	0.1177	0.1177	0.1177	0.1177	0.1177
	1985	0.1599	0.1460	0.1549	0.1509	0.1603	0.1825	0.1490	0.1621	0.1619
	1990	0.1451	0.1430	0.1587	0.1470	0.1648	0.1848	0.0981	0.1910	0.1853
	1995	0.1523	0.1470	0.1618	0.1474	0.1599	0.1638	0.0829	0.2139	0.2080
	2000	0.1419	0.1393	0.1584	0.1437	0.1513	0.1351	0.0809	0.2258	0.2190
REL.	1976	0.0000	0.0000	0.0000	0.0000	0.0000	0.0000	0.0000	0.0000	0.0000
	1980	0.0000	0.0000	0.0000	0.0000	0.0000	0.0000	0.0000	0.0000	0.0000
	1985	0.0000	-8.6857	-3.1124	-5.6135	0.2881	14.1700	-6.7720	1.3849	1.2406
	1990	0.0000	-1.4235	9.4200	1.3130	13.6050	27.3760	-32.3829	31.6735	27.6946
	1995	0.0000	-3.4997	6.2100	-3.2137	4.9451	7.5398	-45.5897	40.4104	36.5484
	2000	0.0000	-1.8188	11.6290	1.2372	6.5732	-4.7990	-43.0117	59.1210	54.2871

Scenarios

B = base run
1 = increased taxation
2 = 1 + increased expenditure on basic needs
3 = 2 + land reform
4 = 3 + improvement in rural-urban terms of trade and agricultural productivity
5 = growth policies
6 = increased aid and capital
7 = base run under internal and external rigidities
8 = scenario 4 under internal and external rigidities

abs = absolute value of variable
rel = percentage deviation from base run value

KENYA MODEL SCENARIO COMPARISON

| | SCENARIO B | 1 | 2 | 3 | 4 | 5 | 6 | 7 | 8 |
	GINI ALL INCOME	GINI ALL INCOME	GINI ALL INCOME	GINI ALL INCOME	GINI ALL INCOME	GINI ALL INCOME	GINI ALL INCOME	GINI ALL INCOME	GINI ALL INCOME
TYPE|YEAR									
ABS. 1976	0.5545	0.5545	0.5545	0.5545	0.5545	0.5545	0.5545	0.5545	0.5545
1980	0.5528	0.5528	0.5528	0.5528	0.5528	0.5528	0.5528	0.5528	0.5528
1985	0.5546	0.5563	0.5557	0.5432	0.5175	0.5191	0.5519	0.5548	0.5183
1990	0.5626	0.5627	0.5619	0.5494	0.5205	0.5482	0.5691	0.5595	0.5208
1995	0.5687	0.5685	0.5675	0.5547	0.5210	0.5582	0.5776	0.5639	0.5202
2000	0.5751	0.5746	0.5734	0.5605	0.5208	0.5663	0.5863	0.5684	0.5191
REL. 1976	0.0000	0.0000	0.0000	0.0000	0.0000	0.0000	0.0000	0.0000	0.0000
1980	0.0000	0.0000	0.0000	0.0000	0.0000	0.0000	0.0000	0.0000	0.0000
1985	0.0000	0.2996	0.1885	-2.0630	-6.6904	-6.4992	-0.4992	0.0220	-6.5516
1990	0.0000	0.0282	-0.1137	-2.3484	-7.4732	-2.5628	-0.0287	-0.5526	-7.4275
1995	0.0000	-0.0446	-0.2217	-2.4688	-8.3891	-1.8582	1.1639	1.5644	-8.5253
2000	0.0000	-0.0893	-0.3078	-2.5445	-9.4510	-1.5263	1.9524	-1.1728	-9.7389

KENYA MODEL SCENARIO COMPARISON

| | SCENARIO B | 1 | 2 | 3 | 4 | 5 | 6 | 7 | 8 |
	GINI DISP INCOME	GINI DISP INCOME	GINI DISP INCOME	GINI DISP INCOME	GINI DISP INCOME	GINI DISP INCOME	GINI DISP INCOME	GINI DISP INCOME	GINI DISP INCOME
TYPE|YEAR									
ABS. 1976	0.5198	0.5198	0.5198	0.5198	0.5198	0.5198	0.5198	0.5198	0.5198
1980	0.5184	0.5184	0.5184	0.5184	0.5184	0.5184	0.5184	0.5184	0.5184
1985	0.5203	0.5186	0.5180	0.5056	0.4792	0.5194	0.5201	0.5204	0.4800
1990	0.5285	0.5255	0.5247	0.5122	0.4826	0.5169	0.5352	0.5253	0.4828
1995	0.5349	0.5315	0.5305	0.5178	0.4835	0.5272	0.5440	0.5299	0.4825
2000	0.5416	0.5379	0.5367	0.5239	0.4835	0.5356	0.5527	0.5345	0.4816
REL. 1976	0.0000	0.0000	0.0000	0.0000	0.0000	0.0000	0.0000	0.0000	0.0000
1980	0.0000	0.0000	0.0000	0.0000	0.0000	0.0000	0.0000	0.0000	0.0000
1985	0.0000	-0.3227	-0.4326	-2.8216	-7.8912	-0.1724	-0.0399	0.0294	-7.7380
1990	0.0000	-0.5799	-0.7235	-3.0930	-8.6826	-2.1979	-2.1960	-0.6031	-8.6426
1995	0.0000	-0.6485	-0.8293	-3.2013	-9.6220	-1.4473	1.6866	-0.9399	-9.7972
2000	0.0000	-0.6802	-0.9066	-3.2756	-10.7354	-1.1148	2.0487	-1.3050	-11.0860

APPENDICES

APPENDICES

Appendix 1 Determination of value added, employment and capital

A1.1 Value added and employment

In the model the Kenyan economy is divided into 14 sectors. These have been chosen with a view to distinguishing, first, between sectors providing different basic needs goods, and second, between sectors having different production techniques and wage levels.

Table A1.1 gives an overview of the 14 sectors and their value added in 1976. In each sector a distinction is made between unskilled labour, skilled labour and self-employed. In some sectors, the self-employed belong to the educated high-income group and are included in the group of professionals; in other sectors they belong to less educated, low-income groups (the informal sector).

The definition of sectors differs from that in the national accounts, which makes it difficult to gauge their value added directly from the national accounts.

Rather than using the value added in the national accounts as reported in the Statistical Abstracts (Republic of Kenya, CBS, various issues), the value added of the input–output table 1976 (Republic of Kenya, CBS, 1979c) was used. In most cases this was consistent with the values given in the national accounts. The one exception is agriculture, for which sector the national accounts and the input–output table report different subdivisions.

The national accounts distinguish up to 1978 between the traditional economy, semi–monetary agriculture and monetary

Table A1.1. Gross domestic product by sector and major employment categories (base year 1976)

Sector	K£ million		Employment (in thousands)				
	GDP	Wages and salaries	Total	Unskilled wage employees	Skilled wage employees	Self-employed modern[1]	Informal sector workers
1. Small-scale agriculture	370.04	293.18	4 176.2	169.4	—	—	4 006.8
2. Large-scale agriculture	134.61	53.11	228.2	189.9	7.2	31.0	—
3. Mining	3.25	1.70	3.8	2.8	1.0	—	—
4. Food manufacturing	94.57	20.65	33.2	15.4	13.0	0.5	4.3
5. Non-food manufacturing	167.71	63.81	99.8	49.3	39.4	1.7	9.4
6. Modern building and construction	46.52	40.92	48.1	26.7	20.3	1.1	—
7. Traditional building and construction[3]	19.45	12.37	—	—	—	—	—
8. Transport and communications	65.10	47.39	49.5	19.9	27.4	2.2	—
9. Modern trade	109.07	79.05	68.8	31.5	28.6	8.7	—
10. Traditional trade and services[4]	49.83	49.83	135.4	—	—	—	135.4
11. Modern services	89.61	62.52	61.9	31.5	24.8	5.6	—
12. Government services (excluding 13)	82.47	81.07	103.4	81.6	21.8	—	—
13. Education and health	98.56	98.56	124.3	24.8	99.5	—	—
14. Ownership of dwellings	75.12	—	—	—	—	—	—
TOTAL	1 405.92	903.77	5 132.6	642.9	282.9	50.8	4 156.0

Table A.1.1 (continued)

	Average annual earnings (K£ per year)				Total sectoral earnings (K£ million)			
	Unskilled wage employees	Skilled wage employees	Self-employed modern[2]	Informal sector workers	Unskilled wage employees	Skilled wage employees	Self-employed modern	Informal sector workers
1. Small-scale agriculture	65	—	—	70	11.05	—	—	282.13
2. Large-scale agriculture	106	1 359	748	—	20.15	9.75	23.21	—
3. Mining	164	1 243	—	—	0.46	1.24	—	—
4. Food manufacturing	271	1 087	2 788	217	4.17	14.15	1.39	0.94
5. Non-food manufacturing	271	1 099	2 789	216	13.33	43.74	4.71	2.03
6. Modern building and construction	222	1 569	2 779	—	5.95	31.92	3.05	—
7. Traditional building and construction[3]	—	—	—	3	—	—	—	12.37
8. Transport and communications	406	1 211	2 786	—	8.10	33.18	6.11	—
9. Modern trade	183	1 724	2 748	—	5.75	49.35	23.95	—
10. Traditional trade and services[4]	—	—	—	368	—	—	—	49.83
11. Modern services	333	1 479	2 772	—	10.48	36.61	15.43	—
12. Government services (excluding 13)	312	2 556	—	—	25.44	55.63	—	—
13. Education and health	318	901	—	—	8.86	89.70	—	—
14. Ownership of dwellings	—	—	—	—	—	—	—	—
TOTAL	178	1 290	1 532	84	113.75	364.87	77.85	347.31

1 Earnings for self-employed have been estimated with the help of the 1974 Tax Report. No sectoral breakdown is available.
2 The earnings of the self-employed are a weighted average of the estimated earnings of the large farm owners and that of the so-called "gap" farms (Crawford and Thorbecke, 1978).
3 Traditional construction only in rural areas. Number of workers asumed to be included in traditional agriculture. (The CBS informal sector surveys report a negligible number of urban informal sector workers in traditional construction.)
4 Traditional services include domestic servants. The total number of domestic servants in 1976 is 55,000, and average annual earnings are K.£192 (Crawford and Thorbecke, 1978; Statistical Abstract, 1978).

agriculture. To arrive at a distinction between small-scale and large-scale farmers we have to take into account the fact that a considerable part of the value added of monetary agriculture comes from small-scale farms. In 1976 small-scale agriculture contributed 51 per cent to monetary agriculture. In order to calculate the total value added of small-scale farms we have therefore added to semi-monetary agriculture (all produced on small farms) 51 per cent of the value added of monetary agriculture. We have also added to small-scale agriculture the traditional economy, with the exception of traditional construction which was allocated to sector 7 (traditional building and construction) in our model, as we discuss below.

The small-scale agricultural sector, which uses mainly traditional methods, produces food crops and export crops, while the large-scale sector produces export crops, food crops and industrial crops. Taking all this into account, 27 per cent of total value added in agriculture is attributed to large-scale agriculture and 73 per cent to small-scale.

The input-output table does not, however, distinguish between semi-monetary and monetary agriculture, nor between small-scale and large-scale. The distribution of intermediate products and final demand components between large-scale and small-scale agriculture is discussed in the context of the construction of the input-output tables for the model (Appendix 3).

Neither the input-output table nor the national accounts figures distinguish between formal and informal production. Such a distinction is, however, important, and two "informal" sectors are incorporated in the model, namely traditional building and construction, and traditional trade and services. In the manufacturing sector (both food and non-food) informal sector workers are distinguished from formal sector workers.

The value added in informal sector activities has been derived as follows: traditional building and construction is taken from the national accounts figures for the traditional sector by deducting traditional farming activities from the total of the traditional sector.

The trade and services sectors are split into a modern and a traditional component. A survey by House (1978) on the informal sector provides figures for value added per worker in the formal and the informal sector. The number of workers in the formal and the informal sector can be derived from a survey on the informal sector carried out annually by the Central Bureau of Statistics. Having obtained a ratio of value added per formal and informal sector worker as well as a ratio of formal and informal sector employment, value added for the formal and the informal components is obtained. Regarding the other sectors, the number of workers as well as their status has been mainly derived from a study by Crawford and Thorbecke (1978). Average earnings for each class of workers in each sector are based upon a comparison of the results presented in the input-output table, the survey of employment and earnings for 1976, as reported in the Statistical Abstracts for 1978 and 1979, various tax reports and the study by Crawford and Thorbecke (1978).

A1.2 Determination of capital stock
and depreciation by sector

Data on capital stock in Kenya are relatively scarce. In order to determine the capital stock for each of the 14 sectors in the model in 1976 we had therefore first to estimate the capital stock according to the usual sectoral national accounts definitions and then determine on that basis the capital stock for the various sectors of the model.

In order to estimate the capital stock in 1976, available capital stock estimates for 1964, as reported by Ryan (1983), were updated to 1976 figures by adding real net investment to the 1964 estimates which were expressed in 1976 values by using GDP deflators. Net investment was determined by subtracting from the gross fixed capital formation each year depreciation of stocks. The depreciation was calculated by applying each year a fixed depreciation rate of the capital stock.[1] The way these depreciation rates are determined is explained below.

The 1976 capital stock for the sectors used by Ryan enabled us to determine a capital-output ratio for the sectors in our model, which are of a slightly different composition to those used by Ryan (1983). Multiplying the output (value added) of each of the 14 sectors of the model with the capital-output ratio determined according to the method explained above,[2] allowed us to determine the capital stock of each sector in the model.

In order to determine the depreciation rates the following method was applied. According to the national accounts as presented in the official input-output tables, the amount of depreciation in 1976 was K.£87.3 million. As is usual in national accounts practices, there is no depreciation on assets held by the public sector. We thought this to be incorrect for economic modelling purposes and first determined depreciation by the public sector. For government services on education and health (model sector 13) we assumed a depreciation rate of 4 per cent and for other government services (model sector 12) we assumed a depreciation rate of 2

273

per cent. Relating this to the respective amounts of capital of these sectors resulted in a total amount of depreciation of K.£5.89 million for model sector 12 and of K.£5.05 million for model sector 13. These amounts were added to the amount of depreciation reported in the national accounts, giving a total amount of depreciation of K.£98.24 million.

Sector-wise depreciation was consequently determined by applying a 4 per cent rate of depreciation in agriculture, a 5 per cent rate for mining and trade, a 7 per cent rate for building, construction and transport, and a 2 per cent rate for services. These figures have been chosen based upon the composition of the capital stock in the various sectors. Applying these rates to non-government activities and adding public sector depreciation, as given above, resulted in a total amount of depreciation of K.£97.67 million, which was deemed close enough to the estimate above, to be included and used for projections in the model. See table A1.2.

Notes

[1] Thanks are due to Jan Vandemoortele for carrying out these calculations.

[2] By doing so we ignored the slight difference in definition of the modern sectors in the model and in the national accounts. For the traditional sectors (7 and 10) information from the earlier cited survey by House (1978) was also used to gauge the value of the capital-output ratio.

Table A1.2. **Capital stock and depreciation by economic sector, 1976** (in K.£)

Sector	Value added	Capital-output ratio	Capital stock	Depreciation
1. Small-scale agriculture	370.04	0.36	133.91	5.32
2. Large-scale agriculture	134.61	0.78	105.31	4.21
3. Mining	3.25	9.92	32.27	1.61
4. Food manufacturing	94.57	2.20	207.27	10.39
5. Non-food manufacturing	167.71	2.20	368.51	18.42
6. Modern building and construction	46.52	2.45	114.00	7.98
7. Traditional building and construction	19.45	1.27	24.69	1.72
8. Transport and communications	65.10	4.38	285.00	19.95
9. Modern trade	109.07	1.65	179.67	8.98
10. Traditional trade and services	49.83	0.80	39.82	0.79
11. Modern services	89.61	0.83	74.48	1.49
12. General government services (excl. 13)	82.47	3.57	294.72	5.89
13. Government services relating to education and health	98.56	1.28	126.30	5.05
14. Ownership of dwellings	75.12	3.91	293.94	5.87

Appendix 2 A comparison between the official 1976 social accounting matrix and the social accounting matrix built for the model

The 1976 Social Accounting Matrix (Republic of Kenya, CBS, 1981) does not distinguish between urban and rural income groups. In the distribution of sectoral value added in the Social Accounting Matrix, however, a distinction is made between various production factors including skilled and unskilled workers (see also Bigsten, 1981).

The economic structure in the model does not correspond exactly to that of the Social Accounting Matrix. In the model a distinction is made between small-scale and large-scale agriculture, while trade and services are also split into traditional and modern components. These distinctions are not made in the Social Accounting Matrix, and consequently these refinements in the model had to be dropped in the comparison.

Table A2.1 presents the comparisons of the actual 1976 values. In the model the definition of skilled and unskilled labour depends on the classifications of the labour force survey. Earnings are derived from the labour force surveys and from the national accounts for 1976. In the case of the traditional economy it is difficult to gauge "profits" or, better, "operating surplus", as this contains to a large extent consumption of own product; also wages are partly paid out in kind. In the basic needs model more value added is allocated to "profits" than in the Social Accounting Matrix, as the basic needs model includes a valuation of other aspects of the traditional economy such as housing.

Furthermore, as agriculture and the traditional economy had to be amalgamated in this comparison, some elements which should have been classified under trade and services in the column relating to value added in the basic needs model are to be found under "agriculture and traditional economy". GDP and profits in agriculture are therefore higher while GDP and profits in trade and services are lower as compared with the Social Accounting Matrix.

Apart from these differences, which are the result of the different definitions of sectors used in the basic needs model and the Social Accounting Matrix, the data sets compare rather well.

Table A2.1. A comparison between the official Social Accounting Matrix (SAM) and the social accounting matrix built for the basic needs model (BNM) (K.£ million), 1976

Sector	GDP		Earnings								Per cent of government consumption		Depreciation		Profits		Per cent of private consumption	
			Unskilled		Skilled		Self-employed and informal sector		Total									
	BNM	SAM	BNM	SAM	BNM	SAM	BNM	SAM	BNM	SAM	BNM	SAM	BNM	SAM	BNM	SAM	BNM	SAM
1. Agriculture and traditional economy (1) (2) (7) (10)	573.9	544.5	31.2	51.0	9.8	7.6	367.5	323.6	396.1	382.9	0.0	0.0	27.4	27.6	481.9	455.9	38.4	35.6
2. Mining (3)	3.3	3.5	0.5	0.7	1.2	1.1	--	0.1	1.8	1.9	0.0	0.0	0.7	0.7	0.3	0.8	0.0	0.1
3. Food manufacturing (4)	94.6	95.9	4.2	5.9	14.2	13.6	2.3	2.3	22.0	21.8	0.0	0.0	7.3	7.3	20.9	26.6	20.2	19.1
4. Non-food manufacturing (5)	167.7	176.0	13.3	16.7	43.8	42.7	6.7	6.3	66.7	65.7	0.0	0.0	17.4	17.7	29.2	50.3	16.3	15.7
5. Modern building and construction (6)	46.5	46.6	6.0	13.2	31.9	24.6	3.0	1.3	40.8	39.1	0.0	0.0	6.0	1.4	2.4	0.0	0.0	--
6. Modern trade (9)	109.1	121.7	5.8	8.0	49.3	45.2	24.0	32.4	79.6	85.6	0.0	0.0	10.9	7.6	31.1	58.4	5.5	5.5
7. Transport and communications (8)	65.1	70.0	8.1	8.9	33.2	32.3	6.1	6.0	47.3	47.2	0.0	0.0	11.7	11.7	6.1	16.2	6.0	5.2
8. Modern services (11)	89.6	105.3	10.5	24.3	36.6	45.9	15.5	4.6	62.8	74.8	0.0	0.0	4.3	6.9	2.2	23.8	2.9	9.9
9. Government services excluding 13 (12)	82.5	84.8	25.4	29.8	55.6	53.1	--	--	82.9	82.9	54.7	54.7	1.6	1.6	--	--	0.5	0.6
10. Education and health (13)	98.6	100.4	8.9	8.3	89.7	91.6	--	--	99.8	99.9	45.3	45.3	--	0.3	--	--	1.6	1.1
11. Ownership of dwellings (14)	75.1	56.4	--	--	--	--	--	--	--	--	0.0	0.0	--	--	67.9	69.8	8.6	7.2
TOTAL	1 405.9	1 405.1	113.8	166.8	364.9	357.7	425.2	376.6	903.8	901.1	100.0	100.0	87.3	87.4	641.0	684.2	100.0	100.0

Appendix 3 The input-output structure of the model

A3.1 Introduction

The input-output table for 1976 published by the Central Bureau of Statistics in Nairobi contains 36 sectors. The intermediate transactions and the final demand categories are further divided into a domestic dimension and an import dimension. The following steps have been taken to fit the original input-output table to the model, retaining the distinction between the domestic dimension and the import dimension.

Two rows and columns were distributed over the rest of the table (namely, "ownership of business premises" and "unspecified"), following a method described by Bigsten (1980). The remaining 34 x 34 table was then aggregated into an 11 x 11 table to satisfy the broad sectoral division in the basic needs model.

Next, it was necessary to split up some of the rows and columns of the aggregate (11 x 11) table in order to arrive at an input-output table which contains the sectors which are not explicitly mentioned in the published table but which are included in the model. The sectors which have been split up are:

(a) traditional economy, into small-scale agriculture and traditional construction;
(b) agriculture, into small-scale and large-scale production; and

(c) trade and services, into modern trade and services and traditional trade and services.

With these six newly created sectors instead of the original three we arrive at a 14 x 14 input-output table. For the mapping procedure see table A3.1.

The following sections describe this in greater detail. The first section describes how the actual figures in the tables are derived in those cases where sectors have been split or amalgamated, while the second section provides methodological notes on the splitting up between sectors.

A3.2 Determination of the various input-output tables used in the model

The traditional economy is split into traditional agriculture, allocated to the small farm sector in the model, and traditional building and construction. Since this sector had no intermediate deliveries except to itself, this presented no difficulty.

The splitting up of the agricultural sector into small-scale and large-scale was more complicated. The intermediate inputs in the original sectors 2 and 3 (agriculture and fishing) were split into 33 per cent for small farms and 67 per cent for large farms, while value added was split into 73 per cent for small farms and 27 per cent for large farms. The split for value added has been discussed in Appendix 1. The split for intermediate inputs was based on more detailed information available on fertilisers: the IRSI survey of 1974, which deals with smallholders only, reported a total fertiliser use of K.£4.723 million by small-scale farmers. In the input-output table total deliveries of chemical products to agriculture amounted to K.£13.918 million. Thirty-three per cent of this amounts to K.£4.593 million, which compares well with the IRSI estimate.

After adding the inputs for small-scale farmers from original sectors 2 and 3 to those for the traditional economy, this resulted in a total of K.£35.5 million and K.£41.5 million for intermediate inputs for small-scale and large-scale farming respectively.

Intermediate deliveries by small-scale and large-scale agriculture have been determined residually after the determination of final demand for small-scale and large-scale agriculture.

According to the consumption expenditure matrix (see Chapter 9), K.£33.7 million of private consumption comes from large-scale agriculture and K.£262.7 from small-scale agriculture. The split of exports between small-scale and

Table A3.1. Mapping of sectors of published 1976 input-output
table on sectors of the model

Original sector of the input-output table	Sector in the model
1. Traditional economy	(1. Small-scale agriculture (7. Traditional building and (construction
2. Agriculture	2. Large-scale agriculture
3. Fishing and forestry	1. Small-scale agriculture
4. Mining	3. Mining
5. Manufacturing food preparations)	
6. " butchery products)	4. Food manufacturing
7. " beverages and tobacco)	
8. " textiles raw materials)	
9. " finished textiles)	
10. " garments, etc.)	
11. " footwear, etc.)	
12. " wood products, etc.)	
13. " paper products)	
14. " petroleum products)	
15. " rubber products)	5. Non-food Manufacturing
16. " paint, etc.)	
17. " other chemicals)	
18. " non-metallic minerals)	
19. " metal products)	
20. " transport equipment)	
21. Electricity supply)	
22. Water supply)	
23. Building and construction	6. Modern building and construction
24. Wholesale and retail trade	(9. Modern trade (10. Traditional trade and services
25. Transport)	8. Transport and communication
26. Communication)	
27. Restaurant and hotel services	11. Modern services
28. Ownership of dwellings	14. Ownership of dwellings
29. Financial services	11. Modern services
30. Miscellaneous services	(11. Modern services (10. Traditional trade and services
31. Government services public administration	12. Government services
32. " " education)	
33. " " health)	13. Education and health
34. " " agriculture)	
35. " " other)	12. Government services
36. Ownership of business premises	See text
37. Unspecified	See text

large-scale agriculture has been determined as follows. Most agricultural exports consist of coffee and tea. If we exclude other crops we arrive at a figure of 74.6 per cent for the share of coffee in total exports and 26.4 per cent for tea (Statistical Abstract, 1978, table 59a). Small farms contribute on average 60 per cent to coffee production and 36 per cent to tea production (World Bank, 1986), which gives a share of 54.3 per cent of total agricultural exports for small-scale farmers, amounting to K.£76.6 million worth of produce, and a share of 45.7 per cent for large-scale agriculture. Gross fixed capital formation in agriculture amounted to K.£5.3 million in the input-output table; this has been allocated to large-scale agriculture in the model. Subtracting the final demand components for small-scale and large-scale agriculture from total supply in small-scale and large-scale farming, which is made up of value added, intermediate inputs (as determined above) and imports (K.£11.4 million in the case of large-scale agriculture), gives the intermediate deliveries of small-scale and large-scale agriculture, amounting to K.£65.4 million and K.£83 million respectively. All intermediate deliveries, which are mainly to the food manufacturing sector, have been split according to the split in total deliveries.

Trade and services had also to be split into a modern and a traditional component. First of all, as discussed in Appendix 1, value added was split according to wage differentials in the traditional and modern sectors. Domestic deliveries were split according to this same ratio. Imported deliveries, however, were all allocated to the modern sector. Deliveries and final demand from services and trade were split according to the assumption that no deliveries existed from the traditional sector in the import dimension of the input-output table and that all exports and capital formation took place in the modern sectors. Since private consumption is known from the consumption matrix, domestic deliveries could be calculated as a residual.

Tables A3.2-A3.4 give the total, domestic and import dimensions of intermediate deliveries, while tables A3.5-A3.7 give the final demand components. Table A3.8 gives the value added components and the supply of resources.

In the model the following matrices of technical coefficients have been used:

[A]   = matrix of domestic intermediate coefficients with

$$a_{ij} = \frac{XD_{ij}}{XD_j} \qquad\qquad [A3.1]$$

[AM] = matrix of imported intermediate coefficients with

$$a_{ij} = \frac{XI_{ij}}{XD_j}$$ [A3.2]

where

XD_j = total domestic supply of sector j

XD_{ij} = intermediate domestic deliveries from sector i to sector j (table A3.3)

XI_{ij} = intermediate imported deliveries from sector i to sector j (table A3.4)

Table A3.2. Input-output table of total dimension, Kenya, 1976 (K.£ thousands)

Sector	1	2	3	4	5	6	7	8	9	10	11	12	13	14	Total
1. Small-scale agriculture	18 343	0	0	47 087	0	0	0	0	0	0	0	0	0	0	65 430
2. Large-scale agriculture	1 361	11 542	0	58 129	10 903	0	0	0	495	123	0	0	193	0	83 028
3. Mining	26	53	1 016	626	113 054	6 906	0	0	0	0	0	267	0	0	121 684
4. Food manufacturing	2 016	4 021	19	84 413	16 187	70	0	2 223	18 253	9 052	1 212	0	0	5	166 674
5. Non-food manufacturing	8 503	16 594	4 450	46 972	223 309	70 830	6 574	60 911	29 338	6 837	12 757	10 595	7 463	112	505 286
6. Modern building and construction	0	0	294	1 188	3 580	19 313	0	0	228	120	273	18 106	10 718	0	44 524
7. Traditional building and construction	0	0	0	0	0	0	0	0	0	0	0	0	0	0	0
8. Transport and communications	281	561	1 210	4 554	8 807	3 451	0	52 419	12 595	4 739	5 007	12 229	2 227	31	106 461
9. Modern trade	2 807	4 363	525	13 117	19 940	7 457	0	9 305	3 572	1 242	2 464	10 695	2 381	22	72 797
10. Traditional trade and services	1 027	1 658	0	5 213	4 040	3 162	0	4 539	1 840	3 178	1 808	6 129	2 036	11	26 476
11. Modern services	1 091	2 177	1 080	6 973	26 922	4 821	0	14 869	17 487	3 929	13 562	3 367	1 045	4 978	97 348
12. Government services (excluding 13)	103	205	0	2	2	6	1	75	9	10	38	240	3	0	692
13. Education and health	0	0	1	324	342	3	0	12	14	7	9	15	6	0	733
14. Ownership of dwellings	0	0	0	0	0	0	0	0	0	0	0	0	0	0	0
	35 558	41 534	8 575	268 658	427 070	116 014	6 574	114 915	83 331	29 237	37 130	61 643	25 072	5 184	1 291 315

Table A3.3. Input-output table of domestic dimension, Kenya, 1976 (K.£ thousands)

Sector	1	2	3	4	5	6	7	8	9	10	11	12	13	14	Total
1. Small-scale agriculture	18 343	0	0	47 087	0	0	0	0	0	0	0	0	0	0	65 430
2. Large-scale agriculture	1 361	10 117	0	58 129	7 616	0	0	15	390	123	0	262	190	0	83 028
3. Mining	0	0	1 016	190	704	6 782	0	0	0	0	0	0	0	0	8 692
4. Food manufacturing	2 004	3 997	19	79 010	14 592	70	0	2 045	28 047	9 052	1 116	10 527	7 394	5	157 878
5. Non-food manufacturing	4 527	9 027	3 733	32 346	119 044	56 774	6 080	54 129	15 926	6 837	10 377	15 649	9 003	112	343 564
6. Modern building and construction	0	0	294	1 188	3 580	19 313	0	94	228	120	273	12 229	2 227	4 978	44 524
7. Traditional building and construction	0	0	0	0	0	0	0	0	0	0	0	0	0	0	0
8. Transport and communications	281	561	1 181	4 526	8 618	3 374	0	43 887	12 328	4 739	4 743	10 113	2 298	31	96 680
9. Modern trade	2 807	4 363	522	13 109	19 876	7 412	0	6 417	3 555	1 242	2 366	5 900	2 027	22	69 618
10. Traditional trade and services	1 027	1 658	0	5 213	4 040	3 162	0	4 539	1 840	3 178	1 808	0	0	11	26 476
11. Modern services	806	1 608	816	6 260	24 685	4 606	0	14 419	14 381	3 929	7 880	1 943	951	25	82 309
12. Government services (excluding 13)	103	205	0	2	6	1	0	75	9	10	38	240	3	0	692
13. Education and health	0	0	1	324	342	3	0	12	14	7	9	15	6	0	733
14. Ownership of dwellings	0	0	0	0	0	0	0	0	0	0	0	0	0	0	0
	31 259	31 536	7 582	243 232	203 103	101 497	6 080	125 632	76 718	29 237	28 610	56 878	24 099	5 184	970 647

Table A3.4. Input-output table of imports dimension, Kenya, 1976 (K.£ thousands)

Sector	1	2	3	4	5	6	7	8	9	10	11	12	13	14	Total
1. Small-scale agriculture	0	0	0	0	0	0	0	0	0	0	0	0	0	0	0
2. Large-scale agriculture	0	1 425	0	4 152	3 287	0	0	0	105	0	0	5	3	0	8 977
3. Mining	26	53	0	436	112 350	124	0	3	0	0	0	0	0	0	112 992
4. Food manufacturing	12	24	0	5 463	1 595	0	0	178	1 291	0	96	68	69	0	8 796
5. Non-food manufacturing	3 976	7 927	717	14 626	104 265	14 056	494	6 782	2 327	0	2 380	2 457	1 715	0	161 722
6. Modern building and construction	0	0	0	0	0	0	0	0	0	0	0	0	0	0	0
7. Traditional building and construction	0	0	0	0	0	0	0	0	0	0	0	0	0	0	0
8. Transport and communications	0	0	0	0	0	0	0	0	0	0	0	0	0	0	0
9. Modern trade	0	0	29	28	189	77	0	8 262	267	0	264	582	83	0	9 781
10. Traditional trade and services	0	0	3	8	64	45	0	2 888	17	0	98	229	9	0	3 361
11. Modern services	0	0	0	0	0	0	0	0	0	0	0	0	0	0	0
12. Government services (excluding 13)	285	569	264	713	2 237	215	0	450	3 106	0	5 682	1 424	94	0	15 039
13. Education and health	0	0	0	0	0	0	0	0	0	0	0	0	0	0	0
14. Ownership of dwellings	0	0	0	0	0	0	0	0	0	0	0	0	0	0	0
	4 299	9 998	1 013	25 426	223 987	14 517	494	18 563	7 113	0	8 520	4 765	1 973	0	320 668

Table A3.5. Total final demand, Kenya, 1976 (K.£ thousands)

Sector	Intermediate deliveries	Exports	Private consumption and stocks	General government consumption	Gross fixed capital formation	Total deliveries
1. Small-scale agriculture	65 430	76 603	262 701	0	0	404 734
2. Large-scale agriculture	83 028	64 575	33 686	0	5 251	186 540
3. Mining	121 684	2 518	937	0	0	125 139
4. Food manufacturing	166 674	33 269	183 787	0	0	383 730
5. Non-food manufacturing	505 286	109 448	148 074	0	133 426	896 234
6. Modern building and construction	44 524	0	424	0	118 707	163 655
7. Traditional building and construction	0	0	0	0	26 014	26 014
8. Transport and communications	106 641	72 634	54 923	0	0	234 018
9. Modern trade	73 979	69 469	50 300	0	9 330	202 078
10. Traditional trade and services	26 476	0	52 541	0	0	79 017
11. Modern services	97 348	19 326	26 268	0	702	143 644
12. Government services (excluding 13)	692	29	4 607	138 915	0	144 243
13. Education and health	733	980	15 129	114 875	0	131 717
14. Ownership of dwellings	0	2 704	77 511	0	0	80 215
	1 291 315	451 555	910 888	253 790	293 430	3 200 978

Table A3.6. Domestic final demand, Kenya, 1976 (K.£ thousands)

Sector	Intermediate deliveries	Exports	Private consumption and stocks	Private consumption only	General government consumption	Gross fixed capital formation	Total deliveries
1. Small-scale agriculture	65 430	76 603	262 701	0	0	0	404 734
2. Large-scale agriculture	74 051	64 575	31 410	0	0	5 106	175 142
3. Mining	8 692	2 518	937	0	0	0	12 147
4. Food manufacturing	157 878	33 269	171 998	0	0	0	363 145
5. Non-food manufacturing	343 564	109 448	98 081	0	0	43 501	594 594
6. Modern building and construction	44 524	0	424	0	0	117 707	162 655
7. Traditional building and construction	0	0	0	0	0	26 014	26 014
8. Transport and communications	96 680	72 634	39 862	0	0	0	209 176
9. Modern trade	69 618	69 469	45 239	0	0	9 292	193 618
10. Traditional trade and services	26 476	0	52 541	0	0	0	79 017
11. Modern services	82 309	19 326	24 887	0	0	699	127 221
12. Government services (excluding 13)	692	29	4 602	0	138 915	0	144 238
13. Education and health	733	980	8 934	0	114 875	0	125 522
14. Ownership of dwellings	0	2 704	79 967	0	0	0	79 671
	970 647	451 555	818 583	0	253 790	202 319	2 696 894

Table A3.7. Imports final demand, Kenya, 1976 (K.£ thousands)

Sector	Intermediate deliveries	Exports	Private consumption and stocks	Private consumption only	General government consumption	Gross fixed capital formation	Total deliveries
1. Small-scale agriculture	0	0	0	0	0	0	0
2. Large-scale agriculture	8 977	0	2 276	0	0	145	11 398
3. Mining	112 992	0	0	0	0	0	112 992
4. Food manufacturing	8 796	0	11 789	0	0	0	20 585
5. Non-food manufacturing	161 722	0	49 993	0	0	89 925	301 640
6. Modern building and construction	0	0	0	0	0	1 000	1 000
7. Traditional building and construction	0	0	0	0	0	0	0
8. Transport and communications	9 781	0	15 061	0	0	0	24 842
9. Modern trade	3 361	0	5 061	0	0	38	8 460
10. Traditional trade and services	0	0	0	0	0	0	0
11. Modern services	15 039	0	1 381	0	0	3	16 423
12. Government services (excluding 13)	0	0	5	0	0	0	5
13. Education and health	0	0	6 195	0	0	0	6 195
14. Ownership of dwellings	0	0	544	0	0	0	544
	320 668	0	92 305	0	0	91 111	504 084

Table A3.8. Distribution of value added, Kenya, 1986
(K.£ thousands)

Sector	1	2	3	4	5	6	7	8	9	10	11	12	13	14	Total
Depreciation	15 330	12 104	699	7 339	17 362	6 029	0	11 673	10 921	0	4 334	1 580	0	0	87 371
Wages and salaries	11 055	40 014	1 854	19 486	59 372	37 820	0	41 200	55 470	0	47 343	81 015	99 450	0	494 079
Profits	342 791	69 905	332	20 946	29 222	1 380	19 440	6 133	31 070	49 780	2 240	0	0	67 923	641 162
Indirect taxes, import duties	0	2 769	141	42 809	48 916	434	0	879	4 286	0	2 973	0	0	6 564	109 771
Interest paid	0	8 816	526	3 907	12 632	978	0	5 096	8 040	0	33 201	0	0	0	73 196
Gross value added	369 176	133 608	3 552	94 481	167 504	46 641	19 440	64 981	109 787	49 780	90 091	82 595	99 450	74 487	1 405 579
Gross output	281 044	298 832	12 147	363 145	594 594	162 655	26 014	209 176	193 618	79 017	127 221	149 238	125 522	79 671	2 696 844
Import CIF	0	10 974	94 255	16 601	259 091	1 000	0	24 842	8 460	0	16 400	5	6 195	544	438 367
Import duties	0	424	18 737	3 984	42 549	0	0	0	0	0	23	0	0	0	65 717
Imports CIF inc. duties	0	11 398	112 992	20 585	301 640	1 000	0	24 842	8 460	0	16 423	5	6 195	544	504 084
Total supply of resources	404 734	186 549	125 139	383 730	896 234	163 655	26 014	234 018	202 078	79 017	143 644	144 243	131 717	80 215	3 200 978

A3.3 Methodology used to split a given sector in an input-output table into two or more subsectors

As the model includes sectors which are not distinguished in the input-output tables, it is necessary to split some original sectors in the input-output table into subsectors. The mathematical procedure is explained below. The economic interpretation remains important, however. Notation in this part of the appendix does not always correspond with the symbols used in the main text and consequently applies only to this section.

If the sector concerned is labelled z, then the total intermediate deliveries amount to $\sum_j a_{zj} X_j$ and final demand to F_z. Total inputs amount to $\sum_i a_{iz} X_z$ and value added to VA_z. The following identity is to hold:

$$\sum_j a_{zj} X_j + F_z - M_z = \sum_i a_{iz} X_z + VA_z = X_z$$

$$i = 1,\ldots,n$$

and similarly for any subsector k.

In splitting up a sector we can either start from the demand side (F_z) or from the deliveries side (value added VA_z). We start with a description of the first method.

Splitting up from the demand side

With knowledge from secondary sources F_z can be split up into several subsectors (in the case of services, for example, into demand for formal business services, for informal services, for education, health, etc.):

$$F_z^k \qquad k = 1,\ldots,h; \quad \text{(h is number of subsectors).}$$

Equally, one usually knows which service sectors use imported final goods and which do not, thus M_z can be split into M_z^k.

The most difficult part is the splitting up of intermediate deliveries, as additional information is often difficult to come by. If no additional information is available, the best solution is to split up all intermediate deliveries $a_{zj}X_j$ in proportion to the split up of final demand (F_z into F_z^k). In fact this means we do not change the technical coefficients but only total output. Thus we get

$$(a_{zj} X_j)^k = a_{zj} X_j * (F_z^k /F_z)$$

and therefore we also have

$$X_z = (\sum_j a_{zj}X_j)^k + F_z^k - M_z^k$$

Some case studies provide information on inputs into the sector (for example, the informal sector will use less input from machinery and more from agriculture, etc.). There are therefore two options for splitting up the input column. The first one is to keep the value added share constant for all subsectors, thus

$$VA_z^k = (VA_z/X_z) * X_z^k$$

for all k. Finally, the inputs $(a_{iz} X_z)^k$ have to be distributed according to additional information, always respecting the equality $\sum_i (a_{iz}X_z)^k = X_z^k - VA_z^k$.

The other option is not to assume equal value added ratios. Then we need to respect

$$VA_z^k + \sum_i (a_{iz} X_i)^k = X_z^k$$

This method will not always guarantee economically acceptable results. As X_z^k is already given by the demand side we may arrive at an unacceptably low value added component after fixing total intermediate inputs. The value added component VA_z^k can in effect be checked against factor payments (mainly labour). Thus as we split up the sectors we also split up employment in the sectors z from L_z into L_z^k. Often having reasonable information about wage payments, we can then gauge VA_z^k and finally again, the inputs $(a_{iz}X_z)^k$ subject to the above restrictions.

Splitting up from the supply side (deliveries)

Often we have good information about how value added in sector z can be split up between the various subsectors.
Recalling that

$$\sum_j a_{zj} X_j + F_z - M_z = \sum_i a_{iz} X_z + VA_z = X_z$$

$$i = 1,\ldots,n; \quad j = 1,\ldots,n$$

we can split VA_z into VA_z^k, and assuming a constant value added ratio for each subsector (unless other information is available) we can also split total intermediate deliveries $\sum_i a_{iz}X_i$ in $(\sum_i a_{iz}X_i)^k$ accordingly.

Then, with additional information on M_z to split it into M_z^k in order to adhere to the above equation, either the total demand for intermediate deliveries and/or the final demand of each subsector can be adjusted for each subsector.

Final check

After all manipulations the following identities must hold:

$$\sum_j (a_{zj} X_j)^k + F_z^k - M_z^k = \sum_i (a_{iz} X_z)^k + VA_z^k = X_z^k$$

$$i,j = 1,\ldots,h$$
(thus including the new sectors)

$$\sum_k F_z^k = F_z$$

$$\sum_k M_z^k = M_z$$

$$\sum_k VA_z^k = VA_z$$

$$\sum_k X_z^k = X_z$$

as well as

$$\sum_k (a_{zj} X_j)^k = a_{zj} X_j$$

and

$$\sum_k (a_{iz} X_z)^k = a_{iz} X_z$$

Appendix 4 Production functions

The main purpose of this appendix is to derive appropriate production functions for the modern sector in the Kenya basic needs model, including the effects of skilled and unskilled labour on production levels.

A4.1 The choice of the production function

We first provide some tests relating to the appropriate formulation of the production function. We would like to know whether economies of scale occur in the different sectors, and whether the elasticity of substitution between labour and capital differs significantly from 1. If there are constant returns to scale and the elasticity of substitution is different from 1, the CES production function is the appropriate formulation; if the elasticity of substitution is equal to 1 the Cobb–Douglas function is adequate.

In order to test for constant returns to scale we carried out the following regression:

$$\ln(Y/L) = a + b \ \ln w + e \ \ln L \qquad [A4.1]$$

where Y = gross value added
       L = number employed
       w = wage rate

This regression is based upon the following production function.

$$Y = C(d_1 K^{-r} + d_2 L^{-r})^{-\frac{m}{r}}$$

where

Y = gross value added
K = capital
L = number employed

the scale parameter is m and the elasticity of substitution is $\frac{1}{1+r}$. C, d_1 and d_2 are constants. By equalising the marginal product of labour to the wage level the following relation emerges.

$$\ln(Y/L) = a + b \ln w + e \ln L$$

with $b = \dfrac{m}{m+r}$

and $e = \dfrac{m-1}{m+r}$

and we have for the scale parameter (s) the following relation.

$$s = 1 + \frac{e}{1 - b}$$

while the elasticity of substitution is

$$\sigma = \frac{b}{1 + e}$$

If we have constant returns to scale, the coefficient e will be equal to zero, and the following equation emerges:

$$\ln(Y/L) = a + b \ln w \qquad [A4.2]$$

where s = 1
      σ = b

If, furthermore, the elasticity of substitution is equal to 1, the equation [A4.2] reduces to:

$$\ln(Y/L) = a - \ln w \qquad [A4.3]$$

Equations [A4.1] and [A4.2] were used in a regression analysis for the seven modern sectors of the Kenyan economy. The estimations are based upon time series covering the period 1968-78.[1]

The regression based upon equation [A4.1] (see table A4.1) provides a good fit. It can be noticed that neither for the modern sector as a whole, nor for any individual sector, is the coefficient (e) of L significantly different from zero, on the other hand, the coefficient (b) of lnw shows acceptable t values.

Table A4.1. Sectoral productivity equations (n = 11)

Sector	a	b	e	R^2
1. Mining	2.105	0.861	−0.850	0.802
	(6.440)	(5.319)	(−2.204)	
2. Food manufacturing	0.652	1.312	0.069	0.894
	(1.056)	(2.075)	(0.146)	
3. Non-food manufacturing	−0.896	1.208	0.572	0.914
	(1.302)	(2.185)	(0.835)	
4. Modern building and construction	1.342	0.530	0.138	0.878
	(8.712)	(2.717)	(0.574)	
5. Transport and communications	0.737	1.343	−0.417	0.954
	(1.098)	(12.835)	(−0.967)	
6. Modern trade	−0.177	1.5502	0.356	0.978
	(−0.770)	(10.552)	(1.187)	
7. Modern services	1.075	1.665	−0.509	0.992
	(4.517)	(8.502)	(−1.467)	
8. Total modern economy	0.582	1.059	0.249	0.993
	(1.834)	(9.031)	(1.123)	

(t values in brackets)

In order to see if the substitution elasticity differs significantly from 1, a regression was also carried out as based upon equation [A4.2], the results of which are indicated in table A4.2.

For the modern economy as a whole we find a substitution elasticity of 1.18. This compares well with a 1967 study, based upon cross-section data (House, 1973b), which found a substitution elasticity of 1.17. Taking the sectors separately, the results can be judged satisfactory, given the limited number of observations. Most sectors show a substitution elasticity higher than 1 (except the more capital-intensive sectors of mining and building and construction). This result would run contrary to the generally accepted ideas of limited substitution in an economy where institutional factors are assumed to play an important role. Bearing this in mind, it seems acceptable to assume a substitution elasticity of 1 for the modern sectors of the economy, and to apply Cobb-Douglas production functions to them.

Table A4.2. Sectoral productivity equations (n = 11)

Sector	a	b	R^2
1. Mining	1.302	0.738	0.747
	(4.348)	(3.292)	
2. Food manufacturing	0.734	1.401	0.893
	(2.827)	(8.194)	
3. Non-food manufacturing	-0.406	1.611	0.907
	(-1.556)	(9.162)	
4. Modern building and construction	1.401	0.630	0.872
	(13.234)	(7.837)	
5. Transport and communications	0.112	1.330	0.949
	(0.622)	(12.821)	
6. Modern trade	0.019	1.688	0.974
	(0.119)	(19.657)	
7. Modern services	0.499	1.190	0.986
	(10.388)	(31.875)	
8. Total modern economy	0.935	1.184	0.992
	(21.212)	(32.918)	

(t values in brackets)

A4.2 The sectoral production functions

The Cobb-Douglas function can be described as:

$$Y = A \ L^a \ K^b \ e^t \qquad [A4.4]$$

where a + b = 1

Since we estimate the production function directly we need to know the value of the capital stock. An estimate of the capital stock was made as follows.

First, the (marginal) capital-output ratio was calculated by regressing the sectoral value added on the cumulated net value of past net investment with a one-year time lag:

$$Y_t = a + b\ V_{t-1} \qquad\qquad\text{[A4.5]}$$

$$V_{t-1} = \sum_{i=0}^{t-1} I_i\ (1-d)^{t-i-1} \qquad\qquad\text{[A4.6]}$$

where

d = depreciation
I = gross fixed capital formulation
with i = 0 for 1964

The slope b of the equation provided the inverse of the capital-output ratios, which are indicated in table A4.3. All capital-output ratios seem to be of reasonable magnitude, perhaps with the exception of transport and communications.

The gross domestic product of 1964 was multiplied by the capital-output ratio in order to calculate the initial capital stock. For consecutive years the Perpetual Inventory was used to gauge the capital stock.

$$K_{64} = \frac{1}{b}\ Y_{64} \qquad\qquad \text{for } t = 64 \qquad \text{[A4.7]}$$

$$K_t = K_{t-1}\ (1-d) + I_{t-1} \qquad \text{for } t > 64 \qquad \text{[A4.8]}$$

Table A4.3. <u>Estimation of sectoral capital-output ratios (equation [A4.5]) (N = 15)</u>

Sector	b	$\frac{1}{b}$ capital-output ratio	R^2
1. Mining	0.103	9.70	0.835
2. Food manufacturing	0.320	3.12	0.971
3. Non-food manufacturing	0.185	5.40	0.981
4. Modern building and construction	0.228	4.38	0.760
5. Transport and communications	0.070	14.29	0.931
6. Modern trade	0.152	6.57	0.403
7. Modern services	0.491	2.03	0.982

Having obtained an estimation of the capital stock, the Cobb-Douglas function can be estimated. For this we used the following formula, in order to avoid multi-collinearity.

$$\ln(Y/L) = a + bt + c \ln (K/L) \qquad [A4.9]$$

where c is the capital coefficient and 1-c by definition the labour coefficient, while b represents technical progress. The results are given in table A4.4.

The coefficient for capital seems in general to be acceptable (perhaps with the exception of modern trade), but the time coefficient, representing the rate of technical progress, seems difficult to interpret for various sectors: for mining the rate is far too high, for modern trade it is insignificant, and for the modern building and construction sector a negative rate appears. This might also be due to the fact that we have determined capital by means of an ICOR and hence implicitly assuming an absence of technical progress. How technical progress has been included in the model for simulation purposes is discussed in the last paragraph of this appendix.

Table A4.4. Sectoral production functions (equation [A4.9])

Sector	a	b	c	R^2	N
1. Mining	2.395 (9.276)	0.68 (4.064)	0.206 (0.787)	0.296	11
2. Food manufacturing	-0.149 (0.504)	0.043 (9.891)	0.486 (2.291)	0.949	10
3. Non-food manufacturing	1.738 (5.673)	0.025 (6.687)	0.264 (1.256)	0.883	15
4. Modern building and construction	2.633 (2.691)	-0.043 (-4.081)	0.131 (1.334)	0.676	14
5. Transport and communications	2.128 (66.966)	0.040 (6.759)	0.200 (1.032)	0.934	15
6. Modern trade	1.075 (6.985)	0.025 (0.613)	0.766 (1.573)	0.740	15
7. Modern services	1.770 (19.801)	0.024 (5.298)	0.484 (3.575)	0.754	15

(t statistics in brackets)

A4.3 Skilled and unskilled labour inputs

In order to gauge the influence of skilled and unskilled labour, time series for employment and for skilled and unskilled workers were constructed for each sector, based upon employment and earnings statistics. These series concerning the 1968-78 period enabled us to estimate sectoral production functions distinguishing these two types of labour input.

Two formulations were used

$$\ln (Y/K) = A + a \ln (LU/K) + b \ln (LS/K) \qquad [A4.10]$$
$$+ c\ t \qquad\qquad + d \quad D$$

$$\ln (Y/K) = A + a \ln (LU/K) + b \ln (LS/K) \qquad [A4.11]$$
$$+ c\ t \qquad\qquad + d \quad D$$
$$+ e \ln(K)$$

The first equation is a normal Cobb-Douglas function written in logarithmic terms, while the second includes a capital term explicitly relaxing the imposition of constant returns to scale. In the first case the value of the capital coefficient is equal to (1-a-b), in the second case to (1+e-a-b). A dummy variable (D) was included to indicate a break in the time series for skilled and unskilled workers between 1975 and 1976, and a time coefficient to pick up technical progress.

The value of the functions are given in table A4.5.

None of the regressions proved satisfactory, however. Another, more restricted, method was therefore used to gauge the coefficients of skilled and unskilled labour - an approach using the data on the wage share of labour in value added, and the share of the unskilled wage bill in the total wage share. These data are reproduced in table A4.6.

The share of wages in value added was used to check the results of the Cobb-Douglas function as given in table A4.4. The rationale for this was that if factors are paid according to their marginal productivity, the share of their rewards in total value added is equal to the coefficient in the Cobb-Douglas function (for example, Cramer, 1969). This check proved to be fairly satisfactory.

A4.4 Determination of the coefficients of the production functions used in the model

On the basis of the outcome of the above analysis, the following procedure was used to determine the coefficients of the production functions in the model.

Table A4.1. <u>Sectoral productivity equations</u> (n = 11)

Sector	A	a	b	c	d	e	$\bar{R}^2$ adj
Mining	−5.955	0.524	0.399	0.056	−0.272	--	0.916
		(0.488)	(0.505)	(0.020)	(0.234)		
	3.412	−0.211	−0.202	0.090	0.145	−1.463	0.975
		(0.328)	(0.318)	(0.014)	(0.168)	(0.378)	
Food manufacturing	−4.127	0.087	0.587	0.027	0.033	--	0.840
		(0.030)	(0.087)	(0.004)	(0.016)		
	−3.803	0.079	0.581	0.031	0.035	−0.057	0.809
		(0.054)	(0.101)	(0.21)	(0.020)	(0.292)	
Non-food manufacturing	−3.853	0.104	0.375	0.030	−0.017	--	0.757
		(0.101)	(0.078)	(0.005)	(0.029)		
	−6.726	0.180	0.452	0.006	−0.034	0.393	0.732
		(0.156)	(0.142)	(0.036)	(0.040)	(0.591)	
Modern building and construction	−2.985	0.224	0.158	−0.052	−0.020	--	0.975
		(0.058)	(0.104)	(0.004)	(0.026)		
	−4.539	0.326	0.205	−0.063	0.033	0.174	0.973
		(0.159)	(0.131)	(0.017)	(0.033)	(0.251)	
Transport and communications	−4.137	0.168	0.315	0.018	−0.015	--	−0.272
		(0.206)	(0.446)	(0.021)	(0.051)		
	13.012	0.168	0.230	0.108	−0.069	−2.702	−0.185
		(0.199)	(0.436)	(0.077)	(0.067)	(2.250)	
Modern trade	1.732	−0.216	0.201	0.069	0.058	--	0.959
		(0.091)	(0.125)	(0.015)	(0.024)		
	−9.805	−0.309	0.016	0.137	0.070	1.401	0.970
		(0.093)	(0.117)	(0.040)	(0.021)	(0.780)	
Modern services	0.403	0.122	−0.235	0.005	0.045	--	0.835
		(0.050)	(0.202)	(0.004)	(0.030)		
	3.571	0.005	−0.326	0.032	−0.020	−0.426	0.857
		(0.101)	(0.199)	(0.020)	(0.033)	(0.309)	
Total modern economy	−0.926	−0.103	0.032	0.012	0.007	--	0.477
		(0.312)	(0.196)	(0.003)	(0.032)		
	−1.215	−0.096	0.033	0.011	0.006	0.034	0.373
		(0.398)	(0.215)	(0.037)	(0.997)	(0.997)	

The coefficient of capital in the Cobb-Douglas function was determined on the basis of the results obtained by the regression analysis as given in equation [A4.9], of which the results are presented in table A4.4. All coefficients appeared to be satisfactory except that of modern trade, which was deemed too high. The capital coefficient of modern trade was thereby based upon the non-wage share in value added of trade, as reported in table A4.6.

Determination of the coefficient of labour was done in two steps following the assumption of nested Cobb-Douglas production functions. First, the overall labour coefficient has to be equal to 1 minus the coefficient of capital. After having determined the overall labour coefficient, the share of the unskilled wage bill in the total wage bill (as reported in table A4.6 and table A1.1 where the wage rates for skilled and unskilled are also given) was used to split up the overall labour coefficient in a coefficient of unskilled and a coefficient of skilled labour in the production function.

Table A4.6. Share of wages in value added
Share of unskilled wages in total wage bill (1976)

	Share of wages in GDP	Share of unskilled wage bill in total wage bill
Mining	0.55	0.27
Food manufacturing	0.44	0.23
Non-food manufacturing	0.44	0.23
Modern building and construction	0.78	0.16
Transport and communications	0.50	0.20
Modern trade	0.45	0.10
Modern services	0.45	0.22

Source. Republic of Kenya, CBS: Statistical Abstract, 1979.

The regression analysis according to equation [A4.9] also provided estimates for technical progress. These were, however, difficult to interpret in many sectors. Furthermore, for those sectors where rates were significant and were within an a priori acceptable range (food manufacturing, 4.3 per cent; non-food manufacturing, 2.5 per cent; transport, 4 per cent; services 2.4 per cent), the rates very much reflected the fast GDP growth Kenya underwent in the 1968-78 period (our period of observation for the estimation). Since growth prospects at present are much more limited, we felt unjustified in using these high rates of technical progress, especially as we found significant and meaningful rates for only a number of sectors. We have therefore applied in the base run as well as in the policy runs, a modest rate of technical progress of 0.5 per cent for all non-agricultural sectors.

Note

[1] Data were obtained from various issues of the Statistical Abstract and the surveys on employment and earnings in the modern sector.

Appendix 5 An analysis of small-scale farming based on rural survey data

A5.1 Introduction

Agriculture is still the largest sector in the Kenyan economy. In 1976 (the base year of the Kenya basic needs model) it accounted for 36 per cent of total GDP and for 31 per cent of direct exports. The majority of Kenyans are dependent on agriculture for their income, as much as 80 per cent of the population according to Crawford and Thorbecke (1978). Of these a large majority – 90 per cent – are engaged in smallholder activities, while the remaining 10 per cent comprise a heterogeneous group of pure pastoralists, landless labourers, and large farm owners.

Smallholders are often referred to as subsistence cultivators, their main reason for farming being seen as providing food and other products directly to their families, with occasional surpluses marketed. Such a notion has come under attack, however, and is now rejected as being generally not a useful concept with which to study smallholder cultivation. Kenya is no exception to this. Over the last decade smallholder production contributed 50–55 per cent of gross marketed farm production. But it is not only the increased share of the smallholder in marketed farm production which casts doubt upon the notion of pure subsistence cultivation. As the Integrated Rural Survey carried out in 1974–75 revealed, smallholder production is intrinsically interwoven with other rural activities. Table A5.1 shows, for example, that farm operating surplus contributed on average

Table A5.1. Percentage distribution of household income by source of income and holding size group, Kenya, 1974-75

	Under 0.5 hectares	0.5-0.9 hectares	1.0-1.9 hectares	2.0-2.9 hectares	3.0-3.9 hectares	4.0-4.9 hectares	5.0-7.9 hectares	Over 8.0 hectares	Total
Farm operating surplus	47.08	54.46	50.17	65.88	57.06	70.25	53.10	51.19	56.98
Non-farm operating surplus	12.35	8.76	7.45	3.65	10.58	6.52	14.98	30.60	9.69
Regular employment	21.11	13.55	20.22	11.97	16.22	8.37	18.85	7.99	15.50
Casual employment	7.36	6.24	8.91	8.68	4.66	6.54	5.79	2.33	6.90
Remittances from relatives	9.97	11.00	11.28	7.50	8.22	6.73	5.53	6.20	8.87
Other gifts	2.13	1.99	1.96	2.30	3.26	1.58	1.76	1.69	2.05
Total household income	100.00	100.00	100.00	100.00	100.00	100.00	100.00	100.00	100.00
Total value of household income (K.sh.)	2 908	3 173	3 209	3 558	3 952	3 874	5 008	5 755	3 652

Source. Republic of Kenya, Central Bureau of Statistics: Integrated Rural Survey, 1974-75 (Nairobi).

308

only 57 per cent of total household income, while non-farm operating surplus contributed 10 per cent, wages 22 per cent, and transfers 11 per cent. Although these percentages vary for different farm sizes, non-farm income is an important part of total income for all farm categories, confirming that smallholder cultivators are, to a considerable extent, involved in non-farm activities.

A5.2 Relation between basic needs and agricultural production

Because of the large number of people involved in farming it is important to spell out in more detail how policies aimed at satisfying basic needs could affect the farming population, and especially the smallholders. Others have already studied aspects of basic needs satisfaction, basing their work on information from the various rounds of the Integrated Rural Survey (Thorbecke, 1980). Their results are briefly mentioned here.

The most crucial of the basic needs is nutrition. An index of food poverty provides important insights into the extent of basic needs satisfaction as in Kenya food consumption appears to be positively correlated with other indicators of basic needs satisfaction. Based upon a locally priced diet providing a recommended daily allowance of 2,250 calories per adult equivalent, 25 per cent of the rural population did not meet their food needs, ranging from 18 per cent in Central Province to 48 per cent in Coast. Table A5.2 shows that provincial rankings with respect to food deficiency are generally consistent with the results of nutrition surveys. Indicators for other needs are given in table A5.3, and their rankings are given in table A5.4, which shows some relation between food deficiency and deficiencies in other basic needs items.

What elements should be included in the agricultural section of a basic needs model so as to incorporate direct government intervention as well as indirect economic effects in order to arrive at satisfaction of all basic needs? Figure A5.1 presents some relationships which may provide a guide for this introductory discussion.[1]

In the left-hand corner the core basic needs are indicated (nutrition, health, education, water and housing). The major question is whether the provision of these basic needs and government expenditure on them should be regarded as investment in human capital and thus be assumed to contribute, indirectly, to economic growth.[2] In the figure this is indicated through the effects on labour, productivity and crop mix.

309

Table A5.2. Percentage households below food poverty
line compared to infant malnutrition by
province (rank in parentheses)

Province	% households below food poverty line		% infants below 90 per cent for height-age and weight-height norm		% infants below 90 per cent on either height-age or weight-height norm	
Central	18.3	(1)	2.9	(1)	39.4	(1)
Coast	48.2	(6)	9.4	(6)	53.9	(6)
Eastern	20.0	(3)	6.1	(4)	48.3	(3)
Nyanza	22.1	(4)	4.7	(2)	53.3	(5)
Rift Valley	19.1	(2)	4.8	(3)	51.0	(4)
Western	42.6	(5)	6.2	(5)	42.8	(2)
National average	25.3		5.2		48.7	

Source. Thorbecke (1980).

A major part of increased basic needs satisfaction results
from increased incomes (indicated by the effect of income on
nutrition and ignoring, for the sake of simplicity, effects on
clothing and other needs). Income in the rural areas, and for
most of the farming population, consists of both farm income
and non-farm income (wages and other business income). Farm
income is determined by various factors, some of which, in
order to guide the discussion, are indicated here, such as
land, labour, capital inputs and productivity under the
conditions of crop mix. The most common hypothesis is that
through the increase in human capital, and with (actual or
desired) government inputs and policies farm production and
farm productivity can increase.

The question thus poses itself whether government
expenditure should be used to increase basic needs
satisfaction and thus increase human capital formation, or to
support other factors of production. This question is,
however, based on the assumption that farming activities are
separate from other activities. This appears not to be the
case in Kenya. Collier and Lal (1980) have therefore put
forward the hypothesis that, in the case of education,

Table A5.3. Rural Kenya: Health, education and housing indicators by province

Province	Health		Education		Housing			
	Population per hospital and health centre	Hospital beds and cots per 100,000 population	Primary enrolment as % of 6-12 year cohort	Secondary enrolment as % of 13-16 year cohort	% with concrete floor	% with pit latrine	% with thatched roof	% with corrugated iron roof
Central	10 034	161	100.8	29.4	12	89	32	57
Coast	7 876	181	65.4	16.4	8	23	92	3
Eastern	10 956	117	99.3	18.8	11	56	63	35
Nyanza	12 725	154	68.0	12.7	7	72	82	18
Rift Valley	7 588	144	75.4	11.8	10	33	76	18
Western	22 950	129	89.9	19.2	6	66	85	14
National average	10 437	143.5	81.0	19.1	9	60	69	27

Source. Thorbecke (1980).

PLANNING FOR BASIC NEEDS

Table A5.4. Rural Kenya: Relative scores of nutrition, health, education, housing and composite indicators by province

Province	Nutrition[1]		Health[2]		Education[3]		Housing[4]		Composite[5]	
Central	1.383	(1)	1.08	(3)	1.39	(1)	1.77	(1)	1.42	(1)
Coast	0.524	(6)	1.30	(1)	0.78	(4)	0.53	(6)	0.68	(6)
Eastern	1.265	(3)	0.89	(5)	1.11	(2)	1.12	(2)	1.16	(2)
Nyanza	1.145	(4)	0.95	(4)	0.75	(6)	0.87	(3)	1.00	(4)
Rift Valley	1.325	(2)	1.19	(2)	0.78	(4)	0.81	(4)	1.12	(3)
Western	0.594	(5)	0.67	(6)	1.06	(3)	0.78	(5)	0.71	(5)

[1] The percentage of households below the food poverty line by province as calculated from table A5.2 is expressed as a ratio of the national average.

[2] The same normalisation was performed on the two health indicators in table A5.3 and the arithmetic average of the two is used here.

[3] The same normalisation was applied to the two education indicators in table A5.3 and again the arithmetic average of the two is used here.

[4] The four housing indicators as in table A5.3 were also normalised and their arithmetic average computed.

[5] This composite index was computed as a weighted average of the four basic needs indices using the following weights: nutrition, 0.5; health, 0.15; education, 0.15; housing, 0.2.

Source. Thorbecke (1980).

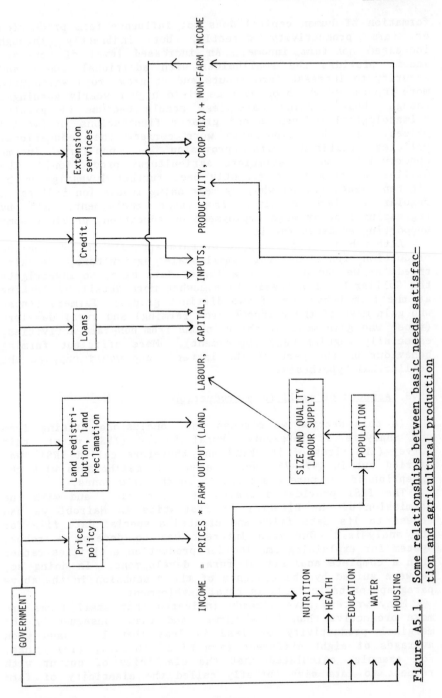

Figure A5.1. Some relationships between basic needs satisfaction and agricultural production

formation of human capital does not influence farm production or farm productivity directly, but indirectly through increased non-farm income. An increased level of non-farm income provides the smallholder with additional funds and security to increase farm inputs and to grow crops which need more inputs and which on average yield higher yearly earnings, though these earnings are less stable because of greater climatological influences and greater fluctuations in (world) prices. If this hypothesis were correct then educational policies combined with provision of non-farm income opportunities would stimulate agricultural production.[3] The Collier-Lal thesis has recently been further investigated by Bigsten (1984, Ch. 6) who, by regressing innovation indices on regular non-farm earnings from wage employment, and by regressing regular wage employment on education, provides some supporting evidence for it.

Although the main purpose of this appendix is to describe production functions for small-scale agriculture, we also tried, as we had access to a larger data base, to investigate the Collier-Lal hypothesis in somewhat more detail by looking at the farm behaviour of two distinct groups: farmers (those who gain most of their income from farming) and rural dwellers (those who gain most of their income from non-farm activities, especially regular wage employment). More efficient farming behaviour on the part of the latter group would support the Collier-Lal hypothesis.

A5.3 Aspects of small farm production

In this section we discuss the conclusions arising from our analysis of Integrated Rural Survey (IRS) data; this survey (the first of its kind and therefore called IRSI) was carried out in 1974-75, and covered all smallholders with the exception of the pure pastoralists in the arid zones.

The IRSI provides a wealth of information, and with the permission of the Director of Statistics in Nairobi we had access to its data files and created a special data file for our analysis.[4] Our main interest was to develop a robust system for explaining smallholder production activities rather than a complete analysis of rural development. In doing so, we were guided by the contents of the discussion in the above paragraph on basic needs in rural development.

Many writers have already indicated that small farms are more productive than large farms, and that consequently the marginal productivity of land is less than 1. Based upon averages of eight different farm sizes, Gunning (1979) has, for example, calculated that the elasticity of output with respect to farm size (briefly called the elasticity of farm size) in the case of crop production varies, according to province, between 0.27 and 0.40. Our own analysis, based upon all recorded inputs, gave the following figures for the elasticity of farm size with respect to various indicators of production (table A5.5).

Table A5.5. Elasticity of farm size

	Household income	Farm operating surplus	Crop production	Livestock production
Elasticity	0.202	0.356	0.372	0.341
R^2	0.047	0.093	0.124	0.053

Source. IRSI data files.

This has consequences, of course, for any policy of land redistribution. In order to gauge such an effect, however, other aspects of production on larger and smaller farms must be taken into account. It was therefore decided to analyse production for three different farm sizes: farms smaller than 1 hectare (group 1), those between 1 and 4 hectares (group 2) and those larger than 4 hectares (group 3). However, as indicated, smallholder activities are interwoven with non-agricultural activities. It is therefore important to single out both farm and non-farm aspects of smallholder activities, particularly in the light of the above discussion on the impact of education on smallholder development. As the major impact of education was said to be (through improved access to wage employment and hence to stable income opportunities) to enable smallholders to engage in more risky farming methods, it was vital to attempt to isolate the impact of wage income.

After experimenting with various indicators we found the most appropriate to be the ratio of farm operating surplus to total household income, with a cut-off point of 0.5. Thus we arrived at a total of six separate groups for which the major indicators are shown in table A5.6. First of these are household size, total household income and its various components, and various farm costs. After that come indicators relating purely to cash crop activities: area of farm devoted

PLANNING FOR BASIC NEEDS

Table A5.6. Farming characteristics for different farm size
groups and for different categories of farmers
(rural dwellers and pure farmers)

Category:	All rural households			
Farm size group:	All	1	2	3
	(1)	(2)	(3)	(4)
Number of farms	1 121 067	356 254	580 712	184 101
Household size	7.28	6.82	7.30	8.094
Total household income (K.sh.)	4 436	3 647	4 336	6 278
Farm operating surplus (K.sh.)	2 886	2 170	2 753	4 689
Non-farm operating surplus (K.sh.)	294	307	237	447
Regular employment income (K.sh.)	577	523	633	502
Casual employment income (K.sh.)	258	212	279	282
Transfers received (K.sh.)	421	434	434	356
Wages to regular labour (K.sh.)	72	70	62	104
Wages to casual labour (K.sh.)	103	56	101	195
Area crops (ha)	1.45	0.49	1.42	3.28
Total area (ha)	2.30	0.55	2.07	6.51
Farm production	3 955	2 894	3 891	6 212
Crop production (K.sh)	2 474	1 725	2 498	3 847
Crop labour, own (K.sh)	1 764	1 365	1 831	2 321
Crop labour, hired (K.sh)	207	94	208	418
Crop input (K.sh)	250	·139	257	439
Livestock production (K.sh)	1 481	1 041	1 169	2 365
Livestock labour, own (K.sh)	1 285	1 175	1 307	1 431
Livestock labour, hired (K.sh)	62	58	51	101
Livestock input (K.sh)	62	32	72	86
Livestock unit (K.sh)	2.4	1.9	2.1	4.0
No. of coffee trees	80	39	99	96
No. of tea trees	279	17	345	572
Volume harvest hybrid maize	227	147	169	562
Education index	0.29	0.24	0.31	0.31
Cash crop index	0.52	0.40	0.54	0.66

<u>Table A5.6</u> (continued)

Category:	Rural dwellers			
Farm size group:	All	1	2	3
	(5)	(6)	(7)	(8)
Number of farms	393 536	145 071	208 530	39 935
Household size	6.84	6.93	6.81	6.65
Total household income (K.sh.)	3 894	3 534	3 843	5 466
Farm operating surplus (K.sh.)	1 053	1 099	1 015	1 083
Non-farm operating surplus (K.sh.)	473	471	324	1 265
Regular employment income (K.sh.)	1 310	967	1 405	2 058
Casual employment income (K.sh.)	362	286	442	223
Transfers received (K.sh.)	695	709	658	835
Wages to regular labour (K.sh.)	106	104	70	304
Wages to casual labour (K.sh.)	127	65	132	328
Area crops (ha)	1.24	0.48	1.30	3.56
Total area (ha)	1.82	0.54	1.92	6.10
Farm production	2 014	1 742	2 057	2 777
Crop production (K.sh)	1 261	1 024	1 354	1 637
Crop labour, own (K.sh)	1 311	1 076	1 462	1 367
Crop labour, hired (K.sh)	243	159	209	726
Crop input (K.sh)	186	137	201	285
Livestock production (K.sh)	752	718	702	1 140
Livestock labour, own (K.sh)	952	905	1 001	862
Livestock labour, hired (K.sh)	93	83	65	277
Livestock input (K.sh)	67	41	84	70
Livestock unit (K.sh)	1.3	1.3	1.1	2.3
No. of coffee trees	57	32	72	68
No. of tea trees	81	17	124	86
Volume harvest hybrid maize	138	129	130	210
Education index	0.36	0.36	0.34	0.43
Cash crop index	0.42	0.37	0.45	0.45

Table A5.6 (continued)

Category:	Farmers			
Farm size group:	All	1	2	3
	(9)	(10)	(11)	(12)
Number of farms	727 531	211 183	372 182	144 166
Household size	7.52	6.75	7.57	8.49
Total household income (K.sh.)	4 729	3 725	4 612	6 503
Farm operating surplus (K.sh.)	3 877	2 905	3 727	5 688
Non-farm operating surplus (K.sh.)	196	194	188	221
Regular employment income (K.sh.)	181	219	201	71
Casual employment income (K.sh.)	202	161	187	299
Transfers received (K.sh.)	273	245	309	224
Wages to regular labour (K.sh.)	53	47	59	48
Wages to casual labour (K.sh.)	89	50	84	158
Area crops (ha)	1.57	0.55	1.5	3.2
Total area (ha)	2.55	0.50	2.1	6.6
Farm production	5 005	3 685	4 919	7 163
Crop production (K.sh)	3 130	2 207	3 139	4 458
Crop labour, own (K.sh)	2 008	1 564	2 038	2 583
Crop labour, hired (K.sh)	190	50	208	333
Crop input (K.sh)	284	141	288	482
Livestock production (K.sh)	1 875	1 477	1 780	2 704
Livestock labour, own (K.sh)	1 466	1 360	1 479	1 588
Livestock labour, hired (K.sh)	45	41	44	53
Livestock input (K.sh)	59	27	65	91
Livestock unit (K.sh)	3.0	2.4	2.7	4.5
No. of coffee trees	92	45	114	105
No. of tea trees	385	17	470	706
Volume harvest hybrid maize	275	160	191	658
Education index	0.25	0.15	0.30	0.28
Cash crop index	0.57	0.43	0.59	0.73

to crops, total farm size, total labour hours per year spent on crops and on livestock, and hired labour hours for the same. The IRSI had some difficulties in valuing changes in livestock, which resulted in some farmers having a large negative income in the year of the survey. In order to avoid distortion by these changes in livestock, all farmers with a negative livestock income have been excluded from the sample. Comparing these with earlier figures which included negative livestock income, we learned that the characteristics of the different groups were not changed by leaving out farmers with negative livestock income.

Looking at farm size, 32 per cent of the farms fall into group 1, 52 per cent into group 2 and 15 per cent into group 3, which indicates a relatively high degree of land inequality (the Gini ratio taken over all groups is 0.46). Of all farms, 35 per cent have a farm operating surplus which is less than 50 per cent of total household income (ratio <0.5), and 65 per cent have a farm operating surplus which represents more than half the household income (henceforth called rural dwellers and farmers, respectively). Looking at household income more specifically, we see that average income for the farmers is considerably higher than for the rural dwellers (columns 9 and 5), although for the rural dwellers on smaller farms income is only 6 per cent lower than that of farmers on the same size holdings.

The structure of incomes also shows an interesting pattern. The major source of income for the rural dwellers is employment income and for farmers farm operating surplus. Regular employment income is for the rural dwellers seven times as high as for the farmers, while farm operating surplus is only 27 per cent compared to that of the farmers; this is accentuated in the case of the largest farm size group, where regular employment income is 29 times higher for the rural dwellers than for the farmers. For the farmers regular employment incomes decrease as farm size increases, while the reverse takes place for the rural dwellers. The farm operating surplus is more or less the same for all groups. The rural dwellers seem to be more linked to the urban areas, given the fact that they receive twice as much in transfers as the farmers, irrespective of farm size.

For our purposes, the most important question is, of course, how effective are the various groups in farming. For that we will look at several indicators. First, we look at total household income and farm operating surplus per hectare (table A5.7).

The fact that smaller farms are more productive per unit of land is clearly demonstrated by these figures. As already indicated, farm operating surplus per hectare is considerably lower for rural dwellers than for farmers. But what is more significant is the fact that income per hectare for all groups of rural dwellers is smaller than for farmers. Thus what rural dwellers lose by abstaining from farming cannot be made up by other incomes.

Table A5.7. Household income and farm operating surplus per hectare (K.sh.)

Farm size	Household income			Farm operating surplus		
	Rural dwellers	Farmers	All	Rural dwellers	Farmers	All
1	6 544	7 450	6 631	2 635	5 810	3 945
2	2 001	2 196	2 095	529	1 775	1 330
3	896	985	964	178	862	720
All	2 140	1 854	1 929	579	1 520	1 255

Source. IRSI data files.

As rural dwellers produce considerably less per hectare they must use land inefficiently compared to farmers. Land inefficiency could be offset by labour efficiency and we look, therefore, at farm operating surplus per man-hour own labour (table A5.8).

The table shows clearly that farmers are far more efficient than rural dwellers. Operating surplus per hour is twice as high for farmers as for rural dwellers; the rural dwellers' inefficiency with land is not offset by a greater efficiency in terms of labour. Although hired labour for both provides only a fraction of total labour (16 per cent for rural dwellers and 9 per cent for farmers), it is interesting to compare the derived wage rates with the operating surplus per hour. All farmers pay their labourers less than their own opportunity costs, which is expected behaviour for a private entrepreneur. Rural dwellers, however, pay more or less the same (except in the case of the first group), indicating that their own labour has about the same opportunity cost as hired labour has. We may conclude that farming by rural dwellers is less efficient.

Table A5.8. Farm operating surplus per hour own labour and wages per hour hired labour (K.sh.)

Farm size	Operating surplus per hour own labour			Wages per hour hired labour		
	Rural dwellers	Farmers	All	Rural dwellers	Farmers	All
1	0.57	1.02	0.84	0.26	0.20	0.23
2	0.52	1.16	0.93	0.63	0.41	0.49
3	0.64	1.78	1.53	0.56	0.38	0.42
All	0.55	1.24	1.00	0.49	0.34	0.40

Source. IRSI data files.

We could further hypothesise that rural dwellers perhaps use more sophisticated techniques, but the evidence is against this too. For all farm size groups the value of purchased inputs is lower for rural dwellers, the number of coffee and tea trees lower, and the cash crop index lower. The volume of hybrid maize and the cattle index is on average (although not uniformly for all farm size groups) lower for rural dwellers than for farmers, despite the fact that the education index (indicating the percentage of household heads with Standard 4 education or higher) is considerably higher for the rural dwellers.

The above evidence thus suggests that for those who earn additional wage income, farming is performed less efficiently and is perhaps regarded as a secondary activity left to those members of the household who are not able to participate in the labour force (as their opportunity costs are lower than the average wage rates).

Our analysis of rural dwellers and farmers might, however, have been influenced by the fact that many landowners do not reside on the plot, but live elsewhere. According to the IRSI file about 20 per cent of owners did not live on their plot (table A5.9).

Total household income for both resident and absentee landowners is about the same for both groups (although household size in cases of absentee ownership is somewhat

Table A5.9. Farming characteristics of absent and non-absent landowners

	All rural households			Rural dwellers		Farmers	
	All	Owner on plot	Owner absent	Owner on plot	Owner absent	Owner on plot	Owner absent
No. of farms	1 121 067	882 950	238 117	267 792	125 744	615 158	112 373
Household size	7.28	7.40	6.81	7.15	6.18	7.51	7.54
Total household income (K.sh.)	4 437	4 444	4 407	3 763	4 173	4 740	4 669
Farm operating surplus (K.sh.)	2 886	3 066	2 217	1 032	1 097	3 951	3 469
Non-farm operating surplus (K.sh.)	294	327	171	642	115	190	233
Regular employment income (K.sh.)	577	456	1 026	1 145	1 660	156	316
Casual employment income (K.sh.)	258	260	251	406	268	196	233
Transfers received (K.sh.)	421	335	742	537	1 032	247	416
Wages to regular labour (K.sh.)	72	65	95	95	129	53	55
Wages to casual labour (K.sh.)	103	96	127	109	167	90	83
Area under crops (ha)	1.45	1.48	1.35	1.20	1.30	1.59	1.4
Total area (ha)	2.30	2.37	2.02	1.81	1.82	2.61	2.25
Farm production (K.sh.)	3 955	4 104	3 405	1 935	2 180	5 047	4 774
Crop production (K.sh.)	2 474	2 564	2 141	1 223	1 342	3 148	3 033
Crop labour, own (K.sh.)	1 764	1 868	1 374	1 378	1 169	2 083	1 602
Crop labour, hired (K.sh.)	207	182	296	203	327	173	261
Crop input (K.sh.)	250	242	279	169	222	273	343
Livestock production (K.sh.)	1 281	1 340	1 264	712	838	1 900	1 741
Livestock labour, own (K.sh.)	1 285	1 348	1 050	960	935	1 518	1 180
Livestock labour, hired (K.sh.)	62	54	91	91	97	38	84
Livestock input (K.sh.)	62	62	59	67	67	61	51
Livestock unit (K.sh.)	2.4	2.6	1.5	1.35	1.11	3.1	2.0
No. of coffee trees	80	83	66	47	78	99	52
No. of tea trees	279	289	236	71	101	385	388
Volume harvest hybrid maize	277	235	193	136	141	279	251
Education index	0.29	0.27	0.35	0.35	0.37	0.24	0.33
Cash crop index	0.52	0.52	0.52	0.38	0.50	0.58	0.56

smaller). Households with absentee owners have a farm operating surplus which is 72 per cent of the farm operating surplus earned by resident owners, and constitutes about 50 per cent of total household income. Family incomes are, however, supplemented by regular employment income and transfers (which are more than double as compared to families with owners residing on the plot). There is also a noticeable difference in the income derived from non-farm operating surplus, which is considerably lower for absentee owners.

Farming characteristics, however, do not seem to differ greatly. The cash crop index is the same; the number of coffee and tea trees and the volume of hybrid maize is lower, but not necessarily so when corrected for area under cultivation.

Differences are more pronounced in the case of rural dwellers. Here absentee ownership (31 per cent of the total) results in higher total household income as a consequence of higher regular employment income and higher transfer receipts, though farm operating surplus is almost identical for both groups. Absentee ownership also results in somewhat more commercial farming activities, with marginally higher returns per man-hour labour used.

A5.4 Farm production functions

We will now take a closer look at the production functions. Table A5.10 gives the elasticities of the various independent variables, together with their level of significance, for the different farming groups. The elasticities are based upon the following multivariate analysis:

$$\ln (FARMOS) = a + b \ln (FARMLAB) + c \ln (FARMAREA)$$

$$+ d \ln (FARMINPUT) + e (EDUC) + f (CASH)$$

where

FARMOS	=	farm operating surplus
FARMLAB	=	farm labour
FARMAREA	=	total area of farm under cultivation
FARMINPUT	=	value of farm inputs used
EDUC	=	education dummy whether received primary education or not
CASH	=	cash crop dummy whether growing hybrid maize, coffee or tea or none of those

What is striking is the difference in results for the rural dwellers and the farmers. The elasticity of operating

Table A5.10. <u>Elasticity of operating surplus with respect to factors of farm production by farm size and farm category</u> (specification without and with dummies, respectively)

Farm size group	Elasticity of labour	Elasticity of land	Elasticity of farm inputs	Coefficient education dummy	Coefficient cash crop dummy	$\bar{R}^2$ adj
<u>All</u>	0.78^1	0.06^2	0.21^1	–	–	0.38
	0.75^1	0.08^1	0.18^2	-0.01	0.23	0.38
1	0.94^1	0.02	0.13^1	–	–	0.39
	0.91^1	0.02	0.12	-0.14	0.13	0.40
2	0.67^1	0.05	0.24^1	–	–	0.29
	0.65^1	0.08^3	0.21^1	0.04	0.18^3	0.30
3	0.65^1	0.03	0.20^1	–	–	0.29
	0.60^1	0.08^2	0.14^1	0.02	0.40^1	0.31
<u>Rural dwellers</u>						
All	0.49^1	0.10^2	0.21^1	–	–	0.28
	0.47^1	0.13^2	0.18^1	0.28^2	0.14	0.29
1	0.56^1	0.06	0.24^1	–	–	0.38
	0.54^1	0.07	0.22^1	0.16	0.16	0.38
2	0.26	0.17^3	0.21^1	–	–	0.14
	0.26	0.17^3	0.16^2	0.35^2	0.06	0.15
3	0.97^1	0.05	0.16^2	–	–	0.34
	0.92^1	0.19	0.06	0.55^2	0.63^2	0.46
<u>Farmers</u>						
All	0.65^1	0.05^2	0.19^1	–	–	0.39
	0.64^1	0.05^2	0.17^1	0.12^2	0.07	0.39
1	0.81^1	0.04	0.11^1	–	–	0.32
	0.80^1	0.04	0.11^1	0.24	-0.10	0.32
2	0.60^1	0.03	0.23^1	–	–	0.39
	0.60	0.04	0.20	0.19^2	0.10	0.40
3	0.49^1	0.05	0.18^1	–	–	0.29
	0.47^1	0.06	0.17^1	-0.02	0.14	0.29

[1] Significant at 0.01 per cent level.

[2] Significant at 0.05 per cent level.

[3] Significant at 0.10 per cent level.

surplus with respect to labour input, for example, is larger
for farmers than for rural dwellers, namely 0.64 compared to
0.47 (col. 1), which implies that farmers can substantially
increase their crop production if they allocate additional
labour.

Labour apart, the other inputs in the production functions
are land and farm inputs.[5] How do the three farm inputs
contribute to total farm output (measured by farm operating
surplus)? For the rural dwellers the scale factor is 0.80
(0.49 + 0.10 + 0.21). For farmers the scale factor is higher,
0.89 (0.65 + 0.05 + 0.19), indicating for both groups a
decreasing return to scale. Taking all groups together the
scale factor is actually somewhat greater than 1:
1.05 (0.78 + 0.06 + 0.21).[6]

The elasticity with respect to land use is in all cases
much smaller than that of labour; at a disaggregated level it
is in some cases hardly significant.[7]

Regarding farm inputs, the elasticities are higher for
rural dwellers than for farmers for farm size 1 and more or
less equal for farms sizes 2 and 3.

Of interest for the present work is the coefficient of the
education dummy.[8] Unfortunately, in most disaggregated
cases the effect of the education dummy turned out to be weak
or not at all significant. Both for all rural dwellers and
all farmers the coefficient is significant; it is higher (but
not much higher) for rural dwellers than for farmers. In the
case of farmers, education would add 0.12 to 7.90 of the
operating surplus (expressed in logarithms), which is equal to
2 per cent. In the case of rural dwellers, education would
add 0.28 to 6.44 or 4.5 per cent. Hence, education can be
seen to have some impact on farm operating surplus, but a
rather limited one. More research into the complex
relationships between education and farm operating surplus has
yet to be undertaken, as discussed in the introduction to this
appendix.

It is also interesting to note that for rural dwellers the
education coefficient increases with farm size, while for
farmers it decreases.

The coefficient of cash crop production turned out to be
significant in only a few cases. It is higher for rural
dwellers than for farmers. For the rural dweller, growing
cash crops will increase crop production by 10 per cent (0.64
contributing to 6.63), while for the farmer cash crops would
add 5.5 per cent (0.40 contributing to 7.51). For the
different farm sizes the coefficients have, both for rural
dwellers and for farmers, an inverted U-shaped behaviour. The
coefficient is lower for the middle group of farms as compared
to the smaller and the larger groups.

A5.5 Indirect effects on production

Finally we look at some possible determinants of what we have labelled indicators of innovation. We look in particular at purchased inputs, the presence of coffee trees and improved cattlestock, and the area planted with hybrid maize, and see how these are affected by the level of education of the household head, by regular wage employment income, and by the amount of transfers received, both for rural dwellers and for farmers. The results are given in table A5.11, which was based upon the following equation:

$$X = a + b \ EDUC + c \ REGWAGE + d \ TRANS$$

where

X	=	PURCHIN or COFFEE or IMPCAT or HYBRID
PURCHIN	=	purchased inputs
COFFEE	=	number of coffee trees
IMPCAT	=	number of improved cattle (weighted)
HYBRID	=	area with hybrid maize
EDUC	=	dummy variable indicating primary education received or not
REGWAGE	=	farm income from regular wage
TRANS	=	transfer received

The influence of education seems to be greater for farmers than for rural dwellers in the case of purchased inputs, improved cattle and the volume of hybrid maize, while the influence was statistically insignificant in the case of coffee trees. This confirms our earlier stated hypothesis that rural dwellers do not benefit more from educational achievement, as far as their farming activities are concerned, than pure farmers.

Surprisingly, too, the income from wage employment does not seem to affect the various indicators any more for rural dwellers than for farmers. The effects of purchased inputs, of coffee trees and of improved livestock all appear to be less, while the effect on hybrid maize cannot be statistically satisfactorily determined. These results again confirm our earlier observations, namely that, on average, regular employment does not enhance more efficient and more modern farming methods.

One might amend this hypothesis if transfers received by the household proved to have a significant influence, as these could be regarded as a source of more stable income, which would make it possible to undertake more risky farming activities. However, almost all the regression coefficients in this case are statistically insignificant.

Table A5.11. Regression coefficients of education, regular
wage employment and transfers received related
to various indicators for innovative activities

	All farmers	Rural dwellers	Farmers
Education			
Purchased inputs	190	141	215
Coffee trees	n.s.	n.s.	n.s.
Improved cattle	0.531	n.s.	0.928
Area with hybrid maize	334	267	400
Regular wage employment			
Purchased inputs	0.054	0.051	0.172
Coffee trees	0.014	0.019	n.s.
Improved cattle	0.0002	0.0002	0.0003
Area with hybrid maize	n.s.	0.038	n.s.
Transfers received			
Purchased inputs	n.s.	n.s.	n.s.
Coffee trees	n.s.	n.s.	0.038
Improved cattle	n.s.	n.s.	−0.0005
Area with hybrid maize	−0.086	n.s.	n.s.

n.s. = not significant at 0.10 level.

Unlike Bigsten (1984, Ch. 6), we have consequently been
unable, by using the data base in a different way, to provide
additional evidence for the Collier-Lal hypothesis: this we
had hoped to do as a "by-product" of studying production
behaviour in the small-scale agricultural sector. Clearly
more refined and detailed analysis is called for.

A5.6 Determination of the coefficients
for agricultural production functions

For modelling purposes the above relations had to be
adopted, and we have re-estimated the production functions for
small-scale agriculture according to the following formula:

$$\ln \frac{VAS}{SIZE} = a + b \ln \frac{LAB}{SIZE} + c \ln \frac{CAP}{SIZE} + d \ EDUC$$

where

VAS = farm operating surplus
LAB = labour used (hired and own)
CAP = capital
SIZE = farm size
EDUC = dummy variable indicating whether primary education received or not

The results of the regression are reported in table A5.12.

Table A5.12. Regression results production functions for small-scale agriculture

Farm group	b	c	d	$\bar{R}^2$ adj	n
1	0.976^x (0.060)	0.060^z (0.039)	-0.026 (0.120)	0.502	340
2	0.748^x (0.068)	0.147^x (0.034)	0.168^y (0.983)	0.265	545
3	0.849^x (0.090)	0.047 (0.039)	0.194^y (0.111)	0.286	284
2+3 combined	0.701^x (0.047)	0.104^x (0.026)	0.196^x (0.074)	0.313	829

x = significant at 0.01 level.
y = significant at 0.10 level.
z = significant at 0.15 level.
Figures in brackets are standard errors.

For farm group 1 we obtained a significant coefficient for labour, but a result of little significance for capital and an inconclusive result for education. For group 2 the coefficients for both labour and capital are significant, while that for education is of little significance. For farm group 3 the capital coefficient is insignificant, that for labour is again significant, and that for education of slight significance. These results led us to combine farm groups 2 and 3, which gave better results. All coefficients are in this case highly significant, with a lower coefficient for labour and a higher coefficient for capital compared to farm group 1.

For modelling purposes the regression results for farm group 1 and for the combined farm groups 2 and 3 have been retained, with the exception of the coefficient of education for farm group 1, which has been put at 0.05 rather than being excluded from the equation.

Information on large-scale farms is more difficult to come by. Rather than using a cross-section analysis, we have applied a time series analysis from 1970 to 1979 in order to obtain the coefficients of the production function for large-scale agriculture. After some experiments we obtained the following regression:

$$\ln \frac{\text{INCOME}}{\text{LAND}} = a + \underset{(0.0713)}{0.4726} \ln \frac{\text{CAPITAL}}{\text{LAND}}$$

$$+ \underset{(0.1739)}{0.4988} \ln \frac{\text{LABOUR}}{\text{LAND}} + \underset{(0.0055)}{0.0109} \text{TIME}$$

where

$\bar{R}^2$ adj = 0.934
figures in brackets are standard errors.

Information for these variables could be obtained from various issues of the <u>Statistical Abstract</u> for the nine-year period 1970-78, where income was defined as farm output minus farm inputs, and where all variables were brought back to 1976 prices by using the deflator for agricultural outputs and inputs.

Notes

[1] This figure is only intended to illustrate the discussion. It does not provide a full description, and some of the relations are not even well defined, such as the difference between factor productivity and non-factor productivity.

[2] As argued elsewhere, linkages also exist between the satisfaction of various basic needs, that is to say satisfaction of one can reinforce satisfaction of another; the total cost can thus be less than the sum of the individual costs. Moreover, as Ghai (1980) has

argued, the Government can more effectively provide basic needs through so-called "basic needs activities". Although important, we ignore this aspect in the discussion for the moment.

[3] The hypothesis implies, of course, certain conditions such as continuous involvement of the rural wage labour force and the rural out-migrants with their original agricultural background and the absence of increased land concentration in the hands of those who have used their non-farm incomes more efficiently.

[4] Thanks are due to Jan Vandemoortele and Eric Zbinden for constructing the data file.

[5] Cattle stock as an explanatory variable invariably gave insignificant coefficients and was therefore excluded from the final analysis.

[6] Another explanation could be that important factors of production have been left out. This does not seem to be the case, however, in this exercise.

[7] This is, of course, partly explained by the fact that the disaggregation was based upon farm sizes.

[8] Earlier attempts to integrate the education variable into the production relations were less successful. At an earlier stage in developing the data base for the Kenya basic needs model, also using the IRS data base, we applied dummy variables relating to three different levels of educational achievement on the part of the head of the household (no schooling, Standard 4 and Form 2). The idea was to detect significance both in the constant term and in the coefficient of regression of household income, farm operating surplus and non-farm operating surplus income from regular employment on farm size, all by adult equivalent. Similar regressions were made with dummy variables indicating distances to health care centres and to marketplaces.

In practically all cases the dummy variables turned out to be insignificant which led us to abandon this way of investigating the effects of educational achievement on farm production.

Appendix 6 Calculation of unit costs of basic needs

For education, the current costs per student are obtained by dividing current expenditure in 1976 on primary and secondary education by the respective enrolment figures for 1976 (Republic of Kenya, CBS, Economic Survey, 1978). Calculation of the capital cost is less straightforward, and the following procedure has been applied following techniques developed by Meerman (1979) and Ritzen and Balderston (1975). For the period 1970–80 the yearly enrolment in primary and secondary education is regressed on the cumulative value of net investments in education, in constant 1976 prices (with a depreciation rate of 5 per cent). The slope coefficient represents the estimated value of the capital–output ratio, so that the inverse is the capital cost of one student year enrolment in primary and secondary education. According to the following formula:

$$X_{t+10} = a + b \left[\sum_{t=1}^{10} I_t (1-d)^{10-t} \right] \tag{A6.1}$$

where

X_t = enrolment rate in year t
I_t = investment in year t

For primary education we found b = 1.62 with a standard error of 0.37 and a R^2 (unadjusted) of 0.70. For secondary education we found b = 0.005 with a standard error of 0.001

331

and a R^2 (unadjusted) of 0.87.

It would be wrong, however, to allocate the capital cost to only one student year. In effect, we have to take into account the fact that capital invested will serve many student years. But in order to keep capital to maintain one student year fully effective, replacement investment has to take place. To calculate the yearly capital cost we took the average life of capital (n) as 20 years and annual replacement investment (d) as 5 per cent of the value of the capital. Hence the yearly capital costs (R) amount to:

$$R = C \frac{(1 + d)^n}{n} \qquad [A6.2]$$

For d = 0.5 and for n = 20 this gives a factor of 0.145.

This comes very close to the heuristic figure of 15 per cent Meerman (1979) used to attribute capital costs in his analysis for Malaysia. Capital cost for primary education turned out to be K.£0.09 and for secondary education K.£29.0.

For calculation of health costs we have first to determine how much should be allocated to in-patient and how much to out-patient services. Such a breakdown is unfortunately not available, so we decided to equate in-patient expenditure with expenditure on curative health, while expenditure on out-patients is then determined as a residual. The number of in-patient days in hospital amounted to 1,779,700. Relating this to current expenditure on curative care, the average cost of one in-patient day could be determined, which amounted to K.£11.90.

Since we do not have long-term series on the number of in-patients, the method used to calculate capital costs for the education sector could not be used. We therefore assumed a constant ratio between capital expenditure and in-patient recurrent expenditure. For the years 1975-80 this gave a ratio of 0.759, implying a capital cost of K.£8.60 for one in-patient day. With 0.13 patient days per capita per person, current expenditure on curative health amounted to K.£1.55 and investment expenditure to K.£1.12 per capita.

As far as out-patients are concerned, medical statistics report an average number of 2.04 out-patient visits per person per year. Relating this to recurrent costs one arrives at a unit cost of K.£0.26. For calculating capital costs of out-patient visits the same method was used as for in-patient care. The ratio of capital costs to recurrent costs was found to be 0.591 and consequently the unit capital cost K.£0.18.

With 2.04 out-patient visits per person per year and 0.13 in-patient days, the total per capita recurrent and capital health costs amount to K.£2.08 and K.£1.48 respectively. The annual capital cost figure for health services was derived by attributing 15 per cent per year of the capital cost according to the method explained above.

The fourth basic needs category is water. Water supply schemes, according to the Integrated Rural Survey and estimates of the Ministry of Water Development, covered 10 per cent of the population in rural areas and 100 per cent in urban areas. Relating these coverage percentages to recurrent expenditure, we arrive at per capita recurrent costs of K.£1.37 in rural areas and K.£1.87 in urban areas. For capital costs the same assumption was made as for health costs, with a factor (capital cost to recurrent cost) of 0.30 for rural areas, and 0.25 for urban areas. Taking the national average the figures are K.£1.45 for recurrent costs and K.£0.45 for capital costs. Of the latter figure, again 15 per cent is attributed to reflect yearly expenditures.

Table A6.1. Unit cost of basic needs (K.£ per person)

	Recurrent costs	Investment costs
Primary education	16.00	0.10
Secondary education	84.00	29.00
Health	2.08	0.22
Water	1.45	0.07

List of variables used

The number in square brackets indicates the number of the formula in the text where the variable is defined; ex indicates an exogenous variable, the number indicating the first formula where the exogenous variable occurs or is defined.

Subscripts

g	= 1,...,8	socio-economic groups
h	= 1,...,4	categories of basic needs
i	= 1,...,14	economic sectors
j	= 1,...,14	economic sectors
k	= 1,...,66	age
s	= 1,2	gender (1 = female; 2 = male)
t	= 1,...,25	model year

AGLABS	agricultural skilled labour supply [105]
AGLABU	agricultural unskilled labour supply [106]
a_{ij}	element of matrix of domestic intermediate inputs [ex A3.1]
am_{ij}	element of matrix of imported intermediate inputs [ex A3.2]
ARRU(s,k)	gender and age-specific rural labour force participation rate [77] [79]
ARUB(s,k)	gender and age-specific urban labour force participation rate [78] [80]

[B]	matrix distributing government expenditure on basic needs h to group g [7]
BINT	domestic public borrowing [143]
BRR	behavioural estimate of fertility in rural areas [45]
BRU	behavioural estimate of fertility in urban areas [47]
[C]	consumption matrix mapping consumption by group in consumption by sector [ex 261]
CBR	crude birth rate, rural areas [49]
CBU	crude birth rate, urban areas [50]
$COMP_i$	compensation for employers in sector i [243]
$COV(g,h)$	number of elements of basic needs category h provided to group g [14]
$COVPER(g,h)$	percentage of relevant population in group g covered by basic needs category h [15]
$COVPERRU(h)$	rural enrolment rate by education type [16]
$COVPERUB(h)$	urban enrolment rate by education type [17]
$CR1R(k)$	completion rate for primary education of person aged k, rural areas [18]
$CR1U(k)$	completion rate for primary education of person aged k, urban areas [20]
$CR2R(k)$	completion rate for secondary education of person aged k, rural areas [20]
$CR2U(k)$	completion rate for secondary education of person aged k, urban areas [22]
D_i	depreciation of capital in sector i [114]
DEBT	total debt [217]
$DIPR_g$	distributed profits received by socio-economic group g [256]
$DISP_g$	disposable income of socio-economic group g [257]
EAP_g	economically active population in group g [224]-[231]
EDUCU	population in urban areas aged 15-65 with education higher than Standard 7 [41]
EDUCR	population in rural areas aged 15-65 with education higher than Standard 7 [40]
ED2R	proportion of rural persons aged 15 and above with education higher than Standard 5 but lower than Form 4 [34]
ED3R	proportion of rural persons aged 15 and above with education higher than Form 4 [35]
EDW2R	proportion of rural women aged 15-49 with education higher than Standard 5 but lower than Form 4 [36]
EDW2U	proportion of urban women aged 15-49 with education higher than Standard 5 but lower than Form 4 [37]

EDW3R	proportion of rural women aged 15–49 with education higher than Form 4 [38]
EDW3U	proportion of urban women aged 15–49 with education higher than Form 4 [39]
EG_i	growth factor of exports in sector i [ex 151], [ex 152]
EMP_i	number of employers/professionals in sector i [223]
ENROLR(s,k)	gender and age-specific enrolment rate in rural areas [26]–[29]
ENROLU(s,k)	gender and age-specific enrolment rate in urban areas [30]–[33]
$ERGR_g$	average wage economically active person in socio-economic group g [262]
EXP_i^*	adjusted exports in sector i [162] [164] [169]
EXP_i	export in sector i [151] [152]
$EXPRFSAV_i$	expected retained profits in sector i [193]
$EXSUP_i$	index of excess supply [173]
$FACABR_i$	factor income paid abroad by sector [218]
FD_i	final demand for product i [128]
FEPR	share of females in primary school enrolment in rural areas [ex 26]
FEPU	share of females in primary school enrolment in urban areas [ex 30]
FESR	share of females in secondary school enrolment in rural areas [ex 27]
FESU	share of females in secondary school enrolment in urban areas [ex 31]
FLEOR	female life expectancy at birth in rural areas [54]
FLEOU	female life expectancy at birth in urban areas [55]
FLPRU	female labour force participation rate in rural areas [70]
FLPUB	female labour force participation rate in urban areas [69]
FORCAP	foreign capital [215]
GAP	foreign exchange gap [212]
GC_i	government consumption of product i [135]
GCBN(g,h)	recurrent expenditure on basic needs category h benefiting group g [5]
GI_i	government investment demand for product i [136]
GIBN(g,h)	capital expenditure on basic needs category h benefiting group g [6]
HFR	binary variable indicating sufficient access to health services in rural areas [53]
HFU	binary variable indicating sufficient access to health services in urban areas [52]

337

I_i	gross investment in sector i [198]
IB_i	investment financed outside retained savings by sector i [190] [192]
$IEXA_i$	intended investment in sector i [186]
IG_i	government investment in sector i [199]
INC_g	expected household income of socio-economic group g [130]
INV_i	private investment demand for product i [128]
INVFUND	expected investible fund [194]
K_i	capital stock, sector i [112]
L_j	total labour employed in sector i [178]
$LANDS_j$	area available for small-scale agriculture, sector j (j=1,...,3) [117]
LANDL	area available for large-scale agriculture [115]
LDS_j	skilled labour demand in sector j [107]
LDU_j	unskilled labour demand in sector j [111]
LIC_i	wage share in sector i [236]
LS_j	skilled labour employed in sector i [180]
LSSRU	skilled labour supply, rural [96]
LSSUB	skilled labour supply, urban [98]
LSURU	unskilled labour supply, rural [95]
LSUUB	unskilled labour supply, urban [97]
LU_j	unskilled labour employed in sector i [180]
M_i^1	import of consumer goods in sector i [145]
M_i^2	import of capital goods in sector i [146]
M_{3i}	imported intermediate goods in sector i [147]
$m_{i,g}^1$	element of matrix of imported consumer goods by socio-economic group [ex 145]
MIG	behavioural estimate of rural-urban migration [57]
MIGR	male rural-urban migrants aged between 20-59 as a proportion of the rural population [66]
MOLABS	non-agricultural skilled labour supply [103]
MOLABU	non-agricultural unskilled labour supply [104]
MPTA	adjusted imports [213]
NIV_j	net investment in sector i [113]
PC_i	private consumption of product i [129]
PC_{ig}	private consumption of product i by socio-economic group g [129]
PCBN(g,h)	private expenditure of socio-economic group g on basic needs item h [8]-[11]
$POPAE_g$	adult equivalent population in socio-economic group g [265]

338

POPGR$_g$	population belonging to socio-economic group g [232] [233]
PRODIS$_i$	distributed profits in sector i [245]
PROFIT$_i$	profits in sector i [244]
PROFSAV$_i$	retained profits in sector i [246]
Q$_i$	domestic supply before convergency [156]
RBORN	number of rural births [82]
RDPR	rural dependency ratio [102]
REP	investment and debt repayment [211]
RP2(s,k)	gender and age-specific rural population [82] [83] [87] [89]
RPOP	total rural population [91]
RPOPS(s,k)	gender and age-specific rural population not in school [75]
RUM	rural-urban migration as percentage of rural population [59]
RUMS(s,k)	age- and sex-specific rural-urban migration rate [62]
SAGR$_g$	household savings socio-economic group g [260]
SAVGAP	savings gap [185]
SERVICE	percentage of urban workers employed in modern services [71]
SERVWAGE	average wage in services [72]
SKCFR	skill coefficient, rural [94]
SKCFU	skill coefficient, urban [93]
SR(s,k)	gender and age-specific rural survival probability [54]
SR3R	proportion of births surviving to age three in rural areas [53]
SR3U	proportion of births surviving to age three in urban areas [52]
STERILE	proportion of married women without any birth [46]
STOCK2(k)	number of males of age k in urban areas who are immigrants [65]
STOCKW2(k)	number of females of age k in urban areas who are immigrants [63]
SU(s,k)	gender and age-specific urban survival probabability [55]
t$_j$	technical progress in sector j [ex 123] [ex 124]
TD$_g$	direct income taxes, socio-economic group g [138]
TDI$_i$	profit taxes, sector i [139]
TEXP$_i$	export taxes, sector i [142]
TIMP$_i$	import taxes, sector i [141]
TIND$_i$	indirect taxes, sector i [140]
TRANF$_g$	household transfers given or received by socio-economic group g [258] [259]
UBORN	urban birth [84]

UDPR	urban dependency ratio [102]
UNC(h)	unit cost of recurrent expenditure for basic needs category h [ex 14]
UNEMP	average unemployment rate in urban areas [183] [184]
UNI(h)	unit cost of recurrent expenditure for basic needs category h [ex 14]
UP2(s,k)	gender and age-specific urban population [85] [86] [88] [90]
UPOPS(s,k)	gender and age-specific urban population not in school [76]
UPOP	total urban population [92]
USAG	unemployment, skilled labour, agricultural sector [181]
USMO	unemployment, skilled labour, non-agricultural sector [183]
UUAG	unemployment, unskilled labour, agricultural sector [182]
UUMO	unemployment, unskilled labour, non-agricultural sector [184]
VA_i	value added, sector i [171]
VAC_j	value added coefficient, sector j [126]
VAL_2	value added per hectare in large-scale agriculture [123]
VAS_i	supply of value added in sector i [118] [122] [124]
$VASA_i$	value added, small-scale farming, sector i after convergency [172]
$VASS_i$	supply of value added per hectare in small-scale agriculture, sector i [119]
W_i	wage bill in sector i [237]
$WAGEGR_g$	labour income received by socio-economic group g [247]-[254]
WMIGR	proportion of urban women aged 15-49 who are immigrants [65]
$WORKU_i$	number of unskilled employees in sector i [220]
$WORKUIN_i$	number of informal sector workers in sector i [221]
$WORKS_i$	number of skilled employees in sector i [222]
ws_j	wages of skilled workers in sector i [239]
wu_j	wages of unskilled workers in sector i [240]
wun_i	wages on income from informal sector worksrs [241]
XS_j	supply of gross output, sector j [127]
Y_g	total income socio-economic group g [255]
YAPAE	household income per adult equivalent in rural areas [263]

YNAPAE   average household income per adult equivalent in urban areas [264]

Z_i domestic final demand before convergency [156]

Bibliography

Adelman, I. 1978. Redistribution before growth: A strategy for developing countries. The Hague, Martinus Nijhof.

———. 1984. "Beyond export-led growth", in World Development, Sep., Vol. 12, No. 9.

Adelman, I.; Taft Morris, C. 1973. Economic growth and social equity in developing countries. Stanford Press.

Ahluwalia, M.S.; Chenery, H. 1974. "The economic framework", in H. Chenery et al.: Redistribution with growth. Oxford University Press.

Ainwick, D. 1979. "An estimate of the minimum cost of a nutritionally adequate and culturally acceptable diet for urban Kenyans", M.Sc thesis. Nairobi; Dec.

———. 1980. "The weight, length and mid upper arm circumference of Kenyan children in Nairobi nursery schools", in Social Statistics Bulletin (Paris, UNESCO), Vol. 3, No. 1.

Aitchison, J.; Brown, J.A.C. 1957. The log-normal distribution. Cambridge, Cambridge University Press.

Alagh, Y., et al. 1984. "Policy modelling for planning in India", in Cohen (1984).

Alfthan, T. 1979. Basic needs satisfaction in ILO member States: Presentation and analysis of national responses to a world enquiry. Geneva, ILO; mimeographed World Employment Programme research working paper; restricted.

Allen, R.M. 1980. "Discussion of social accounting matrix with reference to Kenya", in Statistical News, May, No. 49.

Anker, R.; Knowles, J.C. 1978. A micro-analysis of female labour force participation in Kenya. Geneva, ILO; mimeographed World Employment Programme research working paper; restricted.

---; ---. 1980. "An empirical analysis of mortality differentials in Kenya at the macro and micro levels", in Economic Development and Cultural Change (Chicago), Vol. 29, No. 1.

---; ---. 1982. Determinants of fertility in developing countries: A case study of Kenya. Liège, Ordina.

---; ---. 1983. Population growth, employment and economic-demographic interactions in Kenya: Bachue-Kenya. Aldershot, Gower.

Arellano, J. 1985. "Meeting basic needs: The trade-off between the quality and coverage of the programme", in Journal of Development Economics, May-June, Vol. 18, No. 1.

van Arkedie, B. 1978. "Framework for an analysis of economic structure in Kenya, Sri Lanka and Colombia", paper presented to the Workshop on Organization of Production, Problems of Payment, Income Distribution and Employment, The Hague, ISS, 13-15 July.

Aseto, O. 1977. Capital growth and development policy: The Kenyan experience, Working Paper No. 311. University of Nairobi.

Baji, C. 1975. The Minimum-Needs Programme: A study on social development policy. New Delhi, Centre for Policy Research.

Balassa, B. 1982. "Disequilibrium analysis in developing economies: An overview", in World Development, Nov.-Dec., Vol. 10, Nos. 11-12; special issue on analysing disequilibrium in developing countries.

Barro, R.J.; Grossmann, H.J. 1976. Money, employment and inflation. Cambridge, Cambridge University Press.

Benassy, J.P. 1982. The economics of market disequilibrium. New York, Academic Press.

Berg, A. n.d. "Nutrition, basic needs and growth" (Washington, DC, IBRD; mimeo), as cited by Lewis (1981).

Bhalla, A.S. 1975. Technology and employment in industry: A case study approach. Geneva, ILO.

Bigsten, A. 1977. Regional inequality in Kenya, Working Paper No. 330. University of Nairobi.

———. 1980. Regional inequality and development: A case study of Kenya. Aldershot, Gower.

———. 1981a. The Kenyan labour market: Institutions and policy. Gothenberg, University of Gothenburg, Department of Economics.

———. 1981b. The social accounting matrix and income distribution analysis in Kenya. University of Gothenburg, Department of Economics; Oct.; mimeo.

———. 1983. Income distribution and development theory: Evidence and policy. London, Heinemann Educational Books.

———. 1984. Education and income distribution in Kenya. Aldershot, Gower.

Bigsten, A.; Collier, P. 1980. Education, employment and wages in Kenya, Working Paper No. 366. University of Nairobi.

Blitzer, C., et al. (eds.). 1975. Economy-wide models and development planning. New York, Oxford University Press.

Branson, W.H. 1983. "Economic structure and policy for external balance", in IMF Staff Papers (Washington, DC), Mar., Vol. 30, No. 1.

Casley, D.J.; Marchant, D. 1979. "Smallholder marketing in Kenya", Marketing Development Project.

Chenery, H., et al. 1974. Redistribution with growth. Oxford. Oxford University Press.

Chibber, A.J.; Shah, M.M. 1983. An agricultural policy model for Kenya, Working Paper 83-8. Laxenburg, International Institute for Applied Systems Analysis.

Cliffe, L. 1975. "Underdevelopment or socialism? A comparative analysis of Kenya and Tanzania", in R. Harris (ed.): The political economy of Africa. London, Schenhann Publishing Company.

Cohen, S., et al. 1984. The modelling of socio-economic planning processes. Aldershot, Gower.

Cole, S.; Miles, J. 1984. Worlds apart: Technology and North-South relations in the global future. Brighton, Wheatsheaf Books.

Collier, P.; Bigsten, A. 1981. "A model of educational expansion and labour market adjustment applied to Kenya", in Oxford Bulletin of Economics and Statistics, Vol. 43.

Collier, P.; Lal, D. 1980. Poverty and growth in Kenya, IBRD Staff Working Paper No. 389. Washington, DC, May.

---; ---. 1984. "Why poor people get rich: Kenya, 1969-79", in World Development, Oct., Vol. 12, No. 10.

Collier, V.C.; Rempel, H. 1977. "The divergence of private from social costs in rural-urban migration: A case study of Nairobi, Kenya", in Journal of Development Studies, Vol. 13, No. 3.

Correa, H. 1970. "Sources of economic growth in Latin America", in Southern Economic Journal, July, Vol. 37, No. 1.

Cramer, J.S. 1969. Empirical econometrics. Amsterdam, North Holland Publishing Company.

Crawford, E.; Thorbecke, E. 1978. Employment, income distribution, poverty alleviation and basic needs in Kenya, Report of an ILO Consulting Mission. Ithaca, Cornell University.

---; ---. 1979. "The analysis of food poverty: An illustration from Kenya"; mimeo.

---; ---. 1980. "The analysis of food poverty: An illustration from Kenya", in Pakistan Development Review, Vol. 19, No. 4.

Cuddington, J.T., et al. 1984. Disequilibrium macro-economics in open economies. London, Blackwell.

David, M. 1976. "Allocation by peasant farmers under constrained access to cash and markets. Marketing of food crops and purchase of industrial commodities by Nyanza smallholders, 1970-1971", University of Wisconsin-Madison, SSRI Workshop Series 7615, Sep.

Dervis, K., et al. 1982. General equilibrium models for development policy. Cambridge, Cambridge University Press.

Dick, H., et al. 1983. "The short-run impact of fluctuating primary commodity prices on three developing economies: Colombia, Ivory Coast and Kenya", in World Development, May, Vol. 11, No. 5, pp. 405-416.

Dorfman, R., et al. 1958. Linear programming and economic analysis. New York, McGraw Hill.

Elkan, W. 1976. "Is a proletariat emerging in Nairobi?", in Economic Development and Cultural Change, Vol. 24, No. 4.

Emmerij, L. 1978. "Facts and fallacies concerning the basic needs approach", in Carnets de l'Enfance, Vol. 41.

Fei, J.; Ranis, G. 1964. Development of the labor surplus economy. New Haven, Connecticut, Yale University Press.

---; ---. 1966. "Agrarianism, dualism and economic development", in I. Adelman and E. Thorbecke (eds): The theory and design of economic development. Baltimore, Johns Hopkins University Press.

Fields, G. 1980. Poverty, inequality and development. Cambridge, Cambridge University Press.

Fox, K., et al. 1966. The theory of quantitative economic policy with applications to economic growth and stabilisation. Amsterdam, North Holland Publishing Company.

Frohberg, H.; Shah, M.M. 1980. Food consumption pattern - Rural and urban Kenya, Working Paper WP-80-10. Laxenburg, International Institute for Applied Systems Analysis.

---; ---. 1980. Nutrition status - Rural and urban Kenya, Working Paper WP-80-14. Laxenburg, International Institute for Applied Systems Analysis.

Galenson, W.; Pyatt, G. 1964. The quality of labour and economic development in certain countries. Geneva, ILO.

Ghai, D. 1978. "Basic needs and its critics", in IDS Bulletin

(Brighton, Institute of Development Studies), June, Vol. 9.

Ghai, D. 1980. "Basic needs: From words to action", in International Labour Review (Geneva, ILO), Vol. 119, No. 3.

Ghai, D., et al. 1979. Essays on employment in Kenya. Nairobi, Kenya Literature Bureau.

---. 1979. Planning for basic needs in Kenya (performance, policies and prospects). Geneva, ILO.

Ghose, A.K. 1987. Agriculture-industry terms of trade and distributive shares in a developing economy. Geneva, ILO; mimeographed World Employment Programme research working paper; restricted.

van Ginneken, W.; van der Hoeven, R. 1979. "Vervullen van Basisbehoeften", in Economisch en Statistische Berichten (Rotterdam), pp. 184–191.

Godfrey, M. 1977. "Education, training and productivity: A Kenyan case study", in Comparative Education Review, Vol. 21, No. 1.

Government of India. 1972. 28th Meeting of the National Development Council, 30–31 May 1972. New Delhi, Summary Record, Planning Commission.

Government of India, Perspective Planning Division. 1979. Report of the Task Force on Projections of Minimum Needs and Effective Consumption Demand. New Delhi, Jan.

Government of India, Planning Commission. 1980. Sixth Five-Year Plan, 1980–85.

Greer, J.; Thorbecke, E. 1986. Food poverty and consumption patterns in Kenya. Geneva, ILO.

Griffin, K.; James, J. 1979. "Problems of transition to egalitarian development", in Manchester School of Economics and Social Studies, Sep., Vol. 47, No. 3.

Griffin, K.; Khan, A.R. 1978. "Poverty in the Third World: Ugly facts and fancy models", in World Development, Vol. 6, No. 3, pp. 295–304.

Grosse, R.; Perry, B. 1979. "Correlates of life expectancy in LDCs". Ann Arbor, Michigan (mimeo), as cited in Lewis (1981).

Gunning, J.W. 1979. Income distribution in models for developing countries: Kenya and Tanzania, Ph.D thesis. University of Oxford.

———. 1983. "Rationing in an open economy: Fixed price equilibrium and two gap models", in European Economic Review, Vol. 23, pp. 71-98.

Gupta, S; Togan, S. 1984. "Who benefits from the adjustment process in developing countries? A test on India, Kenya and Turkey", in Journal of Policy Modeling, Feb., Vol. 6, No. 1, pp. 95-109.

Hagenaars, A.J.M.; van Praag, B.M.S. 1985. "A synthesis of poverty line definitions", in Review of Income and Wealth, June, Vol. 31, No. 2.

Harris, J.; Todaro, M. 1970. "Migration, unemployment and development: A two sector analysis", in American Economic Review, Mar., Vol. 6, No. 1, pp. 126-142.

Hazlewood, A. 1978. "Kenya: Income distribution and poverty - An unfashionable view", in Journal of Modern African Countries, Vol. 16, No. 1, pp. 81-95.

———. 1979. The economy of Kenya: The Kenyatta era. Oxford University Press.

Henley, J.S. 1976. "On the lack of trade union power in Kenya", in Relations industrielles, Vol. 31, No. 4.

Henley, J.S.; House, W.J. 1978. "The changing fortunes of an aristocracy? Determinants of wages and conditions of employment in Kenya", in World Development, Vol. 6, No. 1, pp. 83-95.

Herrera, A.O., et al. 1976. Catastrophe or new society? A Latin American world model. Ottawa, IDRC.

Heyer, J., et al. 1976. Agricultural development in Kenya: An economic assessment. Oxford University Press.

Hicks, N. 1979. "Growth versus basic needs: Is there a trade-off?". Washington, DC, IBRD, May; mimeo. Later published under the same title in World Development, Nov.-Dec., Vol. 7, No. 11/12.

———. 1982. "Sector priorities for basic needs: Some statistical evidence", in World Development, June, Vol. 10, No. 6.

Hodd, M. 1972. Aggregate supply in Kenya: Production functions for four major sectors, Working Paper No. 173. University of Nairobi.

---. 1976. "Income distribution in Kenya (1963-72)", in Journal of Development Studies, Vol. 2, No. 3.

---. 1978. "Income distribution in Kenya: A reply", in Journal of Development Studies, Vol. 14, No. 3.

van der Hoeven, R. 1977. Target setting for basic needs with special reference to Africa. Addis Ababa, ILO/JASPA; mimeo.

---. 1980. "Employment, basic needs and industrialisation: Some reflections on the Lima target", in International Labour Review (Geneva, ILO), July-Aug., Vol. 119, No. 4.

---. 1981. A socio-economic framework for basic needs planning: Kenya country study. Geneva, ILO; mimeographed World Employment Programme research working paper; restricted.

Hopcraft, P. 1976. Does education increase farm productivity?, Working Paper 279. University of Nairobi.

Hopkins, M.; van der Hoeven, R. 1982. "Policy analysis in a socio-economic model of basic needs applied to four countries", in Journal of Policy Modeling (New York), Vol. 4, No. 3.

---; ---. 1983. Basic needs in development planning. Aldershot, Gower.

---; ---. 1984. "Economic and social factors in development: A socio-economic framework for basic needs planning", in S. Cohen et al.

Hopkins, M.; Scolnik, H. 1976. "Basic needs, growth and redistribution: A quantitative approach", in Tripartite World Conference on Employment, Income Distribution and Social Progress and the International Division of Labour, Background Papers. Geneva, ILO.

House, W.J. 1973a. "Market structure and industry performance: The case of Kenya", in Oxford Economic Papers, Vol. 25, No. 3.

House, W.J. 1973b. "Wages, employment and productivity in Kenya, some further evidence", in Eastern Africa Economic Review, June, Vol. 5, No. 1.

———. 1975. "Earnings-per-worker differentials in the provinces of Kenya, 1963-1970", in Journal of Developing Areas, Vol. 9, pp. 359-376.

———. 1976. "Market structure and industry performance: The case of Kenya revisited", in Journal of Economic Studies, Vol. 3, No. 2.

———. 1978. Nairobi's informal sector: A reservoir of dynamic entrepreneurs or a residual pool of surplus labour?, Working Paper 347. University of Nairobi, Dec.

———. 1980. "Development strategy and the energy balance: An East African study", in Development and Change, Vol. 11, No. 1.

———. 1981. "Redistribution, consumer demand and employment in Kenyan furniture making", in Journal of Development Studies, July, Vol. 17, No. 4.

House, W.J.; Killick, T. 1978. "Hodd on income distribution in Kenya: A critical note", in Journal of Development Studies, Vol. 14, No. 3.

———; ———. 1980. Social justice and development policy in Kenya's rural economy. Geneva, ILO; mimeographed World Employment Programme research working paper; restricted.

House, W.J.; Rempel, H. 1976a. 1. The impact of unionisation on negotiated wages in the manufacturing sector in Kenya. 2. The role of competitive forces in the determination of wage increases in less developed economies: The case of Kenya. Geneva, ILO; mimeographed World Employment Programme research working paper; restricted.

———; ———. 1976b. "Labour market segmentation in Kenya", in Eastern Africa Economic Review, Dec., Vol. 8, No. 2.

———; ———. 1976c. "The determinants of and changes in the structure of wages and employment in the manufacturing sector of the Kenyan economy, 1967-1972", in Journal of Development Economics, Vol. 3, No. 1, pp. 83-98.

———; ———. 1976d. "The impact of unionisation on negotiated

wages in the manufacturing sector in Kenya", in Oxford Bulletin of Economics and Statistics, Vol. 58, No. 2.

House, W.J.; Rempel, H. 1980. "The determinants of inter-regional migration in Kenya", in World Development, Jan., Vol. 8, No. 1, pp. 25-35.

ILO. 1972. Employment, incomes and equality: A strategy for increasing productive employment in Kenya. Geneva.

---. 1976. Employment growth and basic needs: A one world problem. Geneva.

---. 1983. Increasing the efficiency of planning in Kenya: Concepts, methods and guidelines for reviewing performance and assessing impact. Geneva.

---. 1986. Economically active population, Vol. II, Africa. Geneva.

ILO/JASPA. 1981. First things first: Meeting basic needs of the people of Nigeria. Addis Ababa.

Jamal, V. 1977. Data base for basic needs planning in Kenya: Report of a mission. Addis Ababa, ILO/JASPA; mimeographed.

---. 1982. Rural-urban gap and income distribution: The case of Kenya. Addis Ababa, ILO/JASPA.

Jimenez, E. 1986. "The public subsidization of education and health in developing countries: A review of equity and efficiency", in Research Observer (Washington, IBRD), Jan., Vol. 1, No. 1.

Johnston, B.F.; Meyer, A.J. 1976. Nutrition, health and population in strategies for rural development, Discussion Paper No. 238. University of Nairobi.

Jorgensen, D.W. 1961. "The development of a dual economy", in Economic Journal, June, Vol. 71.

Jorgensen, N.O. 1977. Housing finance for low income groups with special reference to developing countries. Nairobi, General Printers.

Kaplinsky, R. 1975. Technical change and the multinational corporation: Some British multinationals in Kenya, Working Paper No. 228. University of Nairobi.

Kaplinsky, R. 1978a. Readings on the multinational corporation in Kenya. Nairobi, Oxford University Press.

———. 1978b. Trends on the distribution of income in Kenya 1966-76, Working Paper No. 336. University of Nairobi.

———. 1980a. "Technical change in food processing in Kenya", in C. Baron (ed.): Technology, employment and basic needs in food processing in developing countries. Oxford, Pergamon Press.

———. 1980b. "Inappropriate products and techniques in LDCs", in S. Cole (ed.): Issues and analysis of long-term development. Paris, UNESCO.

———. 1981. "Foreign capital employment and accumulation in Kenya", in Development and Change, July, Vol. 12, No. 3, pp. 441-458.

Kaplinsky, R.; Chisti, S. 1976. Technical change and the multinational corporation: Some British multinationals in Kenya and India, Working Paper 266. University of Nairobi.

Kelley, A.C. 1981. "Demographic impacts on demand patterns in the low-income setting", in Economic Development and Cultural Change, Oct., Vol. 30.

Kelley, A.C.; Lillydahl, J. 1976. A re-examination of the concept of economic dependency. Geneva, ILO; mimeographed World Employment Programme research working paper; restricted.

Killick, T. 1976. "Strengthening Kenya's development strategy", in Eastern Africa Economic Review, Dec., Vol. 8, No. 2.

———. 1978. Strengthening Kenya's development strategy: Opportunities and constraints, Discussion Paper No. 239. University of Nairobi.

———. 1980. "Trends in development economics and their relevance to Africa", in Journal of Modern African Studies, Vol. 18, No. 3, pp. 367-386.

———. 1981a. "By their fruits ye shall know them: The Fourth Plan", in T. Killick (ed.): Papers on the Kenya economy. London and Nairobi, Heinemann.

Killick, T. (ed.). 1981b. Papers on the Kenyan economy: Performance, problems and policies. London and Nairobi, Heinemann.

Kinyanjui, K. 1980. Education and development in Kenya: Theories, strategies and practical implications, Working Paper No. 375. University of Nairobi, Institute for Development Studies; Sep.

———. 1981. Education and inequality in Kenya: Some research experience and issues, Working Paper No. 373. University of Nairobi, Institute for Development Studies; Apr.

Klein, L. 1979. "Use of economic models in the policy process", in P. Omerod: Economic modelling. London, Heinemann.

Knowles, J.C.; Anker, R. 1975. Economic determinants of demographic behaviour in Kenya. Geneva, ILO; mimeographed World Employment Programme research working paper; restricted.

———; ———. 1977a. The determinants of internal migration in Kenya: A district level analysis. Geneva, ILO; mimeographed World Employment Programme research working paper; restricted.

———; ———. 1977b. An analysis of income transfers in a developing country: The case of Kenya. Geneva, ILO; mimeographed World Employment Programme research working paper; restricted.

———; ———. 1977c. "Population, employment and income distribution in Kenya: A description of ILO research"; mimeographed.

———; ———. 1981. "An analysis of income transfers in a developing country: The case of Kenya", in Journal of Development Economics, Vol. 8, pp. 205-226.

Koester, U. 1978. Kenya's economic policy with respect to the world coffee market, Working Paper No. 333. University of Nairobi.

Kouwenaar, A. 1986. A basic needs policy model: A general equilibrium analysis with special reference to Ecuador, unpublished Ph.D thesis, Erasmus University, Rotterdam.

Krueger, A. 1982. "Analysing disequilibrium exchange rate systems in developing countries", in World Development, Nov.-Dec., Vol. 10, Nos. 11-12; special issue on analysing disequilibrium in developing countries.

Kuznets, S. 1963. "Quantitative aspects of economic growth of nations: Distribution of income by size", in Economic Development and Cultural Change, Jan., Vol. 11, No. 2, pp.1-80.

Lal, D. 1983. The poverty of development economics. Harvard paperback, Institute of Economic Affairs.

Langdon, S. 1975. "Multinational corporations, taste transfer and underdevelopment: A case study from Kenya", in Review of African Political Economy, Vol. 2.

Lecaillon, J., et al. 1975. "Economic development and the wage share in national income", in International Labour Review (Geneva, ILO), May, Vol. 111, No. 5.

Leipziger, D.M.; Lewis, M.A. 1980. "Social indicators, growth and distribution", in World Development, Vol. 8, pp. 299-302.

Lewis, M.A. 1981. "Sectoral aspects of basic human needs approach: The linkage among population, nutrition and health", in D. Leipziger (ed.): Basic needs and development. Cambridge, Mass., Oelgeschlager, Gunn & Hain.

Lewis, W.A. 1954. "Economic development with unlimited supplies of labour", in Manchester School of Economis and Social Studies, Vol. 22, No. 2, pp. 139-191.

---. 1979. "The dual economy revisited", in Manchester School of Economic and Social Studies, Sep., Vol. 47, No. 3.

Leys, C. 1973. "Interpreting African underdevelopment: Reflections on the ILO report on employment, incomes and equality in Kenya", in African Affairs, Vol. 72, No. 289.

Lijoodi, J.L.; Ruthenberg, H. 1978. "Income distribution in Kenya's agriculture", in Zeitschrift für ausländische Landwirtschaft, 17, Jahrgang, Heft 2, pp. 115-128.

Lipton, M. 1978. Why the poor stay poor: Urban biases in world development. London, Temple Smith.

Lisk, F. 1978. Basic needs activities and poverty alleviation in Kenya. Geneva, ILO.

Livingstone, I. 1986. Rural development, employment and incomes in Kenya, prepared for the International Labour Office, Jobs and Skills Programme for Africa. Aldershot, Gower.

Low, P. 1982. "Export subsidies and trade policy: The experience of Kenya", in World Development, Vol. 10, No. 4, pp. 293-304.

Maitha, J.K. 1973. "Capital-labour substitution in manufacturing in a developing economy: The case of Kenya", in Eastern Africa Economic Review, Vol. 5, No. 2.

Masakhalia, Y.F.O., et al. 1977. National economy and its use as a guide to economic policy, Discussion Paper No. 246. University of Nairobi.

Massell, B.F. 1969. "Consistent estimation of expenditure elasticities from cross-section data on households producing partly for subsistence", in Review of Economics and Statistics, Vol. LI, No. 2.

Mbithi, P.M.; Mwangi, W.M. 1979. The spontaneous settlement problem in Kenya. Nairobi, East African Literature Bureau.

Mburu, F.M. 1980. Sociopolitical imperatives in the history of health development in Kenya, Working Paper No. 374. University of Nairobi, Institute for Development Studies; Nov.

McCarthy, F.D.; Mwangi, W.M. 1979. "Kenya - Agriculture: Towards 2000", draft discussion paper. University of Nairobi and Ministry of Economic Planning and Community Affairs.

Meadows, D., et al. 1972. The limits to growth. A report for the Club of Rome's project on the predicament of mankind. London, Earth Island Limited.

Meerman, J. 1979. Public expenditure in Malaysia: Who gets what and why? Washington, DC, IBRD.

Moreland, R.S. 1984. Population, development and income distribution: A modelling approach. Bachue International. Aldershot, Gower.

Mureithi, L.P. 1974. "Demographic and technological variables in Kenya's employment scene", in Eastern Africa Economic Review, Vol. 6, No. 1.

Mureithi, L.P. Factor intensity in Kenya's industrial sector: An input ratio analysis, IDS Working Paper No. 184. University of Nairobi, Institute for Development Studies.

Narayana, N.S.S.; Shah, M.M. 1982. Farm supply response in Kenya acreage allocation model, IIASA Working Paper No. 82-103. Laxenburg; Oct.

Nugent, J.; Yotopoulos, P. 1978. What has orthodox economics learned from recent experience?, Research Paper 7803. Los Angeles, University of Southern California, Department of Economics.

Nyangira, N. 1975. Relative modernisation and public resource allocation in Kenya. Nairobi, East African Literature Bureau.

Oshima, H.T. 1967. "Food consumption, nutrition and economic development in Asian countries", in Economic Development and Cultural Change, July, pp. 385-397.

Pack, H. 1972. "Employment and productivity in Kenyan manufacturing", in Eastern Africa Economic Review, Vol. 4, No. 2.

Paukert, F. 1973. "Income distribution of different levels of development: A survey of evidence" in International Labour Review (Geneva, ILO), Vol. 108, Nos. 2-3, Aug.-Sep.

Peek, P.; Standing, G. (eds.). 1982. State policies and migration. London, Croom Helm.

Powelson, J.P. 1974. "Employment policies and the informal sector in Kenya", talk before the Lusaka Economics Club, May.

Psacharopoulos, G. 1984. "The contribution of education to economic growth: International comparisons", in J.W. Kendrick (ed.): International comparisons of productivity and sources of the slow down. Cambridge, Mass., Ballinger.

Quibria, M.G. 1982. "An analytical defence of basic needs: The optimal savings perspective", in World Development, Apr., Vol. 10, No. 2.

Ram, R. 1985. "The role of real income level and income distribution in fulfilment of basic needs", in World Development, Vol. 13. No. 5, pp. 589-594.

Ram, R; Schultz, T. 1979. "Life span, health, savings and

productivity", in Economic Development and Cultural Change, Apr., Vol. 27, No. 3, pp. 399–421.

Rattsö, J. 1982. "Different macro closures of the original Johansen model and their impact on policy evaluation", in Journal of Policy Modeling, Vol. 4, No. 11, pp. 85–97.

Rempel, H.; House, W.J. 1978. The Kenya employment problem: An analysis of the modern sector labour market. Nairobi, Oxford University Press.

Rempel, H.; Lobdell, R.A. 1978. "The role of urban-to-rural remittances in rural development", in Journal of Development Studies, Vol. 14, No. 3.

Republic of Kenya. 1979a. Development Plan 1979–1983, Part I. Nairobi, Government Printer.

———. 1979b. Development Plan 1979–1983, Part II. Nairobi, Government Printer.

———. 1980. Economic prospects and policies, Sessional Paper No. 4 of 1980.

———. 1981. National food policy, Sessional Paper No. 4 of 1981.

———. 1983. Development Plan 1984–88.

Republic of Kenya, Central Bureau of Statistics (CBS). 1971. "Input/output tables for Kenya, 1971".

———; ———. 1972a. "Census of Industrial Production, 1972".

———; ———. 1972b. "Employment and earnings in the modern sector, 1968–70".

———; ———. 1972c. "Population projections by district, 1970–80", in Kenya Statistical Digest, Vol. X, No. 3.

———; ———. 1973a. "Employment and earnings in the modern sector, 1971".

———; ———. 1973b. "Surveys of industrial production, 1970 and 1971", in Kenya Statistical Digest, Vol. XI, No. 2.

———; ———. 1974. "Preliminary results of the survey of distribution, 1971", in Kenya Statistical Digest, Vol. XII, No. 2.

Republic of Kenya, Central Bureau of Statistics (CBS). 1975. "Towards a social perspective: A statistical appraisal", in Kenya Statistical Digest, Vol. XIII, No. 3.

———; ———. 1976a. "Employment and earnings in the modern sector, 1974".

———; ———. 1976b. "Quarterly economic report: The household and the holding in Kenya", in Kenya Statistical Review, Vol. XIV, No. 4.

———; ———. 1977a. Integrated rural survey, 1974-75: Basic report.

———; ———. 1977b. "A review of the methodological design, operation and problems of Kenya's multi-purpose national sample", in Kenya Statistical Digest, Vol. XV, No. 4.

———; ———. 1977c. Sources and methods used for the national accounts of Kenya. Nairobi; Dec.

———; ———. 1977d. "Consumer price indices, Nairobi".

———; ———. Economic Survey, 1977-84 issues.

———. ———. Statistical Abstract, 1978-84 issues.

———; ———. n.d. "Urban Food Purchasing Survey, 1977 - Part I".

———; ———. 1978a. "Women in Kenya".

———; ———. 1978b. "A brief review of farming activities", Agricultural Census of Large Farms, 1975 and 1976.

———; ———. 1978c. "Income tax statistics report, year of income 1974".

———; ———. 1978d. "A review of land use changes". Nairobi.

———; ———. 1978e. "Statistics of energy and power, 1969-77".

———; ———. 1978f. Employment and earnings in the modern sector, 1976.

———; ———. 1979a. Crop forecast and crop review, 1979.

———; ———. 1979b. National accounts companion volume 1979 edition. Nairobi.

Republic of Kenya, Central Bureau of Statistics (CBS). 1979c. "Input/output tables for Kenya, 1976".

———; ———. 1979d. "Social accounting matrix, 1976 - A preview".

———; ———. n.d. (c. 1979). Educational trends, 1973-77.

———; ———. (c. 1979). Kenya education sector analysis, Methodological Document No. 1.

———; ———. n.d. (c. 1979). Kenya fertility survey major highlights.

———; ———. n.d. (c. 1979). "Report of the Child Nutrition Survey, 1978-79".

———; ———. 1980a. The national sample survey and evaluation programme, 1980-84. Nairobi; Oct.

———; ———. 1980b. Kenya Fertility Survey, 1977-78, Vol. I, First Report. Nairobi.

———; ———. n.d. (c. 1980). Child nutrition in rural Kenya.

———; ———. 1981. Social Accounting Matrix 1976 (Revised). Nairobi.

Rimmer, D. 1981. "Basic needs and the origins of the development ethos", in Journal of Developing Areas, Vol. 15, pp. 215-238.

Ritzen, J.M.M.; Balderston, J.B. 1975. Methodology for planning technical education: With a case study of polytechnics in Bangladesh. New York, Praeger.

Rodgers, G.B. 1981. "An analysis of education, employment and income distribution using an economic-demographic model of the Philippines", in A. Kahn and I. Sirageldin (eds.): Research in human capital and development: Equity, human capital and development. Greenwich, Connecticut, Jai Press.

Rodgers, G.B. 1984. Population and poverty: Approaches and evidence. Geneva, ILO.

Rodgers, G.B., et al. 1978. Population, employment and inequality: Bachue-Philippines. Farnborough, Saxon House.

Rodgers, G.B.; Anker, R. 1978. Urban employment in the

1980s: The cases of Kenya and the Philippines. Geneva, ILO; mimeographed World Employment Programme research working paper; restricted.

Rowntree, B.S. 1901. Poverty: A study of town life. London, Macmillan.

Rudra, A. 1978. The basic needs concept and its implementation in Indian development planning. Bangkok, ILO/ARTEP.

Ryan, T. 1983. Rural-urban terms of trade. Nairobi, Ministry of Finance and Planning; mimeo.

Sandbrook, R. 1977. "The study of the African 'sub-proletariat': A review article", in Manpower and Unemployment Research, Vol. 10, No. 1.

Seers, D. 1981. "What needs are really basic in Nigeria? Some thought provoked by an ILO mission", in International Labour Review (Geneva, ILO), Vol. 120, No. 6.

Sen, A. 1983. "Goods and people", presented at the plenary session of the Seventh World Congress of the International Economic Association, Madrid.

Sethuraman, S. 1981. The urban informal sector in developing countries, employment, poverty and environment. Geneva, ILO.

Shah, M.M. n.d. "Food demand projections incorporating urbanization and income distribution - Kenya (1975-2000)".

---. 1978. Calorie demand projections incorporating income distribution (Sep.; mimeographed).

Shah, M.M.; Fischer, G. 1981. Assessment of food production potential: Resources, technology and environment - A case study of Kenya, Working Paper 81-42. Laxenburg, International Institute for Applied Economics Research; Mar.

Shah, M.M.; Willekens, P. 1978. Rural-urban population projections for Kenya and implications for development. Laxenburg, Austria, International Institute for Applied Systems Analysis; research memorandum.

Sharpley, J. 1979. "Intersectoral capital flows: Evidence from Kenya", in Journal of Development Economics, Vol. 6.

---. 1980a. Pricing policies and rural incomes in Kenya,

DERAP Working Paper A174. Bergen, Norway, Chr. Michelsen Institute; Apr.

Sharpley, J. 1980b. "Resource transfers between the agricultural and non-agricultural sectors: 1964–1977"; mimeographed.

Sheehan, G.; Hopkins, M. 1979. Basic needs performance: An analysis of some international data. Geneva, ILO.

Singer, H.W.; Reynolds, S.D. 1974. Aspects of the distribution of income and wealth in Kenya, Discussion Paper No. 41. Brighton, University of Sussex.

Skolka, J. 1984. The influence of basic needs policies on sectoral value added shares in input-output tables. Geneva, ILO; mimeographed World Employment Programme research working paper; restricted.

Smith, L.D. 1978. "Low income smallholder marketing and consumption patterns: Analysis and improvement policies and programmes", Marketing Development Project, Phase I.

Spjeldnaes, J. 1980. Updating the input/output for Kenya: A detailed work plan, DERAP Working Paper No. A171. Bergen.

Srinivasan, T.N.; Bardhan, P.K. 1974. "Perspectives of development: 1961–76, Implication of planning for a minimum level of living in poverty and income distribution in India", in P.K. Bardham and T.N. Srinivasan (eds.): Poverty and income distribution in India. Calcutta, Statistical Publishing Society.

Standing, G. 1978. Labour force participation and development. Geneva, ILO.

Standing, G.; Sheehan, G. 1979. Labour force participation in low-income countries. Geneva, ILO.

Standing, G.; Szal, R. 1979. Poverty and basic needs. Geneva, ILO.

Stewart, F. 1985. Planning to meet basic needs. London, Macmillan.

Stewart, F.; Streeten, P. 1971. "Conflicts between output and employment objectives", in Oxford Economic Papers, July, Vol. 23, No. 2.

Streeten, P. 1979. "Basic needs: Premises and promises", in Journal of Policy Modeling, Vol. 1, No. 1.

Streeten, P. 1981. First things first: Meeting basic human needs in developing countries. New York, Oxford University Press.

---. 1982. "Basic needs and the new international economic order", in Mondes et développement, Vol. 10, No. 39.

---. 1984. "Basic needs: Some unsettled questions", in World Development, Sep., Vol. 12, No. 9.

Taylor, L. 1975. "Theoretical foundations and technical implications", Chapter 3 in Blitzer et al. (1975).

---. 1979. Macro models for developing countries. New York, McGraw-Hill.

---. 1983. Structuralist macro economics. Basic Books, New York.

Taylor, L.; Lysy, F. 1979. "Vanishing income redistribution: Keynesian clues about model surprises in the short run", in Journal of Development Economics, Vol. 6, pp. 11-29.

Thorbecke, E. 1980. Attempt at diagnosis of basic needs profile in rural Kenya and potential for improvement. Geneva, ILO, Aug.; mimeographed.

Tinbergen, J. 1952. On the theory of economic policy. Amsterdam, North Holland Publishing Company.

---. 1975. Income distribution analysis and policies. Amsterdam, North Holland Publishing Company.

UNIDO. 1985. Industry and development, Global report, 1985. Vienna.

United Nations. 1985. World population prospects. New York.

University of Nairobi, Population Studies and Research Institute. 1979. "The impact of current and future population growth rates on the short term social and economic development in Kenya". Mimeographed.

Vandemoortele, J. 1983. The public sector and the basic needs strategy in Kenya: The experience of the seventies.

Geneva, ILO, Jan.; mimeographed World Employment Programme research working paper; restricted.

Vandemoortele, J. 1987. The social accounting matrix: A tool for socio-economic analysis: The case of Kenya. Geneva, ILO.

Vandemoortele, J.; van der Hoeven, R. 1982. Income distribution and consumption patterns in urban and rural Kenya by socio-economic groups. Geneva, ILO; mimeographed World Employment Programme research working paper; restricted.

Ward, M. 1978. "Urban-rural data sets", OECD research project (approx. date).

Westlake, M.J. 1973. "Tax evasion, tax incidence and the distribution of income in Kenya", in Eastern Africa Economic Review, Vol. 5, No. 2.

Westley, S.G. (ed.). 1978. The informal sector in Kenya, Occasional Paper No. 25. University of Nairobi.

Wheeler, D. 1980a. "Basic needs fulfilment and economic growth", in Journal of Development Economics, Vol. 7, pp. 435-451.

———. 1980b. Human resource development and economic growth in LDCs, IBRD Staff Working Paper. Washington, DC.

———. 1984. Human resource policies, economic growth and demographic change in developing countries. Oxford, Clarendon Press.

Williamson, C.; Shah, M.M. 1981. Models of expenditure systems for Kenya, Working Paper 81-71. Laxenburg, International Institute for Applied Systems Analysis; June.

World Bank. 1980. Population and development in Kenya, Report No. 2775-KE. Washington, DC, Development Economics Department.

———. 1980. World tables, 1980. Washington, DC.

———. 1983. Kenya country economic memorandum, Report 4689-KE, 5 Oct.

———. 1984. Towards sustained development in sub-Saharan Africa. Washington, DC.

World Bank. 1985. _Staff appraisal report. The Republic of Kenya Sixth Education Project Report 5864-KE, December 23, 1985_. Washington DC; restricted.

———. 1986. _Kenya agricultural sector_, Report No. 4629-KE. Washington, DC; Jan.; restricted.

Author index

Subject index